I0150345

THE MILLIONAIRE'S DIET EATING FOR SUCCESS

How Successful People Feed Body, Mind and Soul

THE MILLIONAIRE'S DIET EATING FOR SUCCESS

How Successful People Feed Body, Mind and Soul

Anton Uhl

FEATHERWING PRESS

Basalt, Colorado • FeatherWingPress.com

Featherwing Press
Basalt, CO

Copyright ©2012 by Anton Uhl

All rights reserved. No part of this publication may be reproduced or transmitted in any form or by any means, electronic or mechanical, including photocopying, recording, or by any information storage and retrieval system, without written permission from the author or his authorized representatives. Brief passages may be quoted for reviews.

Disclaimer: The information and opinions expressed in this book are of a general nature and are not intended as a substitute for professional evaluation or treatment by a competent health care professional. The author, the publisher and persons represented in the interviews in this book specifically disclaim any liability arising directly or indirectly from the use or application of any information contained in this book.

www.millionairesdiet.net

ISBN-13: 978-0615599519
ISBN-10: 0615599516

Library of Congress Cataloguing-in-Publication Data is available upon request.

Cover design by Anton Uhl
Cover image by Leslie Uhl
Author photo by Leslie Uhl

Printed in the United States of America
20 19 18 17 16 15 14 13 12   1 2 3 4 5
TS

Printed on recycled paper

Dedicated to my children, Sage and Griffin.
The way you think is the future of the world.

"Healing may not be so much about getting better as about letting go of everything that isn't you—all of the expectations, all of the beliefs—and becoming who you are. Not a better you but a realer you."

~*Rachel Naomi Remen, MD*

"Everybody is a genius, but if you judge a fish by its ability to climb a tree, it will live its whole life believing that it is stupid."

~*Albert Einstein*

"Success is something you attract by the person you become."

~*Unknown*

"You can't paint a barn red with blue paint."

~*Anton Uhl*

CONTENTS

aligns us with success. Physical alignment of our bodies opens channels for a clear flow of these energies within us.

its highest level as you give your time, talent and resources.
Create the vibration of abundance in fulfilling your purpose.

Diana Stobo
The Raw Truth   **218**
*You may not even know something is missing, but once you
have experienced feeling great, you will never want to go back
to just feeling good. Food is the most direct way to influence
your sense of well-being. Discover the "Naked" lifestyle
through whole raw foods.*

David "Avocado" Wolfe
Choosing The Best Day Ever   **229**
*We have access to more foods today than ever before. Even in
large urban areas we can make the best choices for everything
from superfoods to fresh living water straight from the earth.
With choices we become free.*

Berny Dohrmann
Your Fuel Filter   **238**
*The purpose of food is to nourish. Our greatest responsibility
lies in educating ourselves and our children about how our
food choices not only affect our individual potential but
ultimately determine the future of this planet.*

WHAT IF?

What if there were a simple way to have the life of your dreams, to be the sexiest, most beautiful, most energetic you you have ever been?

What if there were a way to turn back the clock and become younger, to have a faster, clearer mind and never worry about Alzheimer's or heart disease?

What if you could live to be 100 and still be energetic and making love to the very end?

What would it be like to have the best relationships of your life—to fall back in love with your partner, your family, your friends, and yourself?

What if you discovered that your choice of the food you eat was the *only* thing left standing between you and the success of your wildest dreams—in health, in relationships and in money.

If someone could show you how a simple and small shift in your habits and the way you think could change your very *ability* to attract and have wealth in all aspects of your life, would you listen?

In *The Millionaire's Diet – Eating For Success* some of the most innovative thinkers, teachers, and scientists of our time share their secrets with you to show you how the food you eat not only changes your waistline, but affects your energy, your hormones, and the brain chemistry that *defines* your potential, that gives you the very *ability* to imagine and attract anything your heart desires.

PREFACE

While attending T. Harv Eker's Extreme Health Seminar, one of the speakers said something that changed my life in a flash. The light bulb went off. The deed was done. A thought was born that had that distinctive ring of truth—and the need to share that vision.

A handsome and clearly very fit Harvey Mackay, the CEO of Envelopes America, stood on the stage beaming with energy, focus, clarity and a joy that was as infectious as it was awe inspiring. He had just completed his third Boston Marathon—at age seventy-six!

I lost track of what he was actually talking about. I was mystified by the idea of how anyone could run—and complete—the Boston Marathon at age seventy-six. I was more than twenty years younger than him. Even though I was relatively fit, the very idea of running twenty-six miles in a single day was exhausting. Unthinkable. *How does he do it? What is his secret?*

Then another thought occurred to me. A few years earlier when I had had a battle with acute anxiety disorder, a man saved my life and put me back on track simply by changing the food I ate. I looked at Harvey onstage and thought, *I'll bet he eats really good food. I'll bet this clear-headed, light-spirited, physically fit gentleman eats consciously and conscientiously.*

I decided to see if there was a common thread among the speakers at the seminar. This was, after all, Extreme Health. I wanted to know, Does the food they eat have anything to do with their ability to meet the extreme demands of their high-paced, over-scheduled lives, so they can still show up on stage full of life, clarity and energy for their audiences time after time after time? Can I do this in my life?

The best way to find out anything is to ask. Ask those who have gone before you.

I ran out and bought a small hand-held digital recorder and started pulling some of the speakers aside as they came off the stage. I asked them three basic questions:

1. Do you believe food has anything to do with our actual ability to succeed, to achieve our potential?

2. Did you always eat the way you do now, or did something happen in your life to make you change?

3. Do you have any words to share with those people still looking to improve their lives?

Everyone balked at the word *interview*. These are people who are hounded daily to make time for interviews in their already overloaded schedules. But as soon as they heard the topic of my request, they lit up and usually began with something like, "I'm glad you asked!" Resistance quickly gave way to enthusiasm. I had struck a nerve. I couldn't shut them up. These were people who genuinely cared about making the world a better place for all of us, starting with the individual. After all, everything we do affects everyone else in some way; we all live here together.

Astounded by the passion expressed by my first handful of interviewees, I made a list of other highly successful personal development coaches, authors, teachers, actors, and trainers.

Initially, most interview requests were greeted with the same resistance, but as I persisted, *they insisted* on making the time to talk. Interviews became an opportunity for deep and intimate sharing about the relationship between food and success—and word about the book began to spread. In fact, when word got out about the project, some people actually phoned to ask why I hadn't called on them!

Even though I requested just ten minutes to ask three simple questions, the interviews became impassioned conversations, some lasting in excess of an hour. It became obvious that this was a topic that needed to be addressed.

Although food was at the root of all these conversations, each person had a special passion and purpose in his or her life. "Eating for success" became a metaphor for not only how we feed our bodies, but also how we feed our minds and souls with the choices we make every minute of every day.

My life has changed dramatically since beginning this project. I will never go back. I will never be the same. Neither will you, I'm certain, once you discover the many treasures revealed in the pages and between the lines of this book.

There are those who have gone before us who have helped to pave the way. This book is a collection from some of the road crew that have made it possible for you to race across the desert to the land of abundance on a superhighway.

If you are searching for a way to raise up your spirits, raise your income, and change and improve your life, the Universe has said that you are ready and in the right place by putting this book into your hands.

ACKNOWLEDGMENTS

In recent years it has become accepted to put the acknowledgments page at the back of a book, but I believe gratitude is always a better place to start. It lets the Universe know that its efforts have not been wasted, that we are appreciative and ready for more. My entire life has been blessed with such uncanny serendipity that it would be hard even to imagine that the Universe is not paying attention.

Unlike the Academy Awards presentation, there is no orchestra that will interrupt when the thank-yous become endless, but really, there are so many people involved on so many levels in the manifestation of a project of this scale that it might warrant a book in itself just to list everyone.

There are, however, a few key people whose contributions stand out, who made this book become far more than I had envisioned when I began, and without whom this book may never have seen the light of day.

Success is mirrored in every aspect of a person's being. I would like to start by thanking Harvey Mackay, whose brilliant energy and presence revealed a new paradigm to me. It goes to show that, regardless of our intentions, we are always on parade and should never underestimate the impact our mere existence has on this world. I would also like to thank T. Harv Eker for having created a unique and friendly environment for exploration and self-discovery with his Peak Potentials seminars. It was in this supportive atmosphere that the concepts of the Eating For Success project first began to percolate from the depths of my heart.

Without the encouragement and direction offered by my writing coach, Keith Leon, this book may never have gotten out of the starting gate. It was Keith who also supplied me with the initial seed list of interviewees that started the ball rolling. Multiple *New York Times* best-selling author Marci Shimoff lit a disturbing fire that completely changed the direction and quality of this project when she challenged me not to do just a simple collection of transcribed interviews. Thanks to Marci for raising the bar and showing me what's really possible!

The strongest bonds in my life have always been formed through an unbroken chain of relationships. This has remained true on this project. Marci introduced me to her friend and colleague, best-selling author and editor Jennifer Read Hawthorne. As editor of this book, Jennifer was ruthlessly cool in her professionalism and brilliant in her warmth and support as we slogged through some of my swamps and turned them into parks and superhighways.

Janet Bray Attwood could not have been more passionate or supportive in her enthusiasm for this book and could easily have supplied material for the entire book on her own. Janet insisted on connecting me with certain people whose words became some of the best conversations in this book.

John Gray is another person whose conversation could supply enough information for a book (or two) on its own. Thank you for your generosity and the incessant fountain of inspiration that comes from you. The time I spent with you lit a fire within that is a gift of incalculable measure, not only for me, but for all those who are fortunate enough to have found these pages.

The people I approached were so passionate about this topic that they went out of their way to ensure that the words in this book made it into your hands. Berny Dohrmann went miles beyond the mark when he repeated a lengthy interview after the first recordings were lost! This kind of enthusiasm and generosity was typical of the people whose words fill this book. Some of you were old friends and many of you became new friends who have shared meals with my family and me at the table in our home. It is so clear that Eating for Success is a lifestyle you live and not just an outfit you wear. There is definitely proof in this pudding!

In my personal life I would like to thank all the friends who supported and encouraged me through this project, like my writing muse, Tristan Heberlein, who, in his typical, straight-forward approach, never bandies words but still insists that I make each and every day the best ever.

No single person affected the certain outcome of this book seeing the light of day as much as my dearest companion, Mark Robins. After six years on the front lines in Afghanistan, his tolerance for any form of negativity is zero. Thank you, Mark, for giving me the joy and incentive that I live by every day and for seeing in me what I didn't see myself. Thanks for your persistence in endless hours of encouragement and wisdom to help me see this project through.

I would like to thank my family for bearing with me on the many days and nights they were neglected by a man married to his computer. I thank my wife, Leslie, for her unconditional support and belief in this project right from the start; my daughter, Sage, for her inspiration; and my son, Griffin, whose unwavering faith in this project gave me courage to keep on keepin' on when the days seemed long and the lights seemed dim.

Above all, I thank each and every one of you who took precious time out of your busy schedules to share your words and vision. I thank you for the joy and passion you conveyed for this topic and for encouraging me never to lose sight of its importance. Not all the interviews I conducted found their way into the pages of this edition, but everyone's words and actions contributed in some way to what appears in these pages. I have grown. You have changed my life forever and will surely have no less effect on all those fortunate enough to hear your words for many years to come. Without you, there would be no book.

INTRODUCTION

Choosing the food we eat is one of the singularly most consequential acts of our daily lives. We easily dismiss its purpose and have been numbed by the effects of food designed for our fast-paced, highly sensationalized lifestyles. But the cause and effect of what we eat becomes apparent over time—in our bodies, in our minds, and in the world around us.

The Millionaire's Diet is about Eating for Success, both literally and metaphorically. *Everything* that you put into your body, that you *allow* into your body, and everything you create or allow in your life and environment has some effect on you.

Eating is something we do day after day, year after year, for the duration of our lives. Through repetition, patterns become ingrained. Good and bad decisions become habits as our internal circuitry takes the path of least resistance. The quality and type of food we choose to fuel our bodies and minds determines whether our engines will run smoothly and effectively or become gummed up and break down.

So what is food anyway?

Food is usually the central theme of our gatherings with friends and family at the holidays, in our travels, in our courtships, and in our daily lives.

Food is something we put in our mouths when we get hungry. It's something we eat when we celebrate or to make us feel better when we feel blue.

We think of food as something beautiful and delicious. We think of food as something that affects whether *we're* beautiful and delicious.

We know that the food we eat can make us fatter or thinner. A new fad diet appears on the newsstands almost daily that promises *this* is the one that will tip the scales—in the right direction. We are used to hearing that certain foods affect the amount of muscle we can put on for all our hard work at the gym.

We also know that the food we eat can affect our health, our cholesterol levels and whether or not we will have a heart attack. But did you know what a profound influence it has on our hormones and brain chemistry as well?

People like success guru Tony Robbins have been teaching us for years that food is part of the equation in our quest to achieve success in all aspects of our lives. But have you ever thought that your choice of food could be the one factor determining whether you can even *be* successful or not?

What if the food you eat was the *only* thing left standing between you and the success of your wildest dreams?

The first thing to realize is that everything you do, no matter how big or how small, has some effect on your life. The problem is, we often underestimate the power of some of the most ordinary aspects of our lives, like eating, while focusing on some grand scheme to set us free.

Every moment of every day, you are moving either toward success or away from it. Doing nothing is *just as effective* as doing everything. Every *non-action* affects your life just as much as any *action* you take. There is no middle ground. Everything is cause and effect. For every action there is a reaction, just as for every non-action there is a reaction. This takes constant vigilance.

In the following pages, you will see what some of the most successful people and greatest teachers of our time have to say about food and how it affects our lives. Some of their words may hit you like a sledgehammer. Some of their words will ripple to the surface of your awareness months from now in a moment of discovery and enlightenment, triggered by some subtle or profound event in your life.

What is certain, however, is that the cumulative effect of their words will affect the way you think about food. If you're paying attention, it will change your life forever.

How to Read This Book

The Millionaire's Diet is arranged in seven sections:

    I.   State Of Mind
    II.   Forever Young
    III.   Everything Is Energy
    IV.   Getting Centered
    V.   What You Put In
    VI.   We're In This Together
  VII. VII. The Imperative Of Awakening

Even though the primary topic of this book is how food affects our ability to succeed, the very nature of the topic of success invites countless brilliant discussions. The conversations within each topic are presented as interviews.

Each person I spoke with brought his or her own special focus to the conversation. Many of the conversations share the same thoughts, but this only strengthens our sense of their conviction of the importance of what is being said.

You can read this book from front to back, or you can browse the table of contents and skip around at will. This book is not formulaic, nor is it a treatise of sequential steps that build on each other. It is more of a free-flowing conversation with some of the most inspiring and brilliant minds of our day.

Here's what you'll find in each section:

In *State Of Mind* we explore the phenomenal world of the brain. Fascinating new discoveries have been made about how this Control Central of our very being operates, and we'll look at these and the effects that not only food but our very thoughts have on how this most amazing organ operates and affects our lives.

Forever Young reveals that through greater understanding of the effects of food and lifestyle choices, we can literally change our bodies and brain chemistry to predispose us to join the ever-expanding ranks of the lively, loving, and alert centenarians. A new paradigm is evolving about the quality of our lives as we age and how long we can live. Science is showing us that longevity is not just the luck of the draw.

Quantum physics has proven to us that *Everything Is Energy*, from physical matter to the very thoughts in our head. Every type of energy vibrates at a certain resonance. Since ancient times, scientists, and mystics alike have known that we have the power to recognize, control, and align our own energies with the energies in the world around us, and to optimize how we move through this world to our greatest advantage.

Getting Centered is key to empowering ourselves to be the best that we can be. By focusing on ourselves first, we expand what we have to offer. Balance in how we distribute our attention is crucial to having a strong platform from which we operate. Appropriate nutrition is a huge factor affecting our ability to manage any level of business with focus, clarity, and grace.

Ultimately, *What You Put In* will determine what you get out of anything in your life. You really are what you eat, both literally and metaphorically, and what you let into your body and your life will determine what you are able to get out of it. You must set high standards in all that you do, including the way you eat, for only quality begets quality.

In *We're In This Together* there is a consensus that we are all connected; every choice you make affects not only you but those around you and around the planet. In the world of supply and demand, our food choices go far beyond our taste buds or our bodies. This is our world and our time, and we must take responsibility for our choices in order to enjoy the benefits of a good life, now and in the future.

The Imperative Of Awakening is that we cannot stumble blindly through life and hope for good things to come. There must be awareness and a willingness to reach beyond the comfort of what we know. The power of discovery is that once you have experienced the success, beauty, and joy of a life lived deliberately and well, making better choices becomes unforced and automatic. You will never go back.

With more information available to us today than ever before in history, making the best choices in everything that fuels our lives is the foundation for creating the life of our dreams. In *The Millionaire's Diet*, some of today's greatest minds have gathered under one roof to give you the best of their best. When you open your mind before you open your mouth, Eating For Success will set you free.

I.

STATE OF MIND

SHOWING UP

*The quality of relationships determines success. Good relationships
are built on positive qualities that are the direct result of the thoughts
we nurture and the foods we eat.*

John Gray, PhD, is the author of sixteen best-selling books, including
Men Are from Mars, *Women Are from Venus*, the number one best-
selling book of the last decade and the number one relationship book of
all time. In the past fifteen years, over 40 million *Mars and Venus* books
have been sold in over forty-five languages throughout the world.

John is an expert in the field of communication, with a focus to help
men and women understand, respect, and appreciate their differences
in both personal and professional relationships. He provides them with
practical tools and insights to effectively manage stress and improve
relationships at all stages and ages by creating the brain chemistry of
health, happiness, and lasting romance.

Dr. Gray has appeared on *Oprah*, *The Today Show*, *CBS Morning
Show*, *Good Morning America*, *The Early Show*, *The View*, *Politically
Incorrect*, *Larry King*, and others. He has been profiled in *Newsweek*,
Time, *Forbes*, *USA Today*, *TV Guide*, *People*, and *New Age Journal*,
among others.

In addition to being a Certified Family Therapist, Dr. Gray is a consult-
ing editor of *The Family Journal* and a member of the Distinguished
Advisory Board of the International Association of Marriage and Family
Counselors.

John Gray believes that true success is only possible through forming
successful relationships on all levels of your life: with your clients, your
colleagues, your families, your partners, and yourself.

Your ability to have good relationships with anyone is reliant on your energy and the way you think, which is reliant on your brain chemistry, which is a direct result of the foods you eat.

DR. JOHN GRAY: I have written sixteen books on the subject of relationships. One of the key factors in relationships is stress management. When we look carefully at stress management, we realize that what we put in our mouths—what we eat, the nutrition we take in—has a huge impact on how we cope with stress, as well as how we react to things hormonally. People don't realize how hormones dictate our moods.

We want to be successful in life. We want to be optimistic. We want to stay focused. Those are symptoms of certain hormonal balances. If you don't have that hormonal balance because you don't have enough hormones, it's hard to sustain those positive states.

ANTON: What was it that made you realize this is what was going on?

DR. JOHN GRAY: The key turnaround for me was over thirty years ago. I had been teaching weekend workshops, then I started teaching more advanced workshops, four – to five-day and seven-day workshops. People would get really, really inspired and motivated and pumped up—and then they would crash. What was going on, I discovered, is that when people do a lot of positive work, which activates peak performance of the brain, they literally run out of nutrients faster. It's like having a race car: if you don't have the right fuel, it won't run right.

If you're going to be peak performers, have higher ambitions and achieve higher goals, or if you want to lead an extraordinary life and step out of the "normal" lifestyle (the one where people take drugs and get sick and have problems and get divorced and all those things that are average today), you'll need to have more nutrition. If you don't, you'll rise to these peak states and then crash because you've used it all up.

ANTON: By getting more nutrition, you're talking about the quality of the nutrition, not about eating more.

DR. JOHN GRAY: Definitely not eating more. One of the many reasons we eat more is that there's no nutrition in the food we eat. When we started using fertilizers a hundred years ago, it started depleting soil minerals.

If you don't have enough minerals you can't even digest the food you're getting in order to get the limited amount of nutrition that is in that food! We want to find nutrient-dense foods. We also want to find some supplements for certain issues, because often our food just doesn't provide enough for us today.

Every day I take a mineral supplement from a plant source that has all seventy trace minerals in it. It has all the macro minerals in a form that will get right into the brain. Mineral support, in my opinion, is the most important nutritional component, because it activates the enzymes that allow all the digestive processes to take place.

I focus on what's missing most from our diet today to help produce the right balance of hormones, and to dispel a lot of myths. For example, people are afraid of eating fat, and yet there's good fat and there's bad fat. There are good carbohydrates and bad carbohydrates. There are good proteins and bad proteins.

We really need to follow our body's wisdom, but if our body tells us to eat something and it's not good for us, why does it do that? Part of that is imbalance in the body's hormones and brain function. Brain first. Help the brain function better and you will be drawn naturally to healthier foods.

You have to have a foundation if you want clear thinking. Staying motivated and energized is based on understanding how the body works. Expanding our knowledge of how our body works can provide a foundation for success in all areas, particularly in our relationships. Everything about success is about the quality of our relationships, and the quality of our relationships comes from our attitude, our mood, our energy level, and our memory. These things are proven to be directly affected by what we eat.

If people don't eat enough fat, for example, they're not going to make the hormones necessary to support healthy brain function. What is good fat? One of the best fats is coconut oil. Coconut oil is an easy-to-digest fat that actually stimulates more energy and is not stored as fat. It can actually help you lose weight.

ANTON: You always talk about brain chemistry. I hate to say this but, the 1960s proved to me that you can put a pill in your mouth and it can change everything. Your entire perception of the world and your entire behavior.

DR. JOHN GRAY: I'm now sixty years old and I need to wear glasses. Without those glasses the world is really fuzzy. If your mind isn't focused, your mind is fuzzy. People tend to have fuzzy thinking. They don't have the clarity that's possible for them to have. This was true in our generation, but it's more rampant today because we have more peak-performing people and we have a less nutritious diet.

If you look back in history, you see many of the great geniuses were almost bipolar. They would create something great, like a symphony, and then crash and take drugs and become alcoholic until they got enough nutrition from their diet (which was mineral rich at the time) to then rebuild their consciousness back up again. Just up and down. Mozart, for example.

Abraham Lincoln was bipolar. All the great inventors had obsessive-compulsive disorder. Their minds invented things because they couldn't let go. Basically they would get in these peak states and use up all the nutrition. Then the brain would start to malfunction until they got enough nutrition again. The key in making sure that we have a happy, fulfilled life is recognizing that nutrition is a big part of it.

ANTON: Exercise is another aspect. You're living proof of what you're teaching and what you've learned.

DR. JOHN GRAY: I walk my talk. People often ask if that's hard. When you read my books, you'll see that almost everything I recommend is pretty easy. It's just focusing on those things that are most important. For example, the first thing I did this morning was drink a glass of water with lemon and aloe vera in it. Those two ingredients are the most powerful detoxifying ingredients that exist on the planet—and they are so easy. I call it super cleanse. I've been doing it for thirty years. It's an amazingly simple formula.

Aloe vera has an ingredient in it that converts straight into glutathione, which detoxifies the body. Aloe vera alone goes a long way to correct problems with ADD and ADHD. Lemon goes right to the liver and stimulates the production of bile. Bile is what cleans out the liver, metabolizes fat and keeps your arteries clean. People who have heart attacks have no bile.

Some of these things have the simplest remedies. I have a naturopathic book that is a hundred years old, which I bought on eBay. It has over thirty pages devoted to lemon cures. When we shifted to drugs a hundred years ago, we forgot all these natural remedies that were available for people, and the irony is they're more important now than ever before—particularly the ones that have to do with cleansing and detoxifying, because we're living in such a toxic world.

Toxins surround us. The air we breathe has heavy metals in it. There are toxins in our drinking water. Pesticides are in the foods we eat. All of these things affect all aspects of our health. The biggest part of it affects our brain.

Also, if you don't have healthy gut function, you cannot make healthy brain chemicals. There's a very strong relationship between the gut and the brain.

You cannot achieve your full peak potential if, for example, you're experiencing sugar cravings. Sugar craving is one of the symptoms of too much yeast in your gut—candida. The candida wants to eat the sugar so you don't get enough for the brain. The brain needs it, but only tiny, tiny amounts. We find ourselves consuming more sugar because it isn't really getting to the brain. That's one aspect of it.

There are other aspects. Some resistance develops as well. When we're eating too much sugar, insulin resistance develops. That causes high blood sugar, which causes inflammation in the brain. Our memory becomes less, we aren't able to focus, and we don't have the same energy levels. Once you start having insulin resistance, you're on the way to diabetes. One out of three people in the country are in that position right now.

The simple konjac root from China can help reverse that. It's a very fibrous material you take with water before meals. It will prevent your blood sugar from spiking. It slowly releases the sugar into the system, so it starts taking away sugar cravings. More importantly, even if you're addicted to sugar, it doesn't have the negative effects, and gradually you lose that addiction because your blood sugar starts to balance again. It's in a product called PGX that you can find in stores. A huge amount of research is done on it, but very few people know about it.

ANTON: People have this strange conception that once they are millionaires all their problems will be solved.

DR. JOHN GRAY: When I see that one I'll tell you!

ANTON: When your body is functioning well, when your brain is functioning well, when your heart and your joy are functioning well, you don't have to force yourself to change how you eat. You feel so good that you eat better naturally. People are attracted to you, the world turns and comes to greet you. I'm sure you have found that to be true because you're like a magnet when people are around you.

DR. JOHN GRAY: Absolutely everything about success uses the yin and yang of success, the masculine and feminine side of success. We all have the masculine and feminine inside us. One aspect of success is competence, the ability to make a difference. That is the yang aspect, the masculine side of it: Can you solve the problem? Can you make the difference? Do you have something to offer?

I know so many people that are very competent, but they don't have the audience. They don't have the opportunity. They don't get the payment. I also know so many people who are completely incompetent, and yet they get the audience.

How do you get the audience? The audience is the yin side of it, the feminine side, the ability to attract success to you—that shining and the ability to draw it in. The key is to have both competence, something to offer, and also the ability to build trust and attract people in.

ANTON: You have done that in spades, because you're the best-selling author of all time.

DR. JOHN GRAY: In the nineties my book *Men Are From Mars, Women Are From Venus* was actually the biggest-selling book in the world.

I also wrote a book on success called *How To Get What You Want and Want What You Have*. I was talking about the subject you're talking about now. When you talk about good living, clarity, love, positive energy, looking good, and truly being authentic, who you are, you radiate that. That will attract people. Developing the skill of being authentic, you're able to make a difference in people's lives. That creates the foundation of a success that's a fulfilling success.

However, there are many, many people who are successful who do not have that. We see all these really corrupt, deceptive, misleading people. People who are angry or mean or upset or preach fear.

If you preach a lie, people will believe a lie. Bad people prey on people's fears, and they prey on people's hopes and dreams. People will tend to go for it and will be disappointed. The irony is they will do it again and again and again.

If you define success as money, you can certainly make money that way, but you can make money the other way too.

Your path, which I admire, is focusing on being a positive person, a healthy person, a vibrant person, with positive thinking and authenticity. These are the things that create success, that truly make a difference in the world and truly create fulfillment in your life.

ANTON: When we read your books like *Venus On Fire, Mars On Ice*, you have a way of communicating that is so gentle and clear and easy to understand. You're showing us the power in the simplicity of the things you have discovered.

I believe that you have arrived where you are, of course, because you have genuinely given people what they needed, and that is why you have endured so long. Was there ever a time in your life when you were struggling?

DR. JOHN GRAY: I have been on a path of personal development, of self-inquiry since I was nineteen years old. I became the youngest Transcendental Meditation (TM) teacher in America. They thought I was too young to do it. I said I have to do it, I want to do it. Forty years ago I was doing yoga videos, when video just came out, and teaching about fasting and cleansing. I have been doing this my whole life, but have I ever struggled with this?

My whole journey has been a process of success and struggle. Success and challenges. Without a doubt, there were some really hard times in my journey.

Now there are still challenges, there are always challenges, but part of our growth through these challenges is that we become stronger, and when we become stronger our goals become bigger and then our challenges become bigger.

There is an illusion that if you think right and your goals are aligned with helping the world that you're just going to get on the freeway and everything's going to be successful and you'll have support at every step of the way. It's actually the opposite of that. You find the support only when it's needed. The challenges are there and you pull forth greater bits of your potential. Your potential rises up through having to face the challenges.

There is an old Shakespeare quote, "Some men are born great" (and I think that's true of all of us), "some men achieve greatness" (and I think that's true of all of us), "and others have greatness thrust upon them." That is this third part of it. You fully manifest your potential, your greatness, when you face a challenge that pulls it forth. History is filled with ordinary people who were put in challenging circumstances and something great emerged from that.

You have this potential. You put yourself in circumstances, or circumstances just arise and greatness is thrust upon you. You're put in a situation where you have to perform and it happens.

The key to success for me has always been, make your commitment and then show up. It's always easy to say I'll do something. The harder part is in the follow-through. In the moment when you say, "I'll do it," you feel it's possible. That is the moment of inspiration. Then all you have to do from that point on is just keep showing up.

If I say I'm going to write a book, I just have to come and sit in front of the computer and start writing and just keep overcoming. If I say I'm going to put some course together, sometimes in the moment I go, "I don't know how I'm going to do it, but I swear I can do it." Then you just go and you show up. Quite often as you get closer to showing up, your mind is going, "I can't do it! What do I say? What do I do?" And you just say to yourself, "Hey! You said you're going to do it. Just go do it." You take the step.

On one level, 95% of all success is just showing up. Another level is being authentic so you can feel that feeling inside that says you can do it at the moment you make the commitment.

As you follow through it's perfectly normal to have insecurities and doubts, and often people misjudge their own ability to be successful because they have insecurities or doubts or uncertainties. I remember when I started out at nineteen years old becoming a Transcendental Meditation teacher. I was giving talks on it. My first talk I was so nervous and anxious, my knees shook and I fainted. It was that traumatic for me. But I really wanted to do it. I talked for years and years, and I would always have so much anxiety before the talks. But I would show up.

After a couple of years, I was going to stop. I thought, *This is crazy, maybe it's not right for me.* Then I read an article from John Lennon, who said that the reason the Beatles had stopped touring was they had so much anxiety before a concert. I thought, *If they have anxiety, and they were certainly doing what they were supposed to be doing, then if I have anxiety, it doesn't mean that I'm doing the wrong thing.*

However, it wasn't until later in my life that I realized that there are ways to remove anxiety. One of them is to continue showing up. The other is to learn how to process feelings. That is a lot of the gestalt work. In my book *How To Get What You Want*, I teach people journaling techniques where they can journal their feelings to get in touch with where they come from. Once you can go deeper into them, they tend to resolve. That is a whole journey in itself.

ANTON: One of the great gifts you give to all of us is to teach us to look at our own lives. We grew up in this TV era where so many people want to emulate what they see on the screen that they become blinded to the wonders and beauty of their own lives and their own potential. You help rescue people from that mindset.

DR. JOHN GRAY: Drama on TV is a good outlet. It's a good cathartic experience when you're watching a show but you know that it's fiction. That allows you to go through feelings and explore them—as long as long as you know inside that what you're watching is not true.

One of the big problems today (without going into any kind of conspiracy theories, which certainly have some validity in various degrees) is that so much of the news, so much of what we are lead to believe is true, is not really true.

The news is all the good things that are going on in the world as well as all the really bad things. What are the problems and what are the solutions and who are the people solving the problems? What is really going on in our lives? That truth is not revealed on TV. What you get over and over and over is this sort of false truth, and here's the key: whenever you believe something to be true that is not true, it disconnects you from who you are. You become more and more insecure, you become less connected to your authentic self—so it's important to realize that!

I remember in social studies in high school we would get four different newspapers and read a report from four different points of view (back in those days we read newspapers!). What you'd see is there was never one point of view that gave the whole picture, and quite often there was contradictory information. People of intensity cling to what they want to hear, what they want to believe, as opposed to what is real. Looking at what is real in a variety of different ways is what helps us to become more authentic and mobilizes within us the inherent potential to face a challenge and overcome it. It's only by facing the truth that more truth comes forth from us to help make the world a better place.

ANTON: And ultimately everything everyone does is based on one fundamental principle: we want to be happy. Yet, when we are being told what will make us happy, we listen to everything we hear in the media while forgetting to listen to our own hearts.

DR. JOHN GRAY: The big lie on TV is you're constantly seeing people eating junk food who are happy. It's just this amazing hypnosis that causes us to go out and buy. If you see someone eating something and they're happy and there's pretty music, your brain goes, "Oh, go towards that."

ANTON: People are really worried about having to give up their comfort food. What was really remarkable in my own life was when I changed the food I was eating and when my body came back to life, the things that were good for me ended up being what comforted me. It's just previously I had been trained to drink the Coca-Colas and smoke cigarettes.

DR. JOHN GRAY: I was raised on Coca-Cola and it literally caused ADD symptoms. What people don't realize is, high amounts of caffeine and the sugar in Coca-Cola will actually cause ADD and ADHD symptoms.

ANTON: I'm thrilled that you're so engaged with this topic, and I'd love to hear what you have to say about it.

DR. JOHN GRAY: Well, that's my next book. I would love to talk about it.

We are seeing a range of brain issues in our children, which we're calling ADHD, actually an autistic spectrum, including OCD, oversensitivity and ADD. Most women today have much higher blood sugars than ever before in history. What is now proven is that when a mother has high blood sugar, it directly affects the child. Some children are actually being born with diabetes, type 2 diabetes, and adult diabetes!

Because the mother has high blood sugar during the pregnancy, the baby will have high blood sugar during the pregnancy and develop insulin resistance. When your blood sugar is high it causes inflammation in the brain, and inflammation in the brain causes the inhibition of dopamine function, a shortage of which is connected to all those ADD, ADHD, autism, OCD, and oversensitivity symptoms that I just mentioned.

When you have inhibited dopamine function in the brain, due to either high stress in the mother or high blood sugar in the mother, it will interfere with appropriate and normal dopamine function in the child.

If your child who tends to be more sensitive has inhibited dopamine function, that child will become supersensitive, annoyed and irritated by everything. And they're supersensitive to their environment. Things bother them, upset them, they have allergies, and so forth.

For the naturally hyperactive child, or even an active type child, given an inhibited dopamine function, suddenly they are drawn to danger and to risk. They are always busy, always trying something new. If they were to stop, they would be bored to death, so they're always moving from one thing to another.

The more creative, intuitive children are very positive children, but they easily forget things. They make messes. They don't know where they left things. They can't finish their homework. It's hard to organize things, all because of inhibited dopamine function.

So what you get is this one symptom, inhibited dopamine function, causing all these other symptoms. When your dopamine levels are normal or the function is improved, that's when you can be focused on one thing at a time.

We see for women today, they're all experiencing female ADHD. They're hyperactive in their brains. In brain scans you can see that if a woman is stressed, she has eight times more blood flow in the emotional part of her brain, and her brain literally is thinking about all these different things. Women will report, "I'm feeling overwhelmed. I have so much to do! I have to do this and I have to do that!" And you kind of go, "Who says you have to do that?"

It's an inner compulsion due to inhibited dopamine function. They're not able to just relax and do one thing, then move to the next.

When men have inhibited dopamine function, they're unable to maintain comprehension. This is a real challenge. Nine out of ten children with learning difficulties are boys. Inhibited dopamine function prevents them from maintaining focus and continuing to comprehend something that is not really exciting or challenging. It's hard to hold their attention, and hard for them to have a normal conversation and comprehend what they're hearing, particularly with a woman. Their minds will become distracted with bigger problems that have to be solved. This is inhibited dopamine function. It's pervading our relationships and our children.

One simple solution is already here. You can correct it and cure it by taking away inflammation in the brain, and the simplest way to do that is grape seed extract. Double-blind studies have shown that grape seed extract and vitamin C have proven to be equally effective to Ritalin, the drug that doesn't cure anything but, for some children, can give symptomatic relief that ultimately makes the problem worse.

The grape seed extract is working, not because it's treating the symptom, but because it's actually removing the inflammation in the brain so that the dopamine function improves. Now you're curing as opposed to washing over the symptoms. Two studies have been done. Three hundred milligrams a day of grape seed extract and six hundred milligrams a day of vitamin C are enough to start correcting the brain. Amazing. I've seen it work.

ANTON: It's insane that we can sit in front of the television set watching what the pharmaceutical companies are selling us. We look at the people dancing through fields of flowers and the entire time we are hearing disclaimers about the disaster potential in that drug! What's going on here?

DR. JOHN GRAY: Thirty years ago, I was at the Karl Rogers Institute. We were learning about the subconscious mind and working with hypnotism and suggestion. Techniques were developed to get someone to go into a hypnotic trance and be open to suggestion. One of the techniques was to give two contradictory messages simultaneously to the brain. There would be two therapists, one whispering one thing on one side, while the other whispered something of the opposite meaning on the other side. Thus the person received two conflicting messages. The result was that people would go into a state of being open to suggestion.

Practically, one could conclude that if you get two messages that are contradictory, they negate each other so you feel like, "I don't know what the answer is so tell me." That is what happens when you see these drug commercials. These are all well tested. They spend hundreds of thousands, even millions of dollars on this stuff. If you show happy people and show negative symptoms at the same time, the brain just goes neutral and then you're open to suggestion, which, in this case, is to go talk to your doctor and ask him or her to give you these drugs.

The problem with all the drug commercials is that they are constantly creating this mindset that health is not normal and that we need to depend on drugs to live. That is such an illusion.

ANTON: If you cut your finger it doesn't matter what you think or do. Your finger heals itself. Our bodies are constantly building themselves to be the best they can be, and we are so often throwing as much garbage as we can into them to challenge them. It's surprising that they can keep up with us at all.

DR. JOHN GRAY: The body is a miracle, and your example is so perfect: just observe what happens when you have a little cut. It's amazing. We have nothing to do with it; it happens automatically. Now, we can interfere with that process. That's the thing we need to know. There are ways to prevent the body from doing what it's naturally designed to do.

One of the ways we interfere with that process is using fertilizers to grow food, food that doesn't have all the minerals in order to activate the enzymes to digest that food. Not getting enough minerals is one way we're interfering with that process.

We're breathing air that has mercury in it floating over to our country from the coal mines in China. Seven times more comes from China now than even in America. The air is toxic. These heavy metals get into the body, and the body was never designed to get rid of them. It can get rid of stuff, but it's not so easy to do. So we need to help the body get rid of it.

Back in the oldest days, Hippocrates said, "Let food be thy medicine." If there is a challenge to the body, food can help cure it.

One of the major modalities that alternative doctors are using is giving children shots of glutathione. In many cases autistic children are getting great reversals due to taking shots of glutathione. I've helped so many parents with their children by just giving them straight aloe vera instead of the shots. Aloe vera is the ultimate nutritional substance for producing glutathione, which helps the brain release heavy metals.

You can grow a four-dollar aloe vera plant in your garden. Just start growing them and then start re-growing them. Cut off about a one-inch cube of the gel, which is inside the leaf, and put that in some water or a blended shake. Now you have something that is going to help your child more than anything. Put in some lemon and you've got double the benefit.

ANTON: You mentioned children, but on the other end of the spectrum are older people with memory problems.

DR. JOHN GRAY: What they're finding with Alzheimer's is that it's Diabetes III. Your brain has an inability to absorb sugar after a while. Just as with diabetes, you have high blood sugar because your body is not absorbing the sugar. When you have high blood sugar in your brain, your brain is not absorbing it and you get Alzheimer's.

We want to come back to practical ways that we can start balancing blood sugar in our lives so we don't have those problems. Things we can do right now. For memory, one of the latest researches shows that methylfolate is helping tremendously. The reason for this is that folic acid is something that has to convert into folate in order to make brain chemicals. But due to poor gut health we are unable to convert the folic acid in our food into folate.

Methylfolate is already processed for you, since you can't do it yourself. For many people this is reversing their Alzheimer's symptoms. The drug companies would just love to patent it. Now they're calling it medical food so that they can write prescriptions for it. Fortunately, it's still available in health food stores.

There are all these natural vitamins that are supposed to be in our food, but they're just not there or we're not able to extract them from our food. But one thing I've found to be helpful is to make an easy-to-digest shake with undenatured whey and casein protein, at least for a while, to get kids back on track—and anybody whose brain is not functioning optimally.

The key is digestion. Taking enzymes is one thing, but any kind of dairy product that has been processed with heat is indigestible, so they now have "undenatured," which means it's not processed with heat. It's raw in a sense. Whey protein and casein are very good for making brain chemicals right away.

Put into that some chia seed or flaxseed, or take some fish oils on the side. You need some Omega-3. You need some easy-to-digest protein and a little bit of molasses. Molasses is a sweetener that is really healthy because it's rich in minerals. Put in some fruit, a teaspoon or two of coconut oil, and you've got a great smoothie!

I use this smoothie for kids with ADD symptoms and, if they can get along with the mineral supplement, in a week, most of their symptoms are gone. It's amazing how quickly things can turn around if we have easy-to-digest protein and fat.

There is a mineral called lithium and, unfortunately, it has been stolen by the drug industry and made into a drug that has serious side effects. They give it in a form that doesn't really work and thus have to give it in high doses for it to have any good effect—then it has negative side-effects over time.

What most people don't know is that the same mineral, lithium, is in our food, and small doses of lithium are now missing from our food. We need small doses and in a form that will get to the brain, so there is a product called lithium orotate (not lithium carbonate, which is what doctors give). This is available over the counter.

Lithium orotate is necessary to make the brain chemical seratonin. When we eat sugar we deplete our body of lithium, so people today need lithium orotate more than ever. Just 4.5 milligrams. A tiny, tiny bit. There are no side effects ever reported, and no possibility of side effects. Instantly, for many people, depression goes away, as does OCD. When you get the feeling that your partner irritates you and annoys you, you just take one tiny little capsule of lithium orotate and suddenly you've forgotten what was bothering you and you move on because your brain doesn't loop over those things again and again and again.

ANTON: I recommend all your books to anybody who hasn't read them, especially *Venus On Fire, Mars On Ice*, which is kind of an update of the original *Men Are From Mars, Women Are From Venus*. Because as you mentioned, so many things happen in our lives, especially between men and women, that are so simple to adapt to, ways to adjust our behaviors and our diets so that things we think are torturing us, things that actually lead to divorce, suddenly evaporate, just from having knowledge of changes within our power to make. In this politically correct environment we're afraid to say men are like this, women are like that, but they're different.

DR. JOHN GRAY: We are so different, and one insight can make a world of difference. Just this one insight has saved thousands of marriages:

At the end of the day men go to their caves. Many men just want to be alone. They want to relax and forget everything. They just want to do something that doesn't have to do with solving anybody else's problems.

Women will come home from work and they'll feel overwhelmed with everything that has to go on in a house, and they're looking at him happily sitting on the couch and their brain says, "Why does he sit there? Doesn't he care? Doesn't he love me? Does he expect me to do everything?"

Her brain is making up things that are not true: assuming that he doesn't love her, he doesn't care, she is not important, the romance has gone. And then when he actually does get up from the couch he's faced with this woman who's basically kind of annoyed and irritated with him. You go to any indigenous tribe, you will see that at the end of the day men's brains literally turn off. We have an off switch. We relax.

Women's brains never turn off. It's part of the nurturing hormone that women have, which keeps their brain going all the time. Thank goodness.

In *Venus On Fire, Mars On Ice* I show the research that explains the difference in our brains and our hormones. The hormone that men need to survive and thrive is testosterone. Men need thirty times more testosterone in their body than women. The number one cause of heart attacks in men is low testosterone.

So a man rebuilds his testosterone by simply lowering his stress or relaxing his muscles. That's an imperative in his body to survive. He literally becomes tired and exhausted and must sit down in order to rebuild those muscles.

Women become tired and exhausted and their brain just speeds up and says there is more and more to do. So in my book I teach women how they can cope with stress, but also why he's sitting on the couch—one of the most important ways for men to cope with stress.

Then, the second thing is how to motivate him off the couch when he's done, because usually he will sit around having a good time, not realizing that she needs some help. So how to get that help is a new lesson, because women never expected that from men in the past. But women today have a whole new lifestyle, and men don't know what to do. Women don't know what to do.

We all need dance steps to dance to the new music that we're living in.

SIZING UP YOUR BRAIN

The health of your brain is at the foundation of
everything that you are and hope to become.

Dr. Daniel Amen is a physician, child and adult psychiatrist, and leading specialist in brain imaging. His company is the world leader in applying brain imaging science to clinical practice, with the world's largest database of functional brain scans related to psychiatric medicine. He is a distinguished fellow of the American Psychiatric Association and the CEO and Medical Director of the Amen Clinics, located in Newport Beach, San Francisco; Bellevue, Washington; and Reston, Virginia. His clinics have seen patients from ninety countries.

Dr. Amen is also a speaker and prolific author, contributing to countless professional articles and twenty-eight books, including the *New York Times* best sellers *Change Your Brain, Change Your Life* and *Magnificent Mind at Any Age*. Many of his books include some of the most compelling titles of our time, such as *Healing ADD, Healing the Hardware of the Soul, Making a Good Brain Great*, and *The Brain in Love*. He is also the co-author of *Healing Anxiety and Depression* and *Preventing Alzheimer's*. He has written and produced four recent blockbuster fund-raising shows for public television, which raised more than $30 million, and despite the whirlwind of activity that defines his rich and busy life, he remains a warm and dedicated family man.

ANTON: You have so many books that touch on so many different aspects of our lives. After seeing you at Jim Kwik's Superhuman You seminar in San Diego, it became clear that good brain health isn't just about being able to think more quickly and clearly or not becoming forgetful or developing Alzheimer's as we age—it's really the foundation for everything in our lives.

You have a way of measuring and graphically representing the health of our brain.

DANIEL AMEN: We do a study at the Amen Clinics called Brain SPECT Imaging. SPECT looks at blood flow and activity. It's a very sophisticated look at brain function. It's actually pretty easy to understand, because we look for areas of the brain that work well, areas of the brain that are low in activity, and areas of the brain that are high in activity. If we see too little or too much activity, our job becomes balancing the brain. Your brain is involved in everything you do, how you think and feel and act, and how you get along with everybody. So many new insights come from the brain imaging work that we do.

ANTON: You are fifty-seven and you're in great shape. You don't look your age. More and more these days we hear that we no longer have to accept the declines we generally attribute to aging. Through your SPECT scans and other tests, you can find what's responsible for our deterioration and then respond to it.

DANIEL AMEN: I've written a book called *Use Your Brain To Change Your Age*. What happens to the brain over time is it becomes less and less active. As your body undergoes an aging process, the same thing goes on in your brain. But it doesn't have to if you're smart about it.

You can make incredible differences in your life and the lives of others when you do the right thing to enhance brain function. The first thing people have to understand is that they really need, at an emotional level, to *want* to have a better brain, so they will do things that are smarter for their brain.

People tend to have no love, honor or respect for the brain. In our society we let children hit soccer balls with their heads, we cheer at ultimate fighting matches, and we feed our brains non-stop with bad food. Your brain uses 25% of the energy that you feed your body! If you're eating only fast food, you're only going to have a fast-food mind. Avoid eating artificial diets and artificial sweeteners and toxic food. You cannot consume bad things and expect to think right. Eating for your brain is absolutely critical to being the best you that you can be.

ANTON: What does sugar do to us from the brain's point of view?

DANIEL AMEN: It increases inflammation. Inflammation where your body becomes really on fire shrinks your brain. Inflammation is a very bad thing unless it's in response to a quick fix in your body, like an injured knee. But chronic inflammation ages your organs. It also increases erratic brain cell firing. You don't want that. You want to have good judgment, and thoughtfulness.

Sugar is clearly addictive. There was a study where they gave rats cocaine. The rats really liked the cocaine. Then they gave the same rats sugar. They *really* liked the sugar. Then they gave them a choice, and the rats went after the sugar! We have to be very careful.

People say, I can't get over my sugar craving. Of course you can! Just stop it for two weeks and those sugar cravings will go away. It's just like an addiction. If you were an alcoholic we wouldn't tell you that you should have cheat days. How stupid is that? Or if you are a sex addict or you smoke cigarettes, we don't allow cheat days for those, because we know it will cause people to relapse. But people say, everything in moderation, and I say no, that's a bad idea when it comes to addiction. That's just a lie to keep all the bad habits going that you've done over the years. And it gets you hooked back in.

Eating in the way that we talk about it in our program is about abundance, not about deprivation. It's just abundance with things that serve you rather than things that steal from you.

ANTON: We think of ourselves as spirits, but the spirit would be nothing if it couldn't be expressed through a healthy brain.

DANIEL AMEN: It's your brain that actually receives your spirit and integrates your spirit. We've done 70,000 brain scans over the last twenty years, and one of the most interesting things I've found is that when your brain is better balanced, you're more loving, you're more thoughtful, you have better relationships, and you're better at managing your money. Good brain health is reflected in everything you do. It's very exciting, because we can prove it.

We are finishing the world's largest brain imaging study on retired NFL players. These are people who've been hit on the head thousands of times, and when they come to us they often have very damaged brains. When we put them on our program, we can see their brains get better! How exciting is that, to be able to take a brain that's troubled and make it better?

Most people haven't been hit in the head thousands of times, and if they get on a brain-smart program, which isn't difficult, they can dramatically improve the health of their brain. It's as simple as the game I play with my eight year old—this is good for my brain, this is bad for my brain. You want to avoid things that hurt your brain. You want to do things that help your brain, and we tell you exactly what you can do.

ANTON: You're doing a lot of stuff with kids. You and your son-in-law, Jesse, developed a high school program about making a good brain.

DANIEL AMEN: A number of years ago I gave a lecture at the Orange County Department of Education here in Southern California. I thought, *We need to be teaching these kids about brain health.* We're teaching them algebra, which they're not going to use very much, and we're teaching them history, which they may never think about again. I thought we should teach them something that's really practical, such as how to love and take care of their brains.

The administrator of the school district asked if we would help them with this, so I developed a twelve-week course for high school students. We teach kids how to optimize brain function and how to make a good brain great. It is now in forty-two states and seven countries. My son-in-law, Jesse, has taught it on multiple occasions and is actually studying its effect on teenagers. We're very excited. It extends the message that your brain controls everything you do. When your brain works right, you work right. When your brain has trouble, you have trouble in your life.

I have a course for corporations called High Performance Brain, and I'm doing this incredibly cool program at Saddleback Church, one of the largest churches in the world, about getting the world healthy through churches. I got so angry with my own church because the food they served was so bad—I wondered if they were trying to send people to heaven early! It really irritated me. Save them, then kill them with bad food!

I thought, *Come on, you guys, your body is the temple of the Holy Spirit. The New Testament says that. You're treating your bodies like you live in the ghetto, when we really need to get more serious about this wonderful gift that's been given to us. Our body. Treat it with reverence.* I like to say, If you had a million dollar race horse, would you ever feed it junk food? Only if you were an idiot! And you are worth so much more.

ANTON: There was a time in your life when you ate the more traditional American food. What made you change?

DANIEL AMEN: When I learned about the "dinosaur syndrome," I changed dramatically. We just published two studies that show that as your weight goes up, the actual size and function of your brain go down!

ANTON: The size of your brain actually changes.

DANIEL AMEN: It shrinks. As your weight goes up, the size and function of your brain go down. It's a fact. Information causes you to change your behavior. When I read that study, I lost thirty pounds. I thought, *I'm not having a smaller brain!* You know, in my line of work, brain size matters.

A whole school of other studies came out saying exactly the same thing. So being overweight or obese is bad for your cognitive function.

Many people know Pastor Rick Warren, the author of *The Purpose Driven Life*, which was the world's best-selling book four years in a row. He was very obese when I first met him. When I got involved with his church he said, "Getting healthy for my heart just never did anything for me; I never could relate to it. And to live longer? I'm going to heaven. Why would I care about living longer? And to be sexier?

Look at me. I'm already sexy. But when I heard I was going to lose my mind, that made me pay attention! My mind is my influence, it's what I do my mission in life with, and having a mind that doesn't work—now that would not do."

ANTON: Besides the SPECT scans, are there specific things you can measure to indicate someone's brain health?

DANIEL AMEN: Everybody should know their numbers. They should know their Vitamin D level, for example, because when Vitamin D levels are low, people are hungry all the time; optimizing that level in your brain can actually turn down your appetite and give you more control. Know your thyroid and your testosterone, your blood sugar level, and your blood pressure. All these numbers are really important to know, because if they're off, they could be interfering with you getting well.

You want to eat only high quality food. It's never just *eat less, exercise more*. Exercise is really important, but there's so much more to all of this. What we found looking at these brain scans is that one size doesn't fit everybody. There are many different kinds of brains. Compulsive brains, impulsive brains, impulsive-compulsive brains, sad brains, anxious brains. Knowing your type of brain is really important so that you get away from this one-treatment-fits-everybody approach.

ANTON: Testosterone and hormone levels keep coming up again and again when we talk about food. Why are they so important in our lives?

DANIEL AMEN: Testosterone is the hormone that gives us our libido and determines how interested we are in sex. It also helps build muscle, which affects our metabolism, and it's involved in memory and mood, for men and for women. When testosterone levels are low, people can get depressed, they can be stupid, they don't care about sex, and they can't build muscle.

ANTON: There is often a prudish view of our sex drive in this country, but a healthy libido is actually a reflection of many other aspects of our health and functionality. When you tied memory to testosterone, you really caught my attention. As we're now living longer and longer lives, it's frightening to think of being here but not being ourselves, of losing our minds.

DANIEL AMEN: A healthy testosterone level is important, but don't just go out and get a testosterone shot. It's not the first thing you should turn to when you think, I have a problem; let me take a pill for every ill. Think *skills,* not *pills*. Ask yourself, "What are the natural ways I can boost my hormone levels and boost my brain?" You can raise your own testosterone through simple lifestyle interventions.

I've never taken a testosterone precursor or a testosterone charge, and my levels are excellent. This is in large part because I don't eat sugar any more. Sugar drops your testosterone level. So now I think of sugar as the enemy.

ANTON: Imagine what a huge impact it would have if everything that had sugar in it had to carry a warning label that said, "Warning: sugar lowers your testosterone!"

DANIEL AMEN: I have a beautiful wife whom I'm totally in love with. I don't want to have a low libido. It will make her feel bad. I also like working out, and I like having muscle on my body. Working out builds testosterone, and having a great diet can build testosterone. Why would I do something that interferes with my own goal?

ANTON: Are SPECT scans something within reach of everyone?

DANIEL AMEN: A person has many options at my clinics, from getting a scan to a full evaluation. You can also just get one of my books or do the free evaluation on my website. In the end, you want to ask yourself what the cost is if you *don't* have an optimized brain? Too often, we spend money frivolously when we should focus on the things that are really, really important, like eating only whole, high quality foods.

Ask yourself, "What's the value that I put on the health of my brain? I'm less likely to get fired from my job if my brain works right and less likely to get divorced. I am more likely to live a long, healthy, vibrant life with a healthy brain." That's very valuable.

It's always more expensive to be sick than it is to do the right things to be healthy.

MEMORY IS LIFE

The Mediterranean Diet can help avoid Alzheimer's and promote longevity. Education toward awareness is key in helping people adapt to new behaviors that are sustainable.

The number of successful and innovative health systems that Dr. Arnold Bresky has designed and implemented over the decades is enough to fill a catalog on its own. His experience in the medical field has taken him from obstetrician/gynecologist to Alzheimer's and senior care specialist.

He has taught natural medicine to mothers, brought music and humor into the delivery room, opened the first nationally-accredited and state-licensed free-standing birth clinic, and helped popularize the Bradley method of natural childbirth, which revolutionized childbirth by bringing husbands into the delivery room, a practice that is commonplace today.

In 1978, Dr. Bresky helped lay the ground work to launch the wellness movement when he joined a handful of progressive physicians and leaders at the first annual National Wellness Conference held by the University of Wisconsin-Stevens Point.

After many years of being involved in wellness and preventive medicine, owning a hospital, running a hospice-care unit, and realizing that many of the babies he was delivering would live to be more than ninety years old, Dr. Bresky became acutely aware of the need to focus on healthful programs for an aging population.

Dr. Bresky created comprehensive programs for eating and physical exercise, along with mentally stimulating and social activities, including the development of his highly successful Brain Tune Up program. Seniors responded well to his blend of spiritual, mental and wellness therapies, which resulted in improved memory, focus, concentration and attention. Even his dementia patients started to recognize their surroundings and recall recent experiences.

ANTON: Dr. Bresky, you have really rocked the world with your innovative views and approach to health care through the last four decades, including your perspective on brain health and longevity based on years of scientific research and experience.

DR. ARNOLD BRESKY: I was one of the first doctors to join the American Holistic Medical Association. I believe that we are body, mind and soul. Hippocrates, the godfather of medicine said, "Let food be your medicine."

Before medical school I ate just like everybody else. Once I went to medical school and learned how we have to keep our cells and tissues healthy, I stopped eating as much junk food, highly salted food, and sugar.

It was my medical background that helped me in this because, as an internal medical student, of all the patients I had to take care of, 95% were there because of something that had to do with their lifestyle, with exercise and food.

That was a big turning point for me. I decided I wanted a sense of mastery in my life. I didn't need someone else to give me pills and surgery. I knew that I had to exercise every day and eat properly.

Many of today's babies are going to live to be 90 or 100. So I shifted my focus to health and quality of life, and I became an expert on aging.

It became very clear to me that two biomarkers of aging are the brain and the immune system. I want to use food to help both of those organ systems, because that's what aging is about. Over 80% of our immune system lives in our intestinal tract, so if we don't eat the right food and we're under tremendous stress, our immune system is going to fail and we're going to have chronic inflammatory diseases.

For the brain, I started eating the Mediterranean Diet because what is good for your heart is good for your brain.

We have to keep our blood vessels open to get sugar and oxygen to our brain cells and allow the blood to remove toxins. Our lives are filled with toxins today because of the air and the topsoil, so I changed my eating habits. It's made me a more successful and better physician.

I am a scientist. I marry hope to science. I read almost every journal there is about the brain and the immune system and so, when I speak to the public or to hospitals and doctors, I quote the studies that have been done to prove what I'm saying. That's why Medicare covers my Brain Tune Up program (a method of development of cognitive skills), because it's all based on proven science.

ANTON: Medicare covering your program was a big bridge to cross.

DR. ARNOLD BRESKY: Very big. But I have big feet. I try to get people off medication as much as possible.

ANTON: You have found a way to optimize how our bodies work and live without these pills. As a matter of fact, pill popping is probably one of the great dangers to our society.

DR. ARNOLD BRESKY: There is no question about it. I am an integrated doctor, which means I believe pills and surgery are necessary, but not sufficient. Especially as we age. People have to learn the tools they need to preserve their bodies. The government is not going to help you. The medical system is not going to help you. And the pharmaceutical company is not going to help you. There is only one person who is going to help you—and that's you.

The new health care system is going to have to be based on self-care. Knowledge is power, and ignorance is too expensive. So when I'm not seeing patients or writing a book, I spend all my free time educating the public about what they can do to preserve their health, because there are going to be no brain transplants in the future.

I have to help you change your behavior so you will not suffer from chronic inflammatory disease, and the Mediterranean Diet is the key. It has been proven over and over again that if you eat the Mediterranean Diet you lower your risk of Alzheimer's by 40%. Columbia University Medical School just published the study proving that.

I spend as much time on the *why* as on the recipes. Once people understand the why, they will stay with the behavior.

The Mediterranean Diet includes fresh foods like olives, extra virgin olive oil, as many fruits and vegetables as you can, nuts, whole wheat bread, poultry and fish. I even promote red wine because there is resveratrol in it, which is excellent for the brain. It's an antioxidant and anti-inflammatory. One five-ounce glass of red wine is excellent for the brain.

We also promote exercise. The Mediterranean Diet is based on exercise. If you go to Italy or Greece you will see that, while they are eating, the people are having fun and talking and dancing. This works. They have a very low incidence of heart disease and brain disease in and around those countries.

ANTON: And they are not married to their cars like we are. Italian food is actually food that is part of the environment where they live. It's not some concoction made with heart-stopping layers of processed cheese, like what we call Italian food in America.

DR. ARNOLD BRESKY: Exactly. They eat right off the land. If they want to have an apple they walk to get the apple that is not contaminated by pesticides and everything else, like ours are. Theirs is the lifestyle we have to follow because we are going to live to be 90 to 100.

But, it's not how long we live, it's how well we live.

And memory is life.

I teach people that every day. Without memory you have no past. Without memory you have no context for the present, and without memory, you cannot plan for the future. We have to protect our memory.

ANTON: That's a very moving statement to hear you make, because it is so tragic to see people lose themselves to dementia. We have seen this all too often in the people we touch in our personal lives. About two years ago I could still have conversations with one of my best friends who had Alzheimer's, but one day she didn't know who I was, and she hasn't known since.

DR. ARNOLD BRESKY: My whole program is about brain wellness, which is founded on preventive medicine. We have to do preventive medicine.

In 1978 a group of physicians met in Lacrosse, Wisconsin, and we combined holistic medicine with preventive medicine and came up with the wellness movement. I was one of the doctors who pioneered the wellness movement in America.

ANTON: There are some people that twitch when you say *holistic* because they don't quite understand what that word means.

DR. ARNOLD BRESKY: Twenty-five hundred years ago, the Greek philosophers Socrates, Plato and Aristotle said the human being is a body, mind and soul and we have to keep all three healthy if we are going to have good quality of life. Holistic simply means you consider all the aspects together as a whole unit and not as separate aspects of your being.

We now have mind/body medicine.

Twenty-five years ago, in his book *The Relaxation Response,* Dr. Herbert Benson, out of Harvard University, showed that how we think is how our brain changes. Our belief system affects how our brains work and how our immune systems work. Some people think holistic is magical thinking. I am talking about very rigorous science based on quantum physics.

I am a student of quantum physics and, believe it or not, all you and I are is vibrating energy. Think about what I just said. That's the basis of my program: to keep a vibrating energy in balance.

My goal is to get people to protect their brains, and one of the ways is the way they eat. Whatever we do or do not put into our GI tract is who we are.

Every cell in our body is using the nutrients, the minerals, everything that's in our food. So if we eat whole foods, foods that are grown on trees or in earth that is not contaminated by pesticides, our bodies will stay healthier, because we don't have to spend our whole day detoxifying our body from food that we should not have eaten.

We all know what we shouldn't eat. The problem is everyone wants a quick fix, they want the sugar and salt tastes. But in the long run they are going to suffer medically.

MINDFUL PRESENCE

*To have a quick and clear mind, you must be mindful of
what you put in your body. Always be present.
Become aware of what serves you and what doesn't.*

Jim Kwik jokes about the implications his name bears in the life of a speed-reading and memory expert! For two decades, Jim has been a widely sought-after keynote speaker, corporate trainer, business strategist, and advisor to top universities, celebrity authors, and companies in over sixty countries. He has shared the stage with global thought leaders such as Richard Branson and the Dalai Lama. He is the visionary behind Kwik Learning and has taught speed-reading, memory improvement and accelerated learning to thousands of individuals and organizations.

Jim says, "Your two greatest wealth assets are already inside you, in your head and heart. We weren't shown how to use them in school, and neither one comes with an owner's manual, but when you learn to unlock more of their potential, you can make both a dollar *and* a difference. You can live the life you desire and deserve and in the process, help those around you to do the same." Jim's optimism and great humility are a pleasant surprise from a man of his genius and abilities.

JIM KWIK: Eating is so visceral. It's something we do every single day. It's something we need for survival, but then it's also something that brings so much joy and so much flavor to life!

One of my attitudes towards business and towards life, even food, is I'm always curious. For me life is all about lifelong learning. You can learn from everything and everyone—everyone has something to teach me. A parallel for my food is, I consider life in this universe to be like the most amazing all-you-can-eat buffet! My mind, just like my body, is hungry for nutrients and different flavors.

But there's a connection. When people see me on stage, and they see me memorize a roomful of people's names or a list of random numbers or a deck of cards or what have you, I always tell them there are strategies there, such as the strategy of what you put in your body.

The other thing is, I like being present. I think one of the keys to success in life and a certain level of harmony is to be really present in life. In your business, in your relationships. Even when they're reading something, so many people's minds get distracted. And too often people get distracted when they eat. They think eating is just one of the things they do, and so they turn off and distract themselves from their food and the process of eating. They have to have a television on, or they eat very quickly.

I think it's important to be present and mindful when you're eating and to savor everything, really take it in and be present with the food and the people around you at the table.

ANTON: You are so easy to communicate with, and your mind is astoundingly sharp. Your life must benefit from that. A car wouldn't run if you poured maple syrup in the gas tank; it just isn't what the car needs to run well. Our bodies, of course, want certain things that make them run better.

Was there ever a time in your life when you ate differently than you do now?

JIM KWIK: I grew up with a standard American diet, eating fast food and stuff like that, but I have always loved to eat. I used to be a maniac about desserts. People that knew me knew I really loved my sweets. My diet changed and evolved when I got into college; I started to become more conscious about what I put in my body. I realized that, literally, *what I eat becomes me*. You are what you eat.

I started a path of vegetarianism for different reasons while I was in college, but when I start getting into speed-reading and how to improve your memory, how to remember names and faces, and how to stave off senior moments and life pauses, I found out that a lot of geniuses throughout time had had diets primarily of vegetables. People like Einstein and Leonardo Da Vinci.

I ate a vegetarian diet for a good fifteen years and eventually began eating some raw foods. Eleven years ago I met David Wolfe, who is a dear friend of mine, and he started me on superfoods and herbs. Now I'm a little bit more flexible. I don't subscribe to any one way or any one dogma.

We travel a lot with what we do, and I like to try new things. We just got back from the Amazon rainforest, where we got to spend some time with an indigenous tribe. We actually made contact as the first Westerners that they had connected with. It was amazing! It was a small village of seven families, and we completely adopted their diet. It's very natural, very organic. I don't mean organic as in *without pesticides* and such. Organic in that it just came very easily, was naturally part of their world.

One of the biggest things I believe as a result of my experience after seventeen years of teaching people to improve their memory, how to read faster, how to think clearer, is that diet plays a huge role. People talk about ADD and ADHD, and there is a huge epidemic with diabetes. I am not a medical doctor, but when I used to work with children I noticed changes when they changed their diet.

ANTON: There is such an interest and awareness now about the two extremes: children being diagnosed with ADHD and seniors confronting Alzheimer's. What you are doing helps stave off some of that development. Scientifically, we are seeing that the behaviors that you help people joyfully learn strengthen the mind so that the brain can physiologically survive, even thrive, as it ages.

JIM KWIK: People know that there is a mind/body connection. Your *thoughts* affect your body. More and more research is showing that how you treat your body, what you put into your body, affects your mind and your brain. Your brain is only 2-3% of your total body weight, and yet it uses a lot more nutrients than that, a lot more oxygen, a lot more water, and it needs these things. It needs certain vitamins and minerals to be able to perform optimally.

If you are an athlete and you want to be in peak physical condition, you have to do your workouts and exercise for fitness, but you also have to give your body the raw materials it needs to be able to perform at that optimal level. Our brains are certainly no different. The good thing about what we know through studies is that, even though you grow older you can grow better in some ways. There are new ideas and principles coming out like neurogenesis. Neuroplasticity is saying that even as you grow older, you can create more brain cells and you can create more connections. But it's "use it or lose it."

We give people strategies and exercises to improve their brains. I love talking to people like you who are experts about the things you put in your body that are not only good for you but also taste good, that you prepare in creative ways. Because that level of passion, that level of purpose really affects your performance.

ANTON: When you're talking to athletes, diet isn't a big surprise. But when you're talking to top level executives and companies that want their offices to run smoother, their businesses to run smoother, does diet come into the conversation?

JIM KWIK: It does. With my background I don't focus so much on nutrition, because I'm not a registered dietician or nutritionist or medical doctor, but people ask me how I treat my body. Without a doubt, people who are more physically active have stronger brains. They do better at mental acuity tests. I also know what happens when we don't treat our bodies well, such as when we drink too much alcohol. Obviously that affects our brains, but it's no different than eating a really big, fatty meal. How do we feel afterwards? We don't have energy. Our brains need energy, but we know that digestion is one of the biggest energy drains in our system.

ANTON: What I love about talking with you, Jim, is that you make room for exception. You lead your life applying certain general principles, but you are not intimidating yourself and other people into making progress. I think that's why it's such a joyful experience being around you. You address people in a way that makes room for them to learn something new but not feel like "This is the only way. I have to do it Jim's way." It's no wonder you're so persuasive and powerful in your interactions with other people.

JIM KWIK: Everyone is a bio individual, and people find what works best for them. Ultimately, you are the expert. You could try different things, step into a common-sense corner of your brain, for example, and ask, "Does this work for me?" When you eat too much or you eat poorly, you feel it and your brain starts to slow down. You start to have these little memory lapses, and you wonder what's happening. It comes down to the habits of how we're treating ourselves on a daily basis.

I would say, have fun with it. Don't overcomplicate it. There is an elegant way of approaching food. For me personally, it's getting rid of as much as possible of the bad stuff that doesn't serve me, that doesn't give me a higher level of vibration or higher level of authenticity. I would also say, while we're getting rid of some of the bad stuff, add more of the good stuff, as we would in business and in our relationships. You want to be around positive people. You want to get the right people on the bus and the wrong people off the bus. Then you can drive that bus together on a wonderful journey.

I think it's important to stand guard to our brains and our bodies. We need to be careful what goes into our *minds* in terms of what's positive and what's negative, what serves us and what doesn't. We must also stand guard to what goes into our mouths. What has high-vibration nutrients that are actually good raw materials that can help to quench us—not just our bodies, but also our souls, our hearts.

Food is very intimate. It's something that you're putting into your body, and it literally is becoming more of who you are. Stay away from the things that we know don't serve us, whether it's toxins or refined, processed foods, sugars and chemicals, and maybe not too much fried food. Really focus on nature. When I'm thinking about health, I'm thinking about food, I'm thinking about nutrients that have vitamins and minerals and herbs and enzymes, I'm thinking about water and air and light and exercise and sleep and rest and loving relationships.

We were talking about the brain and learning. Your gut is your second brain. You have more nerve cells there than anywhere in your body, outside your own brain. Your gut has an intelligence, and you want to make sure that what you're putting in there really serves you. Be present. Be mindful with your eating, chewing slowly and savoring your food, and making sure you have everything you need. I make sure I have my fruits, my vegetables, lots of different colors—and I have fun with it.

We go to different restaurants, and all of us have different experiences with the foods. My favorite food comes from home-cooked meals from my family—especially my mother and fiancée, because then it has my favorite ingredients, including the love that comes from it. When you put a lot of love in the preparation of your cuisine, it comes through.

I love showing people how to unlock and unleash the genius that everybody has inside them. We're just not taught how to do that in this society, much as we're not taught how to think about how to manage the food and money in our lives. They are such important things, yet they're neglected in today's school systems.

I believe at any moment in time an idea can change your life when it's acted on. One step in another direction completely changes your destination and your destiny. That's why I have such a deep appreciation for what you're doing and all the other thought leaders and authors that you're spending time with. You're here because you're looking to grow, and you're looking to be able to give more to the people around you, to your family, to your coworkers, to your friends. And, you know, the only way to do that is to grow more yourself.

II.

FOREVER YOUNG

FOREVER YOUNG

Your blood tells many stories. Diet dramatically affects how you look and feel and can make you clearer, happier and more energetic in your approach to living a long and fulfilling life.

Dr. Nick Delgado is widely recognized as one of the foremost authorities on anti-aging and a man who walks his talk. At age fifty-three he broke the strength endurance world record for the most pounds lifted in a single hour (50,640 pounds). Nick is the author of ten books and a major contributing author to *Anti-Aging Clinical Protocols* published by the American Academy of Anti-Aging Medicine (A4M). He has appeared on hundreds of radio and television talk shows and has received global fame from sold-out speaking events around the world.

Nick is involved in high-integrity stem-cell research. His Delgado Protocol profiles your exact blood chemistry to provide lifestyle, food and all-natural supplement guidelines designed specifically for you to achieve your ultimate potential in regaining and surpassing the biological and mental qualities of your youth. He himself plans to soar past the age of 100 with his mind and his libido intact.

ANTON: You travel all around the world teaching people what you've discovered from your research.

NICK DELGADO: As a diplomat of the American Academy of Anti-Aging Medicine, I have been fortunate to speak in South Africa, Germany, China, Canada, and Spain. Virtually all major countries have invited me to speak about anti-aging and how to master the aging process.

With every passing decade of age, people are at increasing risk to develop heart attacks, strokes, diabetes and cancer. Even young people are not exempt. The incidence of autism in young people, for example, is at a record high now, and we are seeing problems of brain damage in these children.

It took me thirty years of research, review, study, and application working with doctors, training them in various protocols and then getting the very valuable feedback of test results, both laboratory and physical. During that time we saw increased vitality and the amelioration of many symptoms.

I was the director of the Nathan Pritikin Better Health Program for several years. I worked with Tony Robbins at Master University as one of the master teachers on health, nutrition and education.

For these last thirty years, I have been giving certification courses to train doctors on blood hematology, this incredibly important science of looking at blood under a microscope and seeing the actual evidence of good health habits or poor health habits.

In fact, you were at an event I did where we invited two people to the stage. We wanted to show their blood under our microscope, projected on a big TV screen for the audience. We invited one person who was considered very healthy, who followed all the aspects of quality health, good nutrition, exercise and positive thoughts. We also invited someone who considered himself very unhealthy, eating improperly, not exercising, with little regard for or understanding about how our wonderful bodies operate.

They were dramatically different. You could see the evidence right on stage on the screen, magnified in color over 3,000 times from the microscope.

ANTON: It was exciting to have immediate visual feedback. I did some of the tests you offered, and your group said my blood was some of the best blood they had seen during the entire event, and yet, they were able to look back through time, as it were, in my blood and see some dramatic events of stress in my life. They could also see some hormonal imbalances. So even though my blood looked healthy, there were other factors in there that you guys could read. Then you offered ways for me to correct and adjust that.

NICK DELGADO: I hit the wall around age thirty-eight, when my hormones started declining rapidly. I knew that because my physical performance, my sexual performance, my awareness and other things were just not like they had been in my twenties.

So I studied. I reviewed the literature and started applying the principles of herbs and supplements and nutrition, plus various types of hormone interventions that were all bio-identical or natural to the body. I had some rather dramatic results as my hormone levels were restored.

We introduce you to a whole new way of looking at health and fitness, not just the typical vitamin A and C and antioxidant approach, but whole food antioxidants and nutrition and special ways to exercise that are quick and efficient. It's a protocol that we call the Delgado Protocol.

We look at several different indicators; for example, oxidative stress. The amount of free radical damage in the blood can actually stretch back five, ten, even fifteen years. Your blood shows us what problems evolved or developed due to what factors.

Also, certainly past the age of twenty-five or thirty, individual hormone levels in both men and women start to decline rather rapidly. We have simple ways to measure these to tailor-make a program to rebuild the body and restore hormone levels to useful levels. We don't have to accept hormone levels declining.

ANTON: You have also found great implications for curative results through stem-cell research. Stem-cell research has varied reactions with the public. What can you say to help people understand why you are so dedicated to this and why they don't need to be afraid of it?

NICK DELGADO: The important thing to understand about stem cells is that we all are born with the ability to produce stem cells, particularly from our bone marrow or body fat and various tissues. When we are younger, if we have an injury or illness, we mobilize stem cells quickly to heal quickly. But as we get older, the ability of the body to release stem cells properly is limited.

So one of the things I focus on is whole, natural foods rich in beta-glucans, plus some supplemental products I've created, which release these natural stem cells to improve the healing process, to improve the healing system, to improve the immune system, to improve the quality of life. An amazing amount of research is being published around the world showing that people have improved damaged joints, cartilage, ligaments and soft tissue through the use of stem cells.

I have seen certain health and disease problems being dealt with effectively with a new science of medicine called rejuvenative medicine. In that science, some of the top experts in the world from hematology, oncology and other various medical areas are now recognizing the incredible power and benefit of stem cells and how to utilize them properly. In my book I have written about safe ways to search out, apply and utilize these therapies. I'm not comfortable with some therapies, and I don't really think it's appropriate for people to undergo certain treatments. But other treatments I see benefit from and encourage.

ANTON: There was a whole period where there was great resistance to stem cell research, and it became a very controversial subject. Are we past that point now?

NICK DELGADO: I think the resistance was specifically targeted at embryonic research and embryo stem-cell lines, and that was under the mistaken belief that the only benefit you could gain was from the rapidly dividing stem cell from embryos. We have discovered that *our own autologous stem cells* can work very, very well.

We also know that the use of stem cells from the placenta or umbilical cord can work well. We just have to have the appropriate testing, isolation separation and quality control at a high-end university laboratory or other appropriate facilities, which I have become accustomed to utilizing.

Then I believe the therapies are very, very safe. And potentially very effective.

ANTON: Has new life been at risk in seeking resources for stem cells?

NICK DELGADO: In the past, stem cells were actually coming from fertilization clinics where the mothers were releasing eggs anyway, and they weren't fertilized eggs. It wasn't really ending a life, but, at the same time, there was some talk that in certain countries, unethical practices might have been going on.

So just to remove from that controversy, we reviewed the literature for the last thirty years. It was quite evident that profound results were possible. I wrote about some of these results in our book, of people who have accomplished benefits like rejuvenating bone damage or cartilage or ligaments, or various things that we used to think couldn't be helped. Even nerve damage in some cases.

That's why I started looking at the research for cerebral palsy and for autism and combining that with hyperbaric oxygen, altitude conditioning and special dietary principles. The Delgado Protocol is very sophisticated.

ANTON: You are successful on many levels, including your reversal of the aging process. Do you see any parallels in the way you approach the food you eat and how you approach and manage other aspects of your life?

NICK DELGADO: Absolutely. A healthy diet would include a rich variety of whole natural foods, including fruits, vegetables, brown rice, beans and peas. There are many wonderful cuisines to consider, including Asian, Thai, Vietnamese, Incan from Peruvian history, Spanish and Italian food.

Cuisines such as the Mediterranean Diet and the Okinawa diet from just north of Japan have certain special aspects that have been learned from generation to generation. We are just teaching people how to restore these diets and get past the typical fast-food generation concept. You can still prepare food quickly.

In a blender, we have people prepare whole natural foods, raw fresh fruits and vegetables with a mix of powders that we came out with. This morning I made up several different items, some cooked, some fresh and some raw—combinations of whole natural foods rich in fiber. Don't cook the life out of those foods.

Cruciferous vegetables such as Napa cabbage, bok choy, brussels sprouts and broccoli are rich in very important phytochemicals and enzymes. Over 360,000 different phytochemicals have been discovered, and it's likely more will be found in the coming years.

You can take a mild-tasting baby bok choy, usually seen in Asian cooking, and Napa cabbage, a light, almost yellowish-white cabbage, and blend it with other raw fruits and vegetables. Then mix it with the Delgado Slim Blend, which has fifty-five other whole natural fresh fruits and vegetables, including derivates of seaweed, which are rich in beta-glucans, and activated barley, like the original Roman formula.

The Romans knew how to specially remove the gluten from barley and keep it live and active in a porridge. We put these formulas together in whole organic combinations such as our Delgado Protein Blend. A lot of people think protein, but they use protein products that are inferior to what we've learned humans require to *absorb* quality proteins, from sweet potatoes, hemp, brown rice and cruciferous vegetables. You can get a rich quality balance of protein, fiber, phytochemicals and enzymes, but from the raw state in particular is best.

Doing this reminds a person of that daily habit of good nutrition, of the introduction of live, whole, natural foods rich in complex carbohydrates, low in fat and free of cholesterol. These are just some of the things that you really must do to manage good health.

In the live blood cell analysis we do, you can see dramatic improvements in tens of thousands of people we've worked with. These changes in diet are experienced in how you feel and how you look—basically, how you approach life. Even your mood improves. You feel happy. It's just a great thing to feel clearer and happy and energetic.

Also, exercise good principles of proper food selection at restaurants, being careful to caution them, "Please prepare my food with little or no added oils or fats, and please add some extra fresh fruits and vegetables." In some of my books I've created recipes and guidelines that are really easy to follow. You feel so good that it's just a matter of never wanting to look back after you taste what it is to be healthy.

ANTON: Was there ever a time in your life when you ate differently than you do now?

NICK DELGADO: At one time, like many Americans, I believed in eating a high-protein diet because I was interested in athletics. I was cautioned to avoid sugar, which I did, and to avoid salt, which I did. In my athletic peak I did fairly well. As I continued to stay on that type of diet, and after I stopped some of my sports activities, I gained way too much weight. The concentrated proteins and fats and the cholesterol found in typical meats, eggs and dairy products caused me to balloon up in weight and also to increase my blood pressure to the point where I had a transient ischemic attack, a small stroke!

It was terrifying to me because the doctors had me on blood pressure medications. I thought I was protected, but I still ended up having this warning sign. It's a good thing I found out in time, because then I sought out literature and guidance from a mentor. I met with Nathan Pritikin, and later with other researches and educators, and I adopted these changes. Within six months I lost over fifty-five pounds. I was able to get in top shape. You could finally see the fat just melt away from my body as I adopted a healthier way of eating. I am thankful that I was enlightened before it was too late, before I suffered irreversible damage!

ANTON: How old were you when you had that stroke?

NICK DELGADO: I was twenty-three years young.

ANTON: We think of that happening to people who are much older, but twenty-three!

NICK DELGADO: It was a rude awakening, because here I thought I was sincere and eating healthily, relatively speaking, although I tended to overeat because of another problem I discovered later: a hormone imbalance. I had low thyroid, low cortisol levels and poor adrenal function. I ended up developing low testosterone levels.

It was really interesting that once I learned about the complexity and beauty of restoring natural hormones and eating healthier, it made my exercise become more fruitful. I was able to gain the benefits, and you could see the difference in my body. I just felt completely different.

I am so thankful that I was enlightened, and I've spent the last thirty years training and educating a lot of aging people through programs such as yours, Anton. I am so thankful to have this opportunity, because the legacy that I want people to remember me by is that the Delgado Protocol is one that has been perfected based on worldwide literature and studying the healthiest people in the world.

Look at what Norman Vincent Peale, Napoleon Hill, Jack Canfield, Mark Victor Hansen, and Harv T. Eker do. These people have studied other successful people. You want to model what you do after those that were successful. That's one of the things Anthony Robbins will tell you. Model those who are successful because they leave clues of success.

What I have done is to take a rather complex area that we want to assign disease names to, like cancer, heart disease, diabetes, hypertension, glaucoma, and all of these disease conditions of the digestive gut, the bones, the skeleton, and the organs. I want people to understand that these are diseases that *may* be treated by drugs and surgery, but if you really want to *prevent* them from happening and get to the cause of the problem, go back to the user manual that God gave us. It's amazing how healthy you can be.

ANTON: And you're proving that age is no longer such a limiting factor. I'm looking at a picture of you from your book. It doesn't show your face, it just shows your torso. I'm thinking this guy has got to be in his twenties, at most in his mid-thirties—but it's you in your fifties! You set an athletic world record in your fifties.

NICK DELGADO: I broke the World Strength Endurance record. I hammer curled and pressed overhead 50,640 pounds to raise awareness for autism, to help people know that we are now struggling around the planet with an ever-increasing rate of brain damage in children with the disease of autism.

We believe there are some diseases that might be preventable with just enlightenment and education in the protocols of diet and exercise, nutrition, and hormones.

I started competing in World Strength Endurance Championship competitions, and I actually led team USA in London to the World Strength Endurance Championships in 2007, a three-man team competing against European champions from the UK, Ireland, Germany, Dubai, and other places around the world. We won the world championships.

If you go to our website you can see this demonstrated. You take a set of dumbbells and hammer curl without swinging, then press overhead. In our case, we were using a 45-pound dumbbell in each hand; totaling up the number of lifts, my team, Team USA, was able to win the World Championships. And our team had the oldest person on the stage (me, age fifty-three at that time), the youngest person on stage (my son, only fifteen) and my training partner, Tim Nash, who is a big brute of a guy at 6'3" and 255 pounds. This was the team I led to victory.

I don't think I am particularly gifted to be a world champion. I just know biochemistry. I have been inspired and trained by many of the top athletes, fitness experts and nutritionists in sports medicine. I have worked with some of the top anti-aging doctors in the world and continue to do so. I know dedication and work performance, and it has allowed me to be among the top three in the world and currently the holder of the World Strength Endurance Championship Lifting Competition.

I am currently training to break the World Guinness record for curls, which was set several years ago by Stuart Burrell. He took fifty pounds and curled non-stop for a solid hour, 520 continuous curls. My goal is to stage a public event with the media, not only to motivate people who are past the age of forty (I am fifty-five), but also to break a world record set by people half my age.

With that understanding, my goal is to prove to people that you can take an average body or individual and exceed all human performance records, and again raise awareness to help parents who are struggling to help their children with autism.

There are some great educators and methods, but I think they're just oftentimes overlooked. I think the time has come for us to really get the word out, and my way is by taking action.

It's so important to follow through and take action. It's that next step you take to be the very best you can be. You have to be a role model, not just for yourself, but also for your children, your grandchildren or even your parents. If they are ailing a little bit, it's really important to walk your talk and to get people on track. You have to look in the mirror and recognize what it takes to improve your health and your performance.

That's one of the things I want my legacy to be: that I truly walked my talk and did what I said, that I was able to accomplish things that no other person has done before to motivate others to be their very best.

ANTON: You have a goal to live to be a 100 or beyond.

NICK DELGADO: The world record for aging is 114 in men and 128 in women (Jeanne Calment). I am focusing very specifically on a day-by-day basis to rejuvenate my body and do everything possible to break that existing world record for aging, and I want to do it with grace and with a quality of life unheard of in today's generation.

We probably have more 100-year-olds now than in all of history, but at the same time these people aren't always in the best of health. My goal is not only to be the record holder for longevity, but also to do it with a quality of life that's never been done before.

ANTON: Well, Nick, you are fifty-five. You are almost *halfway* there!

NICK DELGADO: I have a one-and-a-half-year old child, so I've got to last at least another seventy years. I'm not even going to disclose what age I will reach, just like when I set the world record for hammer curl and press. People were asking me, "How many lifts are you going to do? How much weight are you going to lift?" I just said, "I will do my very, very best"—and that night I broke the world record by 10,000 pounds! Even I didn't expect it. At age fifty-five, I lifted 1,994 lifts in one hour, something no human had ever done.

I will do the same with the record for aging.

I will break that record—hear my words very clearly–I will.

DIAMONDS ARE FOREVER

The secrets to staying young: Love life. Love what you do. Love each other. Live in the present. Enjoy food and life using only the best.

Hollywood icon Jill St. John is one of the most beautiful women in the world, even now in her vibrant seventies. Her filmography is punctuated with classics of the silver screen, including her memorable starring role as Tiffany Case in the James Bond film *Diamonds Are Forever. The Jill St. John Cookbook* came out in 1987 and raised the bar on cookbooks, the quality of the food we eat, and our style of eating, setting a standard that endures to this day. In fact, she took over the food segment of the TV show *Good Morning America*, replacing Julia Childs.

Jill and her husband, Robert Wagner, have also raised the bar and set a standard of integrity in marriage. I love being around them! They are the king and queen of optimism and gratitude. They are living examples of the joyous energy expressed by dynamic people truly living their lives to the fullest. They exemplify what Malcolm Gladwell shows us in his book *Outliers*, that the quality of your life and the people in it may be even more important than the food you ingest in order for you to live a long life.

ANTON: Jill, you are truly the most beautiful redhead I know.

JILL ST. JOHN: Well, thanks. It's always nice to be with you, and it's always nice to talk about food.

ANTON: Well, you know, it was so much fun having you on *Cooking With Anton*. It has been one of our most successful shows. People just love seeing you and your husband, R.J. The two of you have such a youthful spirit. You are really inspiring to a lot of people.

JILL ST. JOHN: We love life. It's very important that you love what you do.

ANTON: It shows. And how could you not? You have such a blessed life with your career, and you live in one of the most beautiful places in the world, here in Aspen. You've been here a long time.

JILL ST. JOHN: I remember you when you were a little boy.

ANTON: We won't go into that!

I was watching some very successful people, and I noticed that there's a pattern to how they do things to get the most out of life, including the choices they make in the food they eat.

JILL ST. JOHN: I think it starts very early in life. I always thought there wasn't anything I couldn't do if I worked hard enough. That translated into acting and then a position as food editor for *USA Today*. I was the first food editor for their weekly magazine, *USA Weekend*. I had never done anything like that, although I had cooked on *Good Morning America* and things like that. It never occurred to me that I couldn't do anything. I just jumped in and did it.

ANTON: Well, you were cooking on TV long before this became popular. You and Julia Child and a handful of people.

JILL ST. JOHN: I took over for Julia. I was a guest of hers on *Good Morning America*. I had to cook in front of her, or for her, actually. That scared the hell out of me, but then she went on to write those twelve books and took a sabbatical for four years from *GMA*, and they asked me if I would like to step into her spot. Well, I just said, "Yes, thank you," without really asking myself, Jeepers, can I do this? Well, yes, I could because I believed in myself.

ANTON: It's so clear being around you. You are so focused, and yet you are so light and joyful.

JILL ST. JOHN: Life is good. We have to enjoy what we have. This is all we have. Let's make the most of it.

ANTON: And food plays a big part in that. There are people who are living depressed and curtailed lives that don't realize that a big contributing factor is what they are putting into their bodies.

JILL ST. JOHN: Oh! Absolutely. It's not unusual to see depressed people who aren't even hungry or upset people who are too hungry. Like everything else in life, there has to be a balance. I eat everything I want. There isn't anything I can't have. I just don't have it all at the same time.

ANTON: That's a great point, because we have talked to a lot of people for this book, and we've run the gamut. There was a guy who was happy with the Campbell's-soup-and-beans type of cooking, and others who said the whole world should be vegetarian. There are so many ways of looking at food and how we approach it. But there *was* a common denominator similar to what you just said: you have to have a little bit of sensitivity and pay attention, and then you can eat what you want.

JILL ST. JOHN: Also, you and I live in Aspen, probably the most athletic city in the country, and all of us are doing something physical. We are working out, horseback riding, hiking, skiing, playing tennis, or golfing. We are all doing something, and, of course, that always helps in terms of calories in and calories out. But the average person doesn't realize that if they just got out and took a twenty-minute walk after dinner, they would be surprised! Their food wouldn't be nearly that fattening.

ANTON: We went through this extreme fitness era where people were killing themselves, literally.

JILL ST. JOHN: And now they are paying for it with arthritis and bum knees and shoulders. They did too much. A twenty-minute walk can take care of a lot if it's brisk. I try to do something every day. I love my food and I'm not giving it up. If I have to walk an extra ten minutes the next day, I don't mind.

ANTON: But Jill, I've seen the food you eat. You eat beautiful food. But you also eat food that is actually body friendly.

JILL ST. JOHN: If you're going to have something extra creamy, then you might just have to concentrate a little more on the vegetables along with it. Hey, it's learning to live with yourself and making yourself happy, not expecting other things to make you happy—and a good meal will put a smile on your face.

ANTON: I love you. It's always so much fun to be around you.

May I say how old you are?

JILL ST. JOHN: Of course! I just turned seventy. I am so happy. It's just so wonderful to be at this age, to live where I live, to see the beauty I see every day, to have this wonderful marriage. I feel very, very blessed. But most of all, grateful. I think the problem most of us have is we look back and say, "Those were the good old days." Well, guess what? We are alive and we are here today. *These* are the good old days!

ANTON: Those are words to listen to. You have a wonderful body, and you have a beautiful face, and you look fit, and you've got this high energy! You are seventy years old, and you've got this great loving marriage. When I am around you and R.J., the love and respect between you is so clear.

JILL ST. JOHN: Oh yeah! We're very lucky that way, and being happy like that keeps you alive. So many of my friends are not married, and they're older, and they've taken it upon themselves to make themselves happy. You don't bring anything to the table if you're just waiting for your prospective mate to make your life complete.

ANTON: We came to talk about food, and we're getting life's lessons here.

JILL ST. JOHN: Food! Everyone thinks I got Robert Wagner because I must have been hell in bed or something, but it's my cooking.

ANTON: I bet it is. We had that vodka rigatoni you made on Valentine's Day, your anniversary, for example.

JILL ST. JOHN: Well, I have to compliment you. You got that can of Italian tomatoes we used for that recipe. It was the best I'd ever used, and I went back to the grocery store and got four more cans. They were just a completely different grade level.

ANTON: This is what's neat about working with you: yesterday we were at the farmer's market, where there's all this beautiful local produce. It came from the local farms in Paonia and Hotchkiss. It's really nice to have that in season, but when winter comes and it's no longer available, there's something to be said for having things in cans. There is *good* in cans and there is *bad* in cans. Like anything else.

JILL ST. JOHN: Also some frozen vegetables. I don't use a lot of frozen or canned things, but the things I do are excellent quality.

ANTON: Jill, was there ever a time in your life when you ate bad food, junk food?

JILL ST. JOHN: No, no. I have to tell you I was brought up on fish and vegetables. We had a fruit orchard at my house when we were growing up. There was a swimming pool in the middle of it. Don't think we were wealthy—everyone in California has a swimming pool! I would lie in the pool floating on my back, and I'd see a peach or apricot I wanted, or maybe an avocado, and I'd get out of the pool and climb the tree or stand on a ladder and get the particular fruit in question. Then I'd wash it off in the pool and eat it still floating on my back!

ANTON: Well, you know, that's really significant. As you just pointed out, it really starts out when we're kids.

JILL ST. JOHN: It does. I have enjoyed all different kinds of food, and sometimes I'll go to a restaurant and order something I've never tasted before. You have to expand, you have to experiment, find out what you really like.

A friend of mine was just telling me that she called her doctor and asked for thyroid hormone replacement therapy because she thought it would make her lose weight. He took all her blood tests, examined her and said, "You're fine. Your cholesterol is fine. Everything is fine. I'm not going to give you anything because you don't need it, but do me a favor, cut your portions in half." She did and lost fifteen pounds.

ANTON: I know a few people who are fairly rotund. I will watch them shovel in the food and then, when we have food left on our plates, want to finish it for us! You need to stop when you're full. Part of the problem of overeating comes from choosing less nutritious foods. Because the body isn't getting the nutrition it needs, it tells you it wants more food in an attempt to compensate.

JILL ST. JOHN: You have to stop. And you have to wait a little bit because it takes twenty minutes to feel full.

ANTON: They say that heart attacks usually happen about four hours after dinner. Generally after a dinner of something that has heavy oils and fats in it.

JILL ST. JOHN: Now, don't forget, Julia Child always said, "The flavor is in the fat."

ANTON: Yes, but there's a difference between eating an occassional fresh croissant made with fresh organic farm butter or regularly having French fries on top of a milkshake, on top of a greasy burger, where everything that can clog your arteries has gone in there.

JILL ST. JOHN: You have to be aware.

ANTON: There is such variety of good food available to us these days. You don't have to have food that looks and tastes like sawdust to eat well and stay healthy.

JILL ST. JOHN: The more you get into cooking, the more you realize what you can do. The best food is made of top quality ingredients, prepared simply.

ANTON: That seems to be the key. You see it in your cookbook, too. You have such a beautiful cookbook, *The Jill St. John Cookbook*. The recipes are so clear and simple.

It's the same with love, with food, all of that. Your life can be so simple.

JILL ST. JOHN: Yeah. As we live, so should we eat—but we don't.

ANTON: Well, you live a lifestyle that has potential for high stress, and with the movies and the life you've led, there must have been times when the pressure got pretty high. How did food play into that?

JILL ST. JOHN: You know, after working a twelve- or fourteen-hour day in the studio, I'd still have to come home and make my own dinner. Thirty minutes of cooking was very good for just calming down. I didn't need a drink. I just needed to cook the dinner, enjoy the aromas and eat it. And it was always good.

ANTON: That's one of the main points we try to make on my cooking show. It's not about the recipes as much as it is that the kitchen is your oasis of peace. After a busy day many people think, "Oh geeze! Now I've got to go home and cook on top of all of this!" But, as you just said, that is when you can assimilate and filter your day and get centered.

JILL ST. JOHN: I find it relaxing. Other people may not. We are all different. But it works for me. Sometimes I get burned out on cooking and ask R.J. to take me out when I don't want to cook anymore.

Food is like life. You get out of it what you put into it.

ANTON: You are so clear. It doesn't take a lot of words for you to really hit a powerful note.

JILL ST. JOHN: Life is pretty simple; it's people who make it complicated.

YOUR HEALTH ACCOUNT

Your biological age can be far younger than your chronological age. The thoughts and actions of your lifelong habits have a cumulative effect. Build and sustain good health so you will have a reserve when challenges arise.

Brian Theiss was born with two very weak lungs and a compromised immune system. He had to fight on a daily basis through most of his childhood just to survive. Weak and excluded from life, against all odds, he decided to turn his life around through fitness and education.

In his youth he discovered that by building a stronger body, the systems failing in his body began to respond on a cellular level. Despite enormous setbacks through the years, including accidents and a broken back that would require seven years of physical re-education to relearn life's most basic skills, Brian persisted and came out victorious.

Brian has an indomitable spirit and a joy about him that defies all the years of hardship he has known. Since he personally understood the cost of loss of quality of life, he didn't want others to suffer as he had. He started educating himself to become the change for others that he wanted to see in the world. Through the last twenty-six years he has proven his commitment to change and saved not only his own life, but also the lives of thousands of people around the world.

In 1984 he founded The Theiss Institute, which uses cutting-edge technology combined with a holistic approach to completely revise the concepts of health care and fitness. Brian's *Theiss Health Life System* produces quantitative, measurable results in maximizing a person's potential for better health, greater energy levels, enhanced self-image, overall confidence, fitness and strength at any age.

He is praised and recognized by the world's leading executives, Olympic athletes, military personnel, medical professionals and celebrities as one of the most prolific body engineers in practice today, adding years to their life potential. He is featured in medical trade journals and has been featured in TV specials highlighting his unprecedented success in preventive health care.

ANTON: You have a service that big corporations use as they design and streamline their systems for optimum success. The health of their employees is actually a very serious concern.

BRIAN THEISS: Especially when you're dealing with top-level players. When you have an individual who is responsible for millions or even billions of dollars and they're fighting their health, they can make some very poor decisions—and a poor decision can be very costly.

A company might have a CEO, a vice president, or someone high up in management that they've noticed has gained some weight and whose productivity is starting to slow down. They'll send them to us.

People will come and say, "I'm really not that deconditioned. I think my company is exaggerating." So we do some testing and collect their medical data. The specific needs of an individual client will dictate the type of testing we send out for. Then we sit down with them and say, "Look. This is where you are today." They might be fifty-five years of age chronologically, for example, but biologically ten to fifteen years older than that. Their lungs are functioning like that of a seventy-year-old instead of a fifty-five-year-old. The amount of energy that's required for them to maintain their level of disease is extremely high. Their body is spending too much energy trying to keep them alive.

ANTON: How do you assess a person's biological age?

BRIAN THEISS: We do something called VO2 max testing[1] to measure oxygen exchange, which determines the difference between

---

1   VO_2 max (also maximal oxygen consumption, maximal oxygen uptake, peak oxygen uptake or maximal aerobic capacity) is the maximum capacity of an individual's body to transport and use oxygen during incremental exercise, which reflects the physical fitness of the individual. The name is derived from V - volume, O_2 - oxygen, max - maximum. - *Wikipedia*

their chronological and biological age. Our analyzer analyzes every single breath going in and going out. We also do a complete EKG in the process. We know the lung function, the motor control, and the carbon dioxide release.

Once we assess this information we build a workable, sustainable model for them that will trigger natural biological processes. We provide a system that is catered to each individual specifically, including exercise, cardio programs, meal programs, and working hand in hand with a cardiologist, respiratory specialist, an internist, an endocrinologist, you name it.

Once we establish those biological processes and re-activate them in an organic way, it starts shifting the clock back for them. In twenty-six years we've had over 15,000 successful documented cases doing this.

ANTON: So you're designing entirely new life habits for them to start following?

BRIAN THEISS: I'm building them from the inside out and showing them that I'm getting them back to the health they had ten to fifteen years before. Once that pattern is established, I teach them how to maintain it for themselves.

ANTON: So you're not creating a codependent relationship. You are giving them the fishing pole and teaching them how to fish.

BRIAN THEISS: If I can't educate a person on how to do this for himself, I haven't done him justice. One of the biggest reasons we have such a decline in our health is that people don't really understand the knowledge we have about health and how it pertains to them. That's where I come in.

ANTON: Two of the largest factors you use in regenerating a client's health and life force are specific physical exercises and a focus on the food they eat. If somebody's seventy-something, you don't suddenly have him lifting heavy weights and jogging ten miles, do you?

BRIAN THEISS: I don't even have clients under forty years of age typically lift heavy weights. It's not about that. They have to be committed to living a healthy lifestyle. They have to be concerned, not only about today but also about tomorrow and the next day.

ANTON: There is such an awareness nowadays of having a good-looking body, but you can look great on the outside and not be well on the inside.

BRIAN THEISS: That is so typical of what we have in a lot of sports today because of all the drugs, excessive training and tearing of muscles. There are a lot of people that you think are in great shape, but internally they're falling apart. I see it every day.

ANTON: We already have such stressful lives because we're trying to do too much too fast. An executive lives in a high-stress environment by nature. Can food change his perception and ability to handle that stress?

BRIAN THEISS: Absolutely. Food is very powerful because of the chemical signals it provides us. So the more conditioned you are, the more effective those chemical signals are and the more energy is produced. Once the substrates[2] are digested and broken down in the body, they trigger every single cellular operation in your body.

Food is so powerful. It can either move us forward or it can induce premature disease in the system. How you fuel your system is really going to dictate whether your body is going to move forward or backward.

Once we do the metabolic profile and look at all their medical information, we really know what we're dealing with. Based on what their requirements are, we give that individual only what their body needs. Not everybody has the same food requirements. When people are working really hard on a certain program and it isn't working, a factor that may be sabotaging their progress could be something as simple as eating the wrong foods or wrong combinations of foods.

---

2   In biochemistry, a substrate is a molecule upon which an enzyme acts.

The way we combine food affects the way that it's actually absorbed. Just because certain things are healthy, it doesn't mean we're going to get their full benefit when we eat them all at the same time—they may not be compatible with each other. Food triggers hormonal responses in the body. As soon as you ingest anything, even before you swallow it, just in the process of looking at it, your body already knows what's coming, and it's getting hormonally prepared. Your body produces different digestive enzymes in your saliva before the food even goes down your gullet.

ANTON: So we can create incredible confusion when we go to a fast-food restaurant. The body doesn't know what the heck to think about the protein, the starch, the sugar and the fat all coming in at once.

BRIAN THEISS: It's worse than that. Because that food is so chemically altered, because we are bringing so much garbage into our systems, the body doesn't know what to do with those chemicals. That's one of the key factors accelerating premature aging and disease in the West today. If food is so toxic that it can't really cycle through our system, the body will isolate it to try to take care of it. It starts to turn into a tumor, into a cancer. We're very close to seeing cancer surpass heart disease as the number one killer in the United States. And it's because of how we're eating and our lifestyle.

ANTON: We have foods now that never existed before in history. So the body that knew how to deal with the food we found as hunter-gatherers is being presented with new challenges. It doesn't know what to do with all the over-processed foods we have.

BRIAN THEISS: People in the West spend more of their lives in a diseased state than in a healthy state. One of the biggest reasons is how they eat. When it comes to the body there's no shortcut. We have been programmed through millions of years of evolution.

ANTON: America is the fast-food kingdom of the world. A lot of people in this country, especially in harder economic times, will resort to fast-food restaurants because they think it's a more economical way to feed their families.

BRIAN THEISS: And it's just the opposite. That's why we have one of the highest premature illness, aging and death factors of any country in the world.

I read a report a couple of years ago by a doctor who evaluated the cost of an American hamburger. He was looking at the long-term effect on your health. A ninety-nine cent hamburger, over a long period of time, actually costs fifteen bucks because of all the health problems it creates. Fast food is the most expensive thing you'll ever buy.

ANTON: A lot of us, especially when we're young, live very freely and don't worry about the damage we're doing to ourselves.

BRIAN THEISS: I was very fortunate because I was raised around the medical community. Because I was taught the right way as a child, I thought of eating in the same way as a bank account. For years and years I "made deposits" into my health account. You can literally stockpile your health and reverse premature illness, aging, and death by controlling biological factors pertaining to stress in your system. But eventually we all have to go to that bank and start making withdrawals. You want something to be in there to back you up in times of need. When I got injured I was able to go for a long time and just withdraw a little bit of that reserve every day. That's what saved me.

ANTON: A lot of the things we have talked about in this book have to do with the mechanics of food and hormones and our responses to food, but in Malcolm Gladwell's book *Outliers*, he tells us how people from Rossetto, Italy moved to Pennsylvania, where they created a community that's living long and healthy lives. They don't eat that much differently than we do, and so scientists were trying to figure out what factors were involved there. They discovered one of the most powerful factors involved was a strong sense of family, of community.

BRIAN THEISS: Your family or your tribe is biologically programmed not to let anybody suffer and self-destruct. They are always looking out for you.

ANTON: And that literally changes their body and brain chemistry in a positive way that supports health and long life.

BRIAN THEISS: That's why families are so critical. What happens when a family loses that structure and becomes separated, or a family member is into drugs or becomes a workaholic? Those families fall apart because they have been biologically designed to work in a very specific way. Those people are usually sick more. They get involved in crime more. They are more likely to have dysfunctional families.

ANTON: In our society we have somehow decided that it's normal to start falling apart as we get older—but it's not normal. There are people who, because of their lifestyle choices and the way they eat, are already dying a very slow death.

BRIAN THEISS: We weren't designed to fall apart. There is a death phase of life, but that shouldn't happen until the last eight to sixteen months of one's biological life. It's ridiculous that people have been programmed to believe that's normal. So they accept it when their knees are hurting or they're told they should expect to have a heart attack since that happened to their father when he was fifty-five. It's just crazy!

ANTON: The Theiss Institute is based on preventive health care. In our society and era, we have been trained to wait for disaster before we take initiative to address our challenges.

BRIAN THEISS: There is an intuitive voice in our heads that guides us. Many people avoid listening to that voice and push their physiologies to the point where they know that if they don't change something, their bodies are going to fail. I've got to pull them out and bring them back to life.

ANTON: We live in a hectic and noisy world these days. Sometimes it's hard to hear that inner voice when we're overcome with the stresses of our modern existence.

BRIAN THEISS: When we breathe our first breath and we accept this gift of life, we also accept this thing called stress. We're born with it. We have some good stresses in our body that keep us out of trouble, for the most part. In the first twenty-one years of a person's life, the growth phase, stress is just kind of hanging in there. But once we get into the second phase of life, called "biological aging," stress runs amok and starts to destroy our bodies.

When you start to go into that disease phase, every morning when you wake up, whatever the situation might be, your body has already identified the state of your health and where you stand in relation to the environment, and it needs to know what it has to do with that for the next twenty-four hours.

If you continue to avoid that voice in your head, you're going to get to a place where it's screaming loudly, "This is not where you want to be!" But this is the problem. If you don't take action in your life, that physiology will get to the point where you can't turn it back.

We make big changes by educating people. I hold people to a higher standard than most people do because I believe in people a little bit more. I believe if you can really educate a person and make them understand, you have a better ability to help them.

ANTON: A chain of events happens when we eat. Food triggers chemical reactions in our bodies and those change the hormonal response, and the hormonal response then changes the brain chemistry. We keep hearing that as men get older they lose testosterone. But now we're hearing more and more that we can reverse that. When people talk about libido and how important it is, it's not just a matter of being sexy, it's a reflection of your overall health.

BRIAN THEISS: Libido isn't just for sex. Libido is for vigor and muscle strength, and muscle in turn means vitality of life. You can have these incredible levels of testosterone, 1000, 2000, sometimes even 8000 for body builders, but it's not so much how much testosterone you have, it's how much testosterone is being converted to T3.

T3 is the hormone in our body that builds muscle mass, that gets us bigger, that gives us energy and increases our metabolism. If you get too much testosterone and you're not able to convert that testosterone to T3, it will be converted to estrogen. At that point you're going to get older and start to lose your testosterone.

You can have two identical men the same age, let's say fifty-five. Their testosterone levels can be exactly the same. At 800, they will look different and work, physiologically and biologically, completely differently. One will have a big gut, and the other one will be completely lean and ripped. The reason for that is because the guy who's completely ripped has converted his testosterone into T3, while the other gentleman has taken his testosterone and is converting it into estrogen.

ANTON: And what causes that difference between them?

BRIAN THEISS: It's the combination of lifestyle and genetics. But for the most part, it's lifestyle. How they do everything. How they eat, how they're combining that with the true science of their body, what their metabolism is, what their muscular endurance is, how they're converting that oxygen into working muscle, what their strength curves are, what they're consuming, what their food ratios are, what medications they're taking, what their sleep patterns are. It's very involved.

ANTON: We have this picture in our brains that we set a goal and all we have to do is follow the steps. Then once we get to the goal we can just stop doing whatever we were doing and coast. But that's not the case. It's like saying, if I take a few deep breaths, I've been oxygenated and now I can stop breathing. It doesn't work that way. You give us the tools to stop undermining our efforts so it becomes something that's fun and easy to sustain over time—especially because we start to enjoy the results.

BRIAN THEISS: Yes. And you've got to remember, it's not psychological, it's biochemical. Your body is very smart. If the body is not receiving the benefits it requires internally, it will direct you to do something completely different, because it needs energy to get it done. Our bodies control everything that happens to us, even the way we think and process.

ANTON: So when people are having psychological challenges, they may actually be based in physiological reasons that are coming from the way they're eating and living?

BRIAN THEISS: That's why proactive doctors are all prescribing lifestyle modifications through diet and exercise. There are people that we can help in organic ways, like what we do at the Theiss Institute. There's a second group of people that, no matter what you do with them organically, you cannot change those biological factors. They need a little boost, and you can boost them through the right doctors medicating them conscientiously. Once those natural biological factors are triggered and turned back, you can get them back into an organic state. There is also a group of people that have created so much damage to themselves that, no matter what they do, they're going to need some form of medication to keep those biological factors moving forward or they will die prematurely.

ANTON: So you are supportive of the pharmaceutical industry? You seem to suggest that there is, on some level, a value to what they're contributing.

BRIAN THEISS: It is *how* they control it. If they're doing it to be proactive and change true biological markers, I'm all for it. If they're not, I'm not. A very small percentage of the people on the planet are actually doing that. I only know a few. There are conscientious doctors out there, but generally, when they look at us from a medical standpoint, they look at us as, "At what level of disease are you?" And they bank on that.

ANTON: As we said before, your focus is more on prevention. You want to bring awareness to people before they are overcome with disease.

BRIAN THEISS: I see the devastating side effects of not getting the right information. Dying prematurely is expensive. With whatever years they have left, people really want to have the vitality of their youth, they want to make good decisions, they want to have the strength and endurance and the flexibility to stay involved in life.

The choice is truly ours. There's a small percentage of people that don't have that choice. But they truly are a small percentage. The majority of people just need to know that there *is* a real solution for them.

Most importantly, it has to be sustainable. For it to be sustainable we have to change our behavior, but the behavior has to be changed through education and research pertaining to everyone personally.

I want people to know how to do it right and how to do it for themselves.

III.

EVERYTHING IS ENERGY

EVERYTHING IS ENERGY

*Bio-energy can be measured and influenced by thoughts and the
energy in our food, the people around us, and things visible and
invisible in our environment.*

Everything is energy.

We have heard this phrase so often that we have dismissed the essence
of its meaning. What's important about this is understanding the
implications of what energy can and will do in our lives, and how to
harness and understand energy to serve our better interests.

In the case of Lee Beymer, a holistic practitioner and licensed
acupuncturist, his alternative approach to assessing my condition and
healing me when I was suffering from accute anxiety attacks was based
entirely on the measurement of and exposure to controlled types of
energy. His business in Aspen is appropriately named Radiant Health.
Think "radiate energy."

By measuring the electromagnetic field around my body, Lee was
able to identify failing or compromised organs inside me, deduce
electromagnetic remedies, apply them to me and *immediately* begin a
rapid healing process.

One of the more obvious remedies Lee prescribed for me was a radical
change in the food I would put in my body for sixty days. No sugar,
no yeast, nothing fermented. Plenty of fresh vegetables, whole grains
and above all, plenty of fresh spring water! Not tap water. Not gallons
of chlorinated, fluoridated city water, but gallons of fresh spring water
from an ancient aquifer that produces water from a level and time long
before man's appearance on the earth to muck it up.

The water was readily available. But the candida diet he prescribed was
another story. Nearly everything I reached for or was used to eating

fell into the sugar, yeast or fermented category. I hadn't heard of Diana Stobo or raw food or pH-balanced water at the time.

But after two years of living in a nightmare, I was ready to try anything!

What is astounding is how quickly and powerfully my body responded to being given nutrition that it could actually process and use to its advantage to heal itself, rapidly and thoroughly.

Once my body was back on track, it was easier for my mind to believe that I was going to heal and not leave my children fatherless at a young age (my young age!). When I realized I wasn't going to die, I started to look ahead and dream of the future and, once again, of success.

It was more clear to me than ever that we must eat for success.

Eating good food is not a fad. It is essential. There is no reason to be constantly fighting to paddle upstream. Eating well is one simple, readily available and doable thing.

ANTON: Lee, you are such a generous spirit. You change people's lives every day in the most amazing way. And it fits into our modern age so well.

LEE BEYMER: Everything is energy. The term *radiant health* actually comes from Chinese, which means "health beyond distress, health beyond danger." So Radiant Health has to do with the radiance of energy that is within a person's being.

I'm licensed as an acupuncturist and doctor of Oriental Medicine, practicing since 1997. I got into this line of work actually to heal myself. I thoroughly enjoy the work I'm doing, bio-energetic testing. We test your energy via computer to see what's going on on the acupuncture meridians in your body. In effect, we put a specific frequency of electricity from the computer into your system, then pull it out with a probe with which we can touch on specific acupuncture meridians to find out what's going on specifically in the body.

ANTON: So when there are dysfunctions, malfunctions within our body that affect the way the energy comes out of our body, this machine can measure that.

LEE BEYMER: It's like the computer diagnostics for a car, except that we're a little more complicated than a car. This is a very sophisticated program. It was originally developed in the early 1950s by Dr. Voll in Germany. He was diagnosed with bladder cancer, and he determined that no matter what, he was going to beat it. He was an Oriental medical doctor with a PhD in electrical engineering, and he reasoned that if the acupuncture meridians actually exist, there must be a way to measure them. So he set out to find the measurement, to find the exact frequency to be able to measure the acupuncture meridians. It turns out that the energy that runs through our body in the acupuncture meridians is at about twelve-millionths of an amp. He found a way of measuring it.

ANTON: Something that small is measurable?

LEE BEYMER: You bet! We are very sensitive.

ANTON: When we sit near people, when we touch other people, are we sharing and picking up their energies?

LEE BEYMER: Yes, very definitely. We are much more sensitive than anyone can imagine. Even though we, in our thinking minds, don't necessarily recognize all that is going on in other people, our inner self, our inner being, our intuitive side is picking up clues and feelings all the time.

ANTON: So do we need to be more discriminating in whom we surround ourselves with, or do we have a certain innate power we can use to shield ourselves and maybe project positive energy out to people?

LEE BEYMER: Yes to both of those. Women are often much more sensitive than men. Guys have to learn it. This is a feminine planet. Men aren't as attuned to our environment, but we have the sensitivity as well and can certainly learn this kind of awareness. And it *is* a kind of awareness. As you develop it you come to understand other people very, very well. You become much more sensitive and discriminating, in the sense of assessing what kinds of energies you want to mix with and what you don't want to mix with. This is important because any kind of energy that you have any kind of exchange with over any period of time, you will process out afterwards.

ANTON: So you measure us with this sophisticated equipment, and then you begin to search for remedies. These remedies are not pills, they're not things we swallow.

LEE BEYMER: What we look for initially is any kind of energetic blockages in a person's system, and the way we find them is through looking for an "inverse." A remedy is actually an energetic frequency that is coded into the computer. We find the inverse energetic frequency that balances out that blockage. There are over 40,000 remedy frequencies in the virtual library of this particular system.

There are three primary categories of dysfunction, all energetic. They can be mental or emotional, such as trauma, stress, etc. Or they can be pathogens: bacteria, virus, fungus, parasites or other toxins are typical. There are also over 70,000 kinds of chemicals produced and put into our environment every year, and, unfortunately, we get exposed to a lot of those through the foods we eat and the air we breathe.

ANTON: Considering that these remedies are energetic, I think about all the energies we're exposed to in our modern daily lives. You can tune your car radio to any number of radio frequencies. Those are all blasting through the air and through us at all times. There is radiation coming from the sun breaking its way through our damaged ozone. All sorts of things are happening to us that we're exposed to, even though we don't see them or hear them until we turn on the TV or radio or use our cellphones. So especially when we're sitting there with the cellphone to our ear for an hour, something is going on. We are changing the energy in our bodies, in our balance.

LEE BEYMER: This is true. We are exposed to all kinds of energetic radiation. Most people think of radiation as radioactive, but the practical reality is sunlight is radiation, and it has many different frequencies within it. The energy coming from a cellphone is another kind of radiation.

ANTON: It would be absurd to suggest that we stop any forms of radio communication, like giving up our cellphones, because even if we use our landlines, the signal is ultimately being sent to a station that is blasting it through the air with radio waves. It is inevitable that we'll be exposed to these radio waves and other energies. So then we have to balance the imbalance caused by such exposure. Can you take a perfectly healthy person and help balance their energy to be in equalibrium in a world that's energized like ours?

LEE BEYMER: This is what I'm doing every day. Part of the practical reality is that each person has to become proactive themselves. If we're going to use cellphones, we've got to find a way to make them safer. Not acknowledging the radiation from them doesn't make them safer. We've actually got to take the step of adding something to them that helps neutralize the negative radiation in a way that makes it harmless for you and me to be able to use them.

My initial imbalance in terms of health was due to the mercury in my fillings. I had heavy metals in my body, primarily mercury, which is very susceptible to the radiation from cellphones. Back when I was affected I would use the cellphone for five minutes and often have a headache for two or three hours afterwards.

There are many different products on the market today that are beneficial and help to neutralize the radiation of cellphones. I have a little tab on mine that neutralizes the majority of the electromagnetic radiation that comes out of it. Now I can use my cellphone without really being affected. I also have these tabs on the three computers at my desk, since I am in an electromagnetic field all day long.

ANTON: Ironically, the city of Aspen decided to put some of their strongest broadcast equipment on your rooftop, where you're treating people with energy. You were able to block that with these things that look like little hang gliders stuck up on your ceiling. What are they?

LEE BEYMER: It's a device that actually neutralizes the radiation of the wi-fi tower they put on the roof. I think this one was made by Biomagnetics out of Arizona. This is what you would use where the power comes into your fuse box on the house. It turned out that this one in particular worked very well to shield us from the wi-fi.

ANTON: This sounds like a kind of mysterious magic, but it is astounding. I have seen personally, twice in my family, how some health challenges that seemed impossible to remedy with standard western medicine were cured by controlled exposure to your specific bioenergetic frequencies. They were remedied quickly and completely.

LEE BEYMER: This is a new norm. This is a new form of medicine. Bioenergy medicine is the wave of the future. I let people off the hook who say that it's woo-woo, but it's actually very high tech.

ANTON: So you measure the electromagnetic field around our bodies, and then you radiate pure waters and other things with energy as remedies.

LEE BEYMER: In creating these remedies, we are actually using homeopathic frequencies, which we're transmitting into the water. Water, it turns out, is an amazing container. It is, in effect, a liquid crystal and able to absorb many different kinds of energies. We are specifically putting energies into a vial of water that will help to balance a person. These are known as energetically imprinted homeopathics.

ANTON: We put many quarts of water into our body every day. If your radiation is changing the nature of the water and can produce these miracles, which I've seen first hand, then it makes me wonder about the quality of the water we ingest daily. How important is that?

LEE BEYMER: Very, very important. Nowadays people will actually pay more for water than they will for a gallon of gas, because we're starting to recognize the value of water. This is going to become a great issue in the future.

ANTON: We have so many choices of water. There is controversy about having the water come to us in petroleum-based bottles. People like David Wolfe show us where we can find natural springs near our homes, even near big cities like Los Angeles and New York.

LEE BEYMER: I get my water from Eldorado Springs, which is a huge, ancient aquifer under the Rocky Mountains on the eastern slope. It has all the minerals in it from the glaciers in times gone by. It's very pure.

ANTON: Food is a really big part of what you are doing.

LEE BEYMER: Probably the most common undiagnosed malady in America today is the overgrowth of yeast. Candida. Conventional medicine using antibiotics actually causes it in that the antibiotics kill off the friendly bacteria in the gut, and everyone knows that. The problem is that conventional medicine hasn't found the means to refurbish those friendly bacteria in a way that they can maintain over time. The antibiotics build up in residue in the gut and continue to kill them off.

ANTON: So when our children constantly get sick during the winter and we give them antibiotics, we are actually compromising their ability to heal.

LEE BEYMER: In a certain sense this is true. The first line of defense for a person's immune system is the friendly bacteria in their gut. So when we kill those off, this weakens our immune system.

ANTON: We are so used to looking at outward expressions of illness in our bodies and addressing those with pills, yet it is becoming really clear that it comes back to what's going on inside our gut. There is old stuff living in there, and there is new stuff that needs to be living in there. What exactly is candida?

LEE BEYMER: Candida is yeast. It's a kind of fungus. In one sense, everyone has candida to a small extent. The yeast actually ferments and helps us digest our food; it's supposed to be there, but under control.

Imagine that the friendly bacteria are farmers. When they're controlling the candida levels, all is good and your body's in balance. But when the friendly bacteria are killed off from antibiotics or substances that we ingest that have an antibiotic effect, then the farmers lose control and the yeast starts to grow and then overgrow. This becomes a problem.

ANTON: Do things like alcohol destroy candida?

LEE BEYMER: No, alcohol and sugars feed the yeast. The yeast feeds on sugar, fermented foods and other yeasts, and, of course, alcohol is sugar that is fermented with yeast—so the candida doesn't even have to chew (laughs).

ANTON: When you were treating me and you said to me "no yeast, no sugar, nothing fermented," I went home and said, "Okay," and then suddenly everything I reached for had something like that in it.

LEE BEYMER: Welcome to the world.

ANTON: For the two-month recovery period you didn't even let me eat fruit. You were pretty extreme—I must have been pretty bad off! It was quite a shock. Suddenly I found myself discovering raw foods, fresh foods. For any food that needed a perk, I found that lemons, limes and yogurt were the three things that made it taste better.

LEE BEYMER: Typically when we do a specific candida therapy diet, we can't allow any sugar. The fructose in the fruit will actually feed it. The amount of sugar in the lemon and lime at the levels that a person will use it are minimal, and I've found that they actually help when added to water to really flush the system. Cinnamon is another good thing.

ANTON: We are accustomed to putting spices on our food because we want to experience the flavor. Are you are suggesting that we are actually moderating aspects of our health and well-being with the common herbs and spices we already have in our kitchen?

LEE BEYMER: Absolutely. Every spice has a benefit. When used appropriately it can be absolutely amazing.

A simple guide from Chinese medicine is to let your taste be your guide. What kinds of things do you want? What kinds of foods do you have a taste for? This, of course, is different from always wanting chocolate cake. That's an allergic addiction, more often than not sponsored by candida, which is always craving the same kinds of sugars, yeast or fermented foods.

The foods that candida loves are very difficult to break the cravings for. It will cause you to crave those foods to feed it. When a person has a strong case of candida, they will eat virtually the same kinds of food every single day to appease their candida.

One of the ways that I test people to see if they have candida is to ask what they eat every day. Some people will say, "I eat bread every day" or "I have a glass of wine every day" or I have this or that every single day. That is their candida talking.

ANTON: So when people are having weight problems or are facing potential diabetes, and when people have chronic fatigue, candida could be involved?

LEE BEYMER: Candida is a precursor for over 300 different diseases, including those that you've mentioned.

ANTON: What about adrenal function and kidney function?

LEE BEYMER: That can be different. Candida doesn't affect the kidneys or adrenals too much. It's more the digestive tract, GI tract, liver and so on.

ANTON: Why is there this huge chasm between Eastern philosophy in medicine and our Western medicine?

LEE BEYMER: They come from different routes and they work according to different motives. The Eastern philosophy is actually to help heal and bring the person into balance. Unfortunately much of the Western philosophy comes from the pharmaceutical industry, which wants to sell more drugs. And so we have a very different approach to conventional medicine, which wants to manage a disease by keeping a person on drugs to manage their symptoms for the rest of their lives.

ANTON: In this world we are used to waiting until some disaster befalls us, and then we go to see the doctor. And when the doctor doesn't work we come to see someone like you. But you have clients and friends that come to see you just for regular, preventative checkups to make sure that everything is in balance.

LEE BEYMER: Most people, I would hope, see their regular doctor and do their blood work every year or so. This is the same except we are talking about doing a checkup on an energetic basis. So the parameter and the scope we're looking at is broader and different from conventional medicine.

ANTON: If different foods have different energies, and that is why they affect us differently, what can we do or what can we consider about balancing the energy in our lives with this simple thing that we do every day, eating and drinking?

LEE BEYMER: Well, it's important to appreciate the relative significance of the foods that we take into ourselves. The old adage was that you are what you eat. Now we understand it to be that you are what you actually *absorb*.

This is important. Food, solid food, we can do without for about seventy days. Water, liquid food, a person can do without for about seven days maximum. Breath, gaseous food, we can last about seven minutes max without, and energetic food (the pure energy of the lifeforce itself) about seven seconds. So when we think about food let us also think about energy, because *what we think about* is much more immediate, much more effective, much more powerful in how it actually affects us. This is the highest frequency of food.

Having a positive attitude, for instance, makes all the difference. It has been very well documented that a person with a positive attitude can eat bad food and not suffer. They've even been able to make homeopathic frequency water by putting that positive attitude in the water and giving it to someone who is ill—and it helped to heal them.

Perhaps you are familiar with the work of Dr. Emoto, a Japanese scientist who started photographing frozen water samples to see how thought could influence the environment. The results were profound. The molecules of waters that were exposed to ugly and imbalanced pollution and negative thoughts turned into misshapen forms, whereas water that was exposed to love, where someone consciously projected love onto it, formed the most exquisite and beautiful snowflake patterns at the molecular level.

The homeopathic frequencies that we're putting into these vials of water as remedies are similar in that we are giving specific energetic frequencies to counterbalance a person's problems. Taking these in small doses has a profound effect.

GOOD VIBRATIONS

Music can help align the energies that bring focus into all apsects of our lives, causing good things to happen in our health, relationships and business.

Mark Romero turned from a successful twenty-year career in sales and executive management to changing people's lives with his innovative transformational music. He is the founder and CEO of Mark Romero Music, Inc. and has been featured at some of the most prestigious events hosted by luminaries like T. Harv Eker and Mark Victor Hansen. He is recognized as a global leader in both personal and professional development through his own unique transformational music technology, which has the ability to shift listeners into higher states of consciousness, where they can tap into their unlimited potential.

MARK ROMERO: I was in the semiconductor business for nineteen years. I had ascended up the corporate ladder and finally gotten to that last rung: CEO of my own company.

I had started the company in my garage and, over the course of five years, taken it to a multi-million dollar enterprise. I had come to the point where I was thinking, *I've done everything society says I'm supposed to do. Why am I still not happy?* I had gotten the house, bought a nice car, built up my portfolio and done all those things, yet I really felt something was missing.

I had a really powerful conversation with my wife one night. She said, "I don't really care how much money you're making. I look in your eyes and you are dead. When are you going to go for the dream?"

I really took that conversation to heart. I realized I wasn't getting any younger, and, if I was going to do this, I had to do it now. So I took the leap. I walked away from that company to pursue a career doing traditional motivational speaking. Initially I wanted just to be a speaker who shared information that would help empower people in their journey through life.

I had been playing music since 1980. It was something I did for a hobby and for fun. I had made a CD, really just to cross it off the list of things I wanted to do in my life. That CD ended up getting in the hands of scientists that discovered frequencies in it that can actually help people create more success in their lives, improve their health and wellness, and ultimately improve their quality of life!

From that discussion I found myself in the sound therapy and healing arena, creating a music technology that I call Vibrational Success. This helps people create extraordinary breakthroughs in their lives on mental, emotional, spiritual and physical levels. It really helps people not only realize their unlimited potential, but also become more empowered in their life.

ANTON: You are man of great vision. Do you see any parallels in the way you approach your life and business and in the way you eat?

MARK ROMERO: That's a really interesting question, because it's something that has changed over the years depending on how I was outwardly expressing myself in life.

One of the things that jumped out for me in my own business, what I'm doing today, is realizing that my decisions, my choices, and where I focus my attention have tremendous impact upon how my life unfolds and how things expand in my career—including food. In the past I ate for comfort. I used food as a drug to prevent myself from feeling some of the not-so-wonderful feelings that tend to show up in the human experience.

What's happened over time is that I've become very conscious about the actions I take in life. There is always a reaction. That certainly applies to my food, especially now that I'm not as young as I used to be. Now, more than ever, it's important for me to eat a well-balanced, nutritious diet with high-quality foods and to realize that if I don't, there are going to be repercussions, whether an expanding waistline or health implications.

I started to notice how those decisions also impact the way I feel. Let's say I go out to dinner with my wife. We have a wonderful dinner, and then she wants to have some of that triple chocolate cake (notice I say *she* wants). So I happen to have some triple chocolate cake too, and the next day, I just don't feel that good.

And I realize how important it is, whether it's my thoughts, my beliefs, the foods I eat or where I am focusing my attention, to pay attention when making decisions, because there are repercussions for every decision I make in life. Knowing this has made me much more conscious. I am all about living the empowered life, and the decisions I make in life ultimately impact just how empowered I can be.

ANTON: What I love about that is that you're not just thinking, "This is what they tell me I am supposed to do, and therefore this is the food I'm going to eat." You are actually paying attention to how you feel, paying attention to the responses you have, and then making your decision in the moment. Step by step, day by day.

MARK ROMERO: We are emerging into a time when all of us are going to have to become more feeling based as opposed to logic based. We can always talk ourselves into a good dessert that we probably shouldn't be eating or something like that, but we can never fool with the heart. Emotions and feelings will always give you clear guidance. The heart is what's connected to your soul, and it's the heart that's going to give you the guidance that's in alignment with your higher self, with your higher purpose. When we as individuals can get connected to our hearts, we feel better.

That plays a big part in my decisions as to the types of foods I'm going to eat. I want to eat things that are going to help me feel good, and I know that when I feel good I am in alignment. I know that when I feel good, amazing things are going to happen, not only in my health, but in my business, my relationships, my family time and all those different aspects that are so important.

ANTON: Your music technology deliberately targets and addresses the challenges we face and the aspirations of our hearts. It helps align the energies that bring focus to all areas of our lives. Scientists discovered that your music has a direct affect on our body chemistry. Music directly affects our feelings. These emotions create a response, a chemistry within our bodies, and that chemistry has direct health and sickness repercussions. Some music makes us feel good and some music we like or don't like, but we're specifically, deliberately focusing on creating frequencies that attune people so that the chemistry within their bodies and minds is changing.

MARK ROMERO: Being exposed to the principles of quantum physics was how I got connected to sound therapy. Everything first starts off as energy before it manifests in physical form, and that includes our physical body. We are all exposed to so many discordant energies, like the 80,000 man-made chemicals in our air, food, and water and all the electronic technology that we've surrounded ourselves with. They all impact our energy, along with the thoughts, perceptions and beliefs that govern our lives.

Become aware of those things, because all the physical things that manifest in our bodies first start off in the quantum field of energy. If we want to truly change our lives and our experiences, we start in that place. That's why it's always so hard when we take on diet programs, which are focused purely on the physical. Let's say we want to lose twenty pounds. Until we change the beliefs and the perceptions that are causing extra weight, we are forever going to struggle trying to lose those twenty pounds—it's just too difficult to make right choices about our food. I have experienced it myself. We hear about people's struggles to create long-term, lasting physical change in their eating programs and in their diets and exercise routines. But we have to start within. We have to start from the quantum level, because it's that energy that manifests in our physical body and ultimately shapes our life experiences.

We are emerging into a time when people are starting to get an understanding about energy and realizing how important it is to keep our energy optimized. We do that by eating quality foods and having a well-balanced diet. We do that by exercising. So many people are eating organic foods now and improving the quality of water they drink. That's also important because it impacts our energy.

Music can help shift the beliefs preventing us from taking care of our bodies, help us feel and process our emotions. One of my favorite ways to open this up for people is to demonstrate with my music. If you can help people experience something on a physical level, it's an opportunity also to open their minds. When we play this music and all of a sudden, instantly, they're stronger and have more flexibility, endurance, coordination and balance, people go, "Wow, there is something going on here. There is something to this!"

Five years ago, vibrational medicine or vibrational therapy or sound therapy—healing through sound—was typically viewed as very esoteric. But we are emerging into a time where it's becoming more and more mainstream, and people are becoming more and more open to it. I don't think there's a person on this planet that doesn't know there is something very special about music, any type of music, whether it's Mozart or something else.

Music deeply impacts our lives. When you throw music into the mix, all of a sudden people become much more open to looking at things differently. That's how I have handled some of the naysayers—and myself. I was a huge naysayer about my own work for quite a while. I have really had to merge into it, having come from a very left-brain corporate-type background.

We all deal with a tremendous number of different types of emotions in our lives. Some of those emotions feel really good. Some of them don't. For a good part of my life I used food as a crutch, because it was a way for me to be able to sweep things under the carpet that I didn't want to deal with. My parents got divorced when I was young, and I used food as a way to deal with it—or not deal with it, in reality.

The thing that I want to leave as my legacy is for people to experience their emotions, to get back in touch with their feelings. Whether they feel great or whether they feel yucky, emotions are a tremendous blessing in our lives, because they ultimately have the ability to guide us and to correct us as we move through the life process. I say, feel your emotions, process them, let them flow through. Don't use food as a crutch or as a drug to internalize or not deal with things, because it will put you at a disadvantage. Let's face it, going out for a beautiful dinner is a wonderful experience that can go to a whole new level when we're not adding pressure to our eating experience.

I once heard that emotions are energy in motion, that emotions are actually our perception of energy and that, if we don't deal with our emotions, they get stored. What is body fat but unprocessed energy? When I went through my own transformation physically and lost almost thirty pounds in twelve weeks, I realized how much stuff had gotten stored in my body fat because, as I lost it, I actually experienced the emotion of it.

Emotions and food is a subject that's near and dear to my heart, because it's something I struggled with for so many years. I used my own sound therapy technology on myself to help me break through some of the beliefs that I had had about food and emotions, which ultimately helped me literally transform my physicality in twelve weeks.

ANTON: Everything just shifted for me when you said that, because you are always giving to other people. It never occurred to me that you also gave that gift to yourself.

MARK ROMERO: You are only going to be able to love other people to the degree that you can love yourself. It starts there. If you can love yourself, who and what you are, and appreciate yourself, you can be a bright beacon out there in the world. It comes back to energy. Our lives and what we experience, whether on a physical level or other levels, are all predicated on who and what we are being in life, and when we shift that, we transform our experiences.

THE RESONANT FLOW OF ALIGNMENT

*Everything has a vibrational frequency. Finding resonance with
the foods and everything else we bring into our lives aligns us with
success. Physical alignment of our bodies opens channels for a clear
flow of these energies within us.*

Chiropractor Dr. Dave Jensen wants to change the world by contributing to a shift in consciousness from sickness to wellness. He has worked in sports medicine with great organizations like the Dallas Cowboys and Miami Dolphins, and Olympic athletes during the 1996 Centennial Olympic Games in Atlanta. He has worked in the Mayo Clinic Minneapolis Research Department. His WIN Health Institute approaches nutrition on a cellular level. They combine the latest cutting-edge technology with ancient holistic practices to help people maximize their greatest health potential.

ANTON: You have this magic touch when I come to see you. Recently I threw out my back when I fell rollerblading. Sometimes I think you're just touching me to assess where the problem is, but you're actually fixing it. It is amazing that you have that insight to realign my body, but you also always talk to me about other aspects of my health. You're helping to realign all of me when you treat me.

DAVE JENSEN: At the WIN Health Institute, our main premise is to create a balanced approach to health. There have been great accomplishments in medicine over the years, but true medicine comes in foods and *real goods* (natural, unprocessed or minimally processed products). These actually change a person's body naturally, as opposed to chemically with a drug or surgery. We want to educate and empower people to move forward in their own health care quest.

The WIN Health Institute near Aspen is our flagship. We have a dream of organizing health care in a way that can then be modeled and replicated around the world. We bring together Western medicine and the latest technology advancements with Eastern philosophies and Old World medicine.

We really want to change health care through a shift in consciousness, by getting people to think about taking care of their health from a progressive standpoint versus a reactive standpoint. It's a huge premise.

ANTON: The WIN Institute includes chiropractic, acupuncture and food awareness, as well as some very high-tech cutting-edge technologies. You founded this business with your wife, Dee.

DAVE JENSEN: Part of our balance comes from taking advantage of male and female energy. Dee brings in a lot of very insightful things that I overlook and vice versa. It's a great combination. Dee brings in the food aspect.

We do free educational cooking awareness classes (through our non-profit) one-on-one, right there in people's homes, to teach them about food and alternative ways to eat. That way they can actually see firsthand how great things can happen and how much progress can be made when you're not eating poorly.

One of the things we cover is not cooking with non-stick or aluminum pans and materials that off-gas heavy metals, which contaminate the food we eat with certain toxins that we still don't understand fully.

ANTON: Everybody is talking about predictions of all sorts related to energetic, political and other disasters, including the end of the world in 2012. What do you think about that?

DAVE JENSEN: I am writing a book with my wife called *Bridging the Gap of 2012*. It's about the secret of bridging that gap between the things we thought were reliable constants that are actually changing right now.

We are going through a major shift in the new millennium. We are going through major turmoil both politically and physically in people's bodies and worlds. I don't think there will be some significant single catastrophe that will take people out; I think there are many things at work all at the same time, converging on us right now.

Think of the way medicine is helping some people but killing many people. Then think about the way our food industry is helping some people but mainly killing many people. We've already gone through a giant cycle of change. The year 2012 will be a significant year, with people experiencing a lot of loss and major lifestyle changes to come in the next twenty-year cycle.

For example, think about the pride of the American Indian and how we've practically eradicated that culture. We've got to revitalize things like that culture and a lot of our own planet, because we've taken over too much and consumed at too great a cost. We have to change our ways in our own economic uses, get some forward momentum, and get into smaller communities to grow our own foods again and not transport them halfway across the planet. Just get real foods back in our bodies so we can actually change the ways people think and how they operate.

We live on thirty-five acres in this magical valley outside Aspen in Colorado. Even at this altitude, we grow much of our own food.

ANTON: We have seen times in winter when the pass between Denver and Aspen, the I-70 corridor, has been closed, and literally within about a day the shelves in the grocery store started to look empty. We are huge producers, with great food resources in America and many parts of the world, but if a disaster befell our food supply, if for some reason that was compromised, we would probably feel the impact of that very quickly.

DAVE JENSEN: If they run out of diesel fuel, for instance, that's going to shut down the shipping, the trucking and the trains, and then we're going to be out of food within three days in the large cities.

ANTON: How do you think food plays into our potential for success?

DAVE JENSEN: I look at food, ultimately, as a resonance that actually builds our body. What you put in your body fuels what you get back out of your body—what you can produce through that support.

Everything in life has some type of vibration, and certainly that includes living foods. We call that a *resonance.* All humans operate at a similar resonance, yet a little bit different from one another. Just as we look a little different, we all function at different frequencies. That's why a lot of the new medicines coming out are based on frequencies.

Foods have a resonance. Real foods and manufactured foods. Resonance makes a giant difference in how we feel day to day, how we perform and how well our brains perform. It assists us in connecting to the Great Spirit and understanding how we're going to move forward in our culture.

ANTON: Science has verified that everything is energy and that the frequencies at which those energies vibrate are measurable. We have devices that can accurately measure the electromagnetic field of your entire body to reveal fluctuations that can precisely indicate which internal organs are stressed or failing. These same machines can produce electromagnetic resonance fields that serve as remedies for the diseases they reveal. Many of the ancient practices of China and the East are only now being recognized in the West because they're being validated by science.

DAVE JENSEN: Now they're figuring out that you can make a giant difference in people's health just by turning a part of the body on or off. Acupuncture, for example, can do this.

Putting the right resonance foods in your body can change your entire being. A tomato that was grown in your backyard, that you loved and nurtured, has a much different effect on you than one that came all the way from Bolivia.

ANTON: And these frequencies shift from day to day within us. In other words, we couldn't eat the same food every day and expect life to go on at its peak level.

DAVE JENSEN: The best way to understand that is in cravings. You have good cravings and you have bad cravings. Once you become toxic enough, you have these bad cravings that just maintain that toxicity level. But as that changes, you can also have good cravings for good foods. These frequencies are constantly changing in all of us.

I certainly cheat on my diet and do things that I probably shouldn't do. I have a glass of wine here and there and things like that. You still have to live and enjoy your life, but it doesn't have to be super hardcore.

ANTON: Did you ever eat differently than you do now? Is there something that promoted all of this wellness to come into your life and made you decide to be conscious in this way?

DAVE JENSEN: I was brought up in a great family with whole foods. I never really knew much different; I thought that's just the way things were until I lived in the real world and saw how much junk was out there. Then I understood what our world was up against. I have never taken an antibiotic in my whole life. There are lots of positive things that come out of living that way since you were born.

ANTON: We're so used to the idea that at some point we're going to get shot up with some antibiotics, but you are a healthy strong man and you've not only made it this far but thrived in your life without them. Why is that?

DAVE JENSEN: We have antibodies living and working inside us at their highest ability all the time. Plenty of good, clean, healthy water and good, clean, healthy food makes almost all the difference. Good food, water and exercise are the foundations. You have to exercise, and you have to do things that you enjoy and that stir your spirit as well.

ANTON: There is a certain flow that comes with that resonance. Just a flow in life in general. Your chiropractic work is focused on opening up that flow, because when something is tweaked and pinched, it's hard to move and it's also hard to think. You help the tight places release, and suddenly it feels as if a pipe has been unplugged.

DAVE JENSEN: Lots of people don't even know what that is. They are out of alignment, clogged up energetically their whole life, and then they wonder why they live with sciatica or headaches or some problem they think is normal for their body—which is completely ridiculous! They have to realize the ramifications further down the line.

If you have some problem in your mid-back, those nerves run through your heart and your lungs. It will eventually create dis-ease in your heart and your lungs. Your whole body is built that way. Little babies all the way to full adults who get adjusted regularly are somewhat bullet-proofed against people's normal ailments.

ANTON: You just said disease as if it were two words: dis-ease.

DAVE JENSEN: It is not a disease. It's actually dis-ease. Our bodies should live in ease in a nice homeostasis, smoothed out. But that changes when something enters the body from a bad food or an accident or a person trying to attack you energetically, through anger, for example. We get pulled off to the side of this road we're going down called life, and that can create what normal medicine calls disease. I always call it dis-ease.

ANTON: That word homeostasis keeps coming up. Please define that for us.

DAVE JENSEN: Homeostasis is the state of perfect centering where every cell in our body is happy, everything is flowing totally normally. Multiple other things go along with homeostasis, such as proprioception, which is your balance and integrity in sport. Your digestion's working perfectly. You wake up exactly at the right time. Everything. Just your consciousness in general. That is homeostasis.

HAPPY CELLS

Just like every cell in your body, with higher consiousness and clear observation, you must move towards what supports you and move away from what does not.

Richard Duree and his wife, Shanti, have been pioneers in the field of Somatic Energy[1] Psychology and Kineseological Energy Medicine for over three decades. Their programs are taught worldwide at professional schools of complementary medicine. Richard has served as the head of research and development for Dr. John Thie, the creator of the Touch For Health program. He also works with Olympic and world-class athletes at the International Sports Medicine Institute in Los Angeles.

Some of the Durees' research has included studying the effects of muscle balancing and energy psychology on stress and aging at the Renaissance Clinic in the Bahamas. They serve on the board of directors for the Neuroenergetic Psychology Foundation, a California based non-profit corporation for education, research and enhancing public awareness of somatic psychology and its benefits.

RICHARD DUREE: I have been in the Neuroenergetic business for about thirty-five years. I started working with a healer after a motorcycle accident up in Grants Pass, Oregon, with whom I ended up studying for about a year. He worked on me, then told me one morning that I should go and meet a man named John Thie down in Pasadena, California. So I went and became part of creating a program called Touch for Health, which developed internationally.

---

1   The somatic system is the part of the peripheral nervous system that is responsible for carrying motor and sensory information both to and from the central nervous system.

I led the research and development department for Dr. Thie. I was researching applied kinesiology[2]. We taught at different chiropractic colleges, LACC [Los Angeles City College], Western States. My wife was a colleague of mine at Touch for Health for years, and then we started having a relationship. We just had our thirty-third anniversary; we are still enjoying our life together.

I started focusing on working on Olympians around that time, working with Dr. Thie's partner, Leroy Perry, who owns the International Sports Medicine Institute here in Los Angeles. As I worked with these athletes, I started to understand how much psychology influenced their musculature and how their biology functioned. I started moving more in that direction.

ANTON: There are two different systems that operate within our body, one of which we can control and one of which is doing its own thing no matter what we do. It never occurred to me that, even though this is going on anyway, we could somehow influence this unconscious process.

RICHARD DUREE: A lot of times when we were studying the body we had the idea that we're made of separate pieces—body, mind, etc. But it's a biological organism, so everything that it experiences is expressed somehow throughout the body. We don't get it. We think it's all about the brain, but everything I ever learned, I learned with my body.

ANTON: We are trained to think of the eye specialist, the liver specialist, the heart specialist. We don't see that the body is an entirely integrated system.

RICHARD DUREE: I'll give you an example. I wear glasses and so I have some vision issues. I'm almost sixty. About ten years ago I went on an alkaline diet. At that time I was starting to exhibit a little bit of arthritic stuff that is in my family. I started eating more things

---

2   The study of the anatomy, physiology and mechanics of body movement, especially in humans.

that make alkaline ash in the body. All of a sudden, I didn't have any arthritic issues or pains or aches or anything. And what was even more interesting was that suddenly I couldn't see out of my glasses. So I went to the optometrist. I said, "I guess I'm getting older and maybe I need stronger glasses." She said, "No. You're going the other way. You need a weaker prescription!"

So in my own life I've seen that manifest. Changing the way I eat changed my vision.

ANTON: We're so used to thinking that once the degeneration starts, we're on a downhill slide. You just illustrated that there are conditions we can improve or even reverse.

RICHARD DUREE: I'll be honest. I've gotten younger. I will be sixty in three months.

ANTON: You certainly don't look it.

RICHARD DUREE: I looked older when I was forty-five than I do now.

ANTON: And how did you feel? Did you feel older?

RICHARD DUREE: I've been in the health business my whole life, but I did feel older then than I feel now. I feel I'm progressively getting younger. I've got students who have tracked me for ten or fifteen years. If you talk to them, they will tell you the same thing, that I've gotten progressively younger every year.

ANTON: So this relates directly to food and diet?

RICHARD DUREE: It's a truth. I stay away from refined carbohydrates just because I don't react to them well. The only grains I really eat are quinoa and millet, because they have more of an alkaline ash effect in the body. The majority of my diet is vegetable oriented, but I do eat chicken and I eat fish.

For fourteen years I was vegetarian and for seven of those I was vegan. For me it didn't work. My hair started getting brittle, and a friend, one of my students who's a doctor said, "Hey, man, come on, you need to alter your eating pattern a little bit." So I started adding some more protein in at that point. I'm pretty rigorous about the way I eat. I eat a lot of superfood types of foods. Actually, I use a product from L.A. called Superfood. I eat a live mix in the morning with a vegetable concentrate, blue-green algae and different stuff. And I don't eat a lot.

I used to have to eat a lot more when I ate food that wasn't as nutritionally packed as the food I eat now. In fact, I ate three times the amount of food I eat now. Quality of food versus quantity. If you're not getting the nutrition you need, you eat more because your body wants to get the nutrition.

ANTON: How did that change or affect your energy levels?

RICHARD DUREE: You have more energy when you spend less time on digestion.

ANTON: You work with Olympian athletes, so we're talking about people that are trying to optimize every aspect of their lives and their body functionality.

RICHARD DUREE: They eat food a little differently than I do. We give them 10% better efficiency out of their musculature. Athletes have a huge psychological component as well. If they're worrying or competing with other people, you have to get their psyche straightened out in order for them to compete at optimum levels. Otherwise they don't perform as well, or they get injuries and they fall down.

I started training them just to compete with themselves—to not even think about the other person, just what they were doing and where they needed to go. And they performed better.

ANTON: That is such a remarkable paradigm shift, not to compete with others but to compete with yourself, even in competition.

RICHARD DUREE: Just do the best they can. These people are highly tuned. When you are talking about the end of a race and everybody is only two or three *hundredths* of a second apart, we are talking about that 1% or 10% or whatever gives them the edge, because everybody out there is tuned to about the same level.

ANTON: This implies that they were not always at a super level. In other words, they were like normal people on some level and had to train and grow into this. Was the food they ate one of the things they changed to give them that edge?

RICHARD DUREE: Certainly. With those kinds of people it depends on the event they're doing. Sometimes they have to carbohydrate load, because they burn a lot of calories.

ANTON: Was there ever a time in your life where you ate junk food or where you didn't eat the way you do now?

RICHARD DUREE: Oh, absolutely. When I was a kid I ate trash just like everybody else. My family just ate whatever was there.

ANTON: What happened to cause you to make a change? Was it something that hit you like a sledgehammer? Or was it something you grew into?

RICHARD DUREE: Actually, that change happened for me at sixteen. I started realizing that I needed to put better fuel in my body. I started eating whole grain bread at that point. I just made a decision within my family unit that I was going to eat this kind of bread and I wasn't going to eat the same way they were eating anymore.

ANTON: But what would even cause you to think of that?

RICHARD DUREE: I was reading some things as a kid and felt it would make me healthier, it would make me better. I wouldn't be tired.

ANTON: And at sixteen, why would you want to be healthier and better? Was there something that wasn't healthy or better?

RICHARD DUREE: I was overweight. I was probably a couple hundred pounds at sixteen. That doesn't seem that strange for someone who is as tall as I am, but I felt I was grossly overweight at that point. I had to carry it around. That was an experience for me, and I thought, *Okay, calories in, calories out, there must be something I'm doing wrong.*

ANTON: The efficiency of our bodies to keep this cellular level of us going and alive becomes inhibited.

RICHARD DUREE: Imagine that in our bodies we have all these cells and they're individuals and they're all out doing whatever they do with their own purpose in the biological system. What I realized is that if I can learn how to feed the cells properly, my cells are happy, and happy cells make happy bodies. So as I ate better, I got happier. I go along with the Dalai Lama's idea that the purpose of your life is to be happy.

ANTON: Happy cells sounds a little bit airy fairy.

RICHARD DUREE: Well, I'm not that at all. I'm a scientist.

ANTON: We are truly talking about joy and happiness?

RICHARD DUREE: Absolutely.

What are the things that make me feel conflicted? That's what I want to look at. If my body is agitated because I'm putting something into it that causes me stress, then the cells are going to come from a stressed place.

Cells under a microscope only make three movements. They move towards things they want. They move away from things that are toxic. Or they have no opinion and they stand still. Those are the only three motions they make underneath a microscope.

When I decided that I wanted to pay attention to my cells, I could feel myself moving towards things or away from things or not caring about things. I started paying more attention to how I *felt* about what was going on rather than the intellectual part of it. That part of us is so small.

That part that thinks is such a little part of our neurology, and we let it control the whole show.

Amassing information for the left brain is like building a filing cabinet full of information. But the real information comes from the right side, where you get the full gestalt of it. You use the other information to fill it in or break it down into usable components.

So how do you use these two different things in a way that is functional for you and allows you to have access to your vitality? When you give cells food that's actual food, they respond to that by moving towards it, by absorbing more of it, by replicating properly. When they go into a stasis where they're pulling away, they don't replicate the same way.

ANTON: We tend to think of food as something tasty and superficial and filling, but you're talking about true nourishment.

RICHARD DUREE: Yes, the nourishment that's inside the food you're eating.

ANTON: Not just to make us feel, "Okay, I needed to eat, I'm full now, I'm good to go."

RICHARD DUREE: A lot of people do it that way, and unfortunately what happens when you eat in a way that's not vital for your body is that you become numb. So you're not even aware that you're feeling bad. You're just dealing with things like gas or acidity or inflammation or other symptoms, and you're not associating it with the fact that, if you changed what you eat, you might not be having these symptoms.

Let's say I have a really highly efficient muscle car. It just won't run on that 89-octane gas. It pings and knocks and does all this stuff that damages the engine, because I didn't put the right quality of fuel in it. How is the body any different from that?

I am a firm believer that people should eat the way people ate a couple of thousand years ago, when there was no processed food. When food gets processed, however that gets done, they pull nutrients out of the food.

You eat the food that grows out of the ground, or, if you eat animals, you eat the animals that eat that food. I don't even know that humans were designed to eat grain that much, you know; a lot of people have problems with different grains.

ANTON: What about the combinations of food we eat? Earlier in history, unlike today, everything wasn't available at all times, all in one place. Food grew regionally and it grew seasonally. Food combinations and the responses that our body has to them affect whether the internal system can handle it, whether it is actually flowing and functioning.

RICHARD DUREE: It's certain that some foods are not meant to be mixed. Melons for instance. It's better to eat them alone or leave them alone because of the type of enzymes they contain and what they do. If you eat melons with other food it causes a digestive disturbance. But if you eat them alone they digest very well.

The body has to react differently to different combinations of food. In other words, when I'm sending the stuff in, the body is saying, "Okay, you've got starches in there, I need to put this enzyme in it." Then I'm throwing in all this other stuff at the same time and the body is saying, "How do I sort all of this out?"

I try to get people to pay attention to their bodies rather than ignoring them. I say learn how to live in your body rather than living up in your head all the time. Pay attention to your body. If you eat something and you get a bad reaction, why would you want to eat it again—unless you want to support the antacid industry. Usually the people who are taking antacids, their hydrochloric acid levels are down too low anyway, and that's why they're having a gastric disturbance.

ANTON: Richard, you are a very successful man. The other aspects of your life clearly tie into the food you eat. If you were going to leave a key gift for the people that are still trying to find their way through all the confusion and all the information we're bombarded with, what would you like to leave behind? Something that your kids, your grandkids and humanity after you could benefit from?

RICHARD DUREE: When I first got involved in this industry, I realized that it was a vehicle for raising people's consciousness and for giving them more control over their own health care. I don't want to make other people the authority for my health care.

I am not against allopathic medicine at all. I have had my life saved more than once by medical doctors. I have had Lyme's disease. I had malaria when I worked in Africa. I had a hernia operation. I've had my finger sewn back on. They are really good at trauma.

Where they have not been good is in chronic illness, because chronic illness is an illness of lifestyle. What I would encourage people to do is to look at the things in their lives that aren't working. Do they need to learn how to communicate? Do they need to learn how to interact with or how to cook food?

In the health care industry, I would like to see a new profession that had an overall understanding of all the modalities of health care that are used, so they could channel people into the appropriate things they need at a given time.

Some people need to learn how to cook food. They just don't know how.

When I worked for Dr. Thie we did a study on congenital illness, where we thought that people had congenital problems because they were showing up in a family group. What we realized after studying them for three years was that it was because of the way they ate! They had certain preferences and choices that came from their family or cultural background. They were simply missing certain nutrients they needed.

ANTON: Stop adding the pills, change the way you eat.

RICHARD DUREE: If you need a pill, take it. Intervention is necessary in a lot of cases. But it's not necessary in all cases, and I think we are overusing pharmaceuticals and people are getting liver damage as a result. Every week there is a new drug on TV that is now killing people. We have turned our health care over to industry.

We are simply not taking responsibility for ourselves. That's what it's really about.

YOUR HOLOGRAPHIC UNIVERSE

All of you shows and is multiplied in everything you do, so know yourself and take care of yourself first, so you can live on purpose and contribute from a place of abundance and overflow.

Terry Tillman's 22/7 is an internationally networked company that excels in teaching and facilitating the key skills of leadership, teambuilding and development, cooperation, confidence, inspiration, risk-taking, and self-esteem to individuals and organizations. He is a serial entrepreneur and has done leadership and teambuilding seminars in ninety-four countries for companies such as Ford, Ericcson, International Paper and countless others.

At fifteen, he designed the rocker-style track hurdle with Nike founder Bill Bowerman. He shares a Grammy Award with The New Christie Minstrels, a hugely popular musical group from the sixties that still plays to audiences today.

George Bernard Shaw once said that *"reason* enslaves all those who are not strong enough to master her." On his website, Terry says, "Many of the most rewarding, creative, fulfilling and enduring solutions, dreams, victories and results are accomplished through unreasonableness and intuition—beyond rationality, outside the mind, from the heart and soul." From ski instructor to pilot, Terry leaves no rock unturned in being a living example of living life to its full potential.

TERRY TILLMAN: Back when I was about twelve years old, Adelle Davis said, "You are what you eat." In my work I say you are what you think, you are what you do. There is an essence inside that manifests in many ways. It's holographic.

In junior high school, my grandfather gave me a book describing how holographic photography worked. It was only discovered in the late forties, and I first ran into it in the mid-fifties. Let's see if I can simplify it.

A holographic image is a three-dimensional image. We see them on credit cards and in other places now, but the way they're taken is by shining laser light off the object you're photographing and reflecting it back onto a photographic plate in a certain way. Then you reproduce the image by reflecting light off the photographic plate.

A real hologram can be three-dimensional in free space. You can walk around it and try to touch it, but you'll reach right through it. That's pretty amazing. But the most amazing part to me is that if you take the photographic plate, drop it on the ground and break it into little pieces, then pick up any one piece and shine the laser light off that piece, the same whole image will be reproduced!

When I first saw that, lights went off in my head, because it demonstrated that *the whole is in every part*.

Author Robert Heinlein coined the term *grok* in his best-selling 1961 book, *Stranger In A Strange Land*. In Heinlein's view, *grokking* is the intermingling of intelligence that necessarily affects both the observer and the observed. It means more than understanding: it's more like "get it completely."

If I want to grok anything—anything—like the existential questions of life, I can pick up any one part of a question, and if I become thoroughly acquainted with it, I will understand everything about it. It doesn't matter if I want to be a football player, a rocket scientist, a lawyer or someone who makes paper. If I get into whatever it is and get into it completely, to the point where I understand all there is to understand about it, *all of life* will show up there!

ANTON: Another way to understand a hologram is that you can take a DNA sample from a piece of someone's hair or spit or a flake of their skin, and no matter what part of the original it is taken from, in that DNA you have all the information that represents the entire human being. Every part of you has all the information needed to make all of you.

TERRY TILLMAN: Exactly! That's fascinating to me. So let's look at it regarding eating, which is a fascinating approach. I eat very much the way I do life.

My wife has a degree in nutritional medicine, so, by osmosis, I absorb an awful lot about eating well and healthily. I have had a fascination with it most of my life, although I got way off course for quite a while. Now I eat very well. I don't think I've shopped at a Ralf's or Safeway in years because I look at what's on the shelf—and it isn't food. It's processed down to where it looks pretty and it sells and it makes somebody money.

I see in that a problem that's showing up everywhere, like in the BP oil spill, or the banks. You look at the major issues we see around us today, and they're happening because somebody got greedy and placed money ahead of people.

I see the same thing with food. Most of the food isn't food. It's not alive and fresh. It's transported from thousands of miles away. It's wasteful.

One of the things I teach, and which I've tried my best to do in my own life, is to take care of myself first, so that I can give to the world and contribute from a place of abundance and overflow, not from a place of lack. If I don't take care of myself first, when I go to any other relationship or project, there's part of me that's needy. It needs to take instead of give. With food, eating well is simply a fundamental of taking care of myself—and living well as a result—so I can be of service to others because of the abundance and overflow in my life, so that I have something to give to make this world a better place.

ANTON: There was a time in your life when you didn't eat and think the way you do now. What happened that prompted you to make a change?

TERRY TILLMAN: When I got out of college I assumed I was supposed to be a "successful" businessman. I am putting quotes around *successful* because I hadn't taken the time to figure out what that meant. But I assumed it meant making and accumulating lots of money.

I also bought into the idea that it takes hard work to make money and that it was important to be efficient. Efficient meant there was no waste of time. So for fifteen years after college I started, ran and groomed six different businesses. I didn't take a vacation for fifteen years. Literally. I had a couple of three-day weekends, but the whole time I would be thinking about business or worrying about it, and the result showed up everywhere in my life.

I would get up in the morning. I would warm up some leftover coffee. I would grab a couple of donuts and eat them in the car on the way to the office. I built my own office building, and one of the tenants was a coffee importer, so I always had a cup of coffee on my desk. I probably drank ten or twelve cups a day—and I wondered why I had a bleeding ulcer and was nervous all the time!

I thought that the way to get energy was from the outside. I thought that everything I needed had to come from outside me: more money, a bigger house, a newer car, a new title. I thought that I had to get it from the outside and bring it in. That's exactly opposite of what I'm doing today.

What I've figured out and what I teach is that life works best from the inside out. Back then, I didn't even take time to eat properly. I'd drink to relax. In the evening I'd have a couple of cocktails. Now I'm the polar opposite from that. At that time, a meal was a time to do business. Otherwise it was something I had to hurry through.

ANTON: And now what do you look for in a meal? What is the essence of the type of food that you're putting in your body now?

TERRY TILLMAN: First of all, it has to be nourishing. It's very important that the food I put into my body is alive and nourishing and healthy. Healthy means organic and fresh. I don't eat entirely raw, but I eat a lot of raw food, a lot of green foods and a minimum of fried foods.

I am sixty-seven and still climbing mountains and running. My body is healthy, and a lot of that is because of nutrition I get from what I eat. The reason we have such a high incidence of cancer and heart problems now at increasing rates is because of the toxins people are putting into their bodies. It isn't *just* from food, but it's largely from food. The hormones and pesticides that go on the plants and in the crops and the animals, that's poison. That might sound radical to some people, but they're the ones getting sick.

ANTON: The incidence of cancer and heart disease is increasing exponentially year after year. When I was a kid, the numbers were much smaller. Now, younger ages, even kids are starting to suffer. There has to be some underlying cause.

TERRY TILLMAN: Your habits are cumulative, so if you've got healthy habits in your eating, that accumulates. It's always seemed common sense to me. If you've got unhealthy habits, you may not see or experience the effect right away, but eventually it will be the last straw on the camel's back. At some point the body won't be able to handle it any more and it will break down.

ANTON: I always say you can't paint a barn red with a can of blue paint. People are trying to do that. They want to have health and success, and yet they're ingesting poison continuously.

What advice about food and success would you like to leave in your legacy for the people who are still searching to grow and improve their lives?

TERRY TILLMAN: Take care of yourself first. It's okay to be selfish, not in terms of *keep it for yourself and don't share* but selfish in terms of *you come first*. That's the opposite of what I was taught. I had to unlearn that and then learn a better way.

Take care of yourself first, nutritionally. Learn how to do that. Information is more readily available now. Don't learn from the new food pyramid that the government put out. It's way off. You've got to dig a little deeper.

You don't have to do this alone. It's hard to do it alone and, I would say, stupid. I did the stupid approach a lot of years. I thought I had to figure it out myself. There are people who have been down the road ahead of us who have done well. I'm not interested in listening to somebody who got theory out of a book. I'm just interested in listening to somebody who has demonstrated through experience the results in their lives of good eating habits.

There are people who eat well, and "well" doesn't mean it has to be boring. There is some really great healthy food. Good tasting. Find somebody who has been down the road and learn from them. Find a mentor, find a group that has a common focus that can support you.

ANTON: On improving your life and finding your life's purpose, you once said, "It's not an analytical process. It's not a mental process at all. It's an *awareness* process."

TERRY TILLMAN: It's an inside-out process. The most enduring advice has been to follow your heart. Follow your bliss. You've got to find that inside you first.

Before you do anything else, you've got to answer the questions Who am I? and Why am I here? If you don't have that, you won't be able to live purposefully. You will spend a lot of time off purpose, and it's hard when we are off purpose.

I've wasted—well, I wouldn't say *wasted*, because I learned a lot—but I've spent a lot of years looking for what I wanted *outside*, and it's not there. Anything I gained outside corrupts or decays. It doesn't endure. But the invisible stuff inside is always there, and it endures. So you start there.

ANTON: You said you were a scout. A scout explores and has experiences so that they can report back and share their discoveries with others.

TERRY TILLMAN: Scouting is my North Star; it's my compass, it has guided me. As long as I'm scouting, my life works really well.

Most people are good people and don't want to create difficulty or harm. Be responsible to you first.

IV.

GETTING
CENTERED

BEWARE THE WOBBLY TABLE

*As we grow, we become stronger in some aspects of our lives
while neglecting others, creating an imbalance and instability that
undermines our potential for success. We can recover balance
through the way we nourish ourselves.*

Barbara De Angelis, PhD, is one of the most influential teachers of our time in the field of relationships and personal growth. She was one of the first people to popularize the idea of self-help in the 1980s and is the author of fourteen best-selling books that have been published in twenty languages.

She is a popular television personality and sought after motivational speaker who has been a frequent guest on *Oprah*, *The Today Show*, *Good Morning America*, *The View*, *Geraldo*, and *Politically Incorrect*. She is also a regular contributor to *E! Entertainment* and *Eyewitness News* in Los Angeles. She is currently president of a company dedicated to bringing transformational education to the world through all electronic and print media.

Barbara DeAngelis is a wonderful woman who helps people discover and improve their relationships with themselves and the people in their lives, be they children, parents, clients or lovers. Her inherent calm, energy, and joy make you believe anything is possible.

When you are face to face with Barbara, no one else exists in her world but you—despite the thousands of faces that pass through her life. You open your heart to her because she is giving you her undivided attention. She sees you. She hears what you say. She will not allow anything to distract her. It's an amazing thing to see and experience.

Who would not fall in love with someone that treats us this way? If we could all learn to do just this one thing in life, to give those in our lives at the moment our undivided attention, our lives would change dramatically, quickly, profoundly.

Barbara is one of the most published authors on the planet. Her books have lived in the #1 spot on *New York Times* best-seller lists. Her titles include books that are impossible to put down, such as *How Did I Get Here? Finding Your Way to Renewed Hope and Happiness When Life and Love Take Unexpected Turns.*

You know how we open books to an arbitrary page to see if there's a special message in there just for us? Then we get carried away and do it again? And by the third or fourth time we're pushing the limits, and the magic of the exercise stops working? With Barbara's books, no matter what page I turn to, no matter what day or how often, I'm thinking, *Oh, my God, she's talking to me.*

That's actually how she writes. She says, "When I write a chapter, I turn to any page over and over to see if I have that same response, and if I don't, I go back and re-write it." Her dedication to truth and the quality of what she brings into our world is without compromise.

ANTON: Barbara, do you see any parallels in the way you approach the food you eat and the way you manage all the other aspects of your life?

BARBARA DEANGELIS: When I teach and work with people, I try to get them to understand that not only are there parallels, but it's the same consciousness that makes all of the choices. One of the problems I see in the world is that so many of us have the pieces of our lives compartmentalized.

Maybe we have excellence in our business but not in our relationship. Maybe we have excellence in our spiritual life but not with how we honor our body. Until we really understand that everything is just a different expression of the same Source, we can only be compartmentalized. We become what I call *wobbly*, where one part of us is strong and the other part is a little shaky. That does not create wholeness.

When I work with people, as I have for forty-something years, I have always talked about them up-leveling everything, and bringing consciousness to everything, and not just looking like they have mastery in one area and then saying, "Don't look over there, just look over here. Over here I've really got it together, but please don't ask me about that over there."

From the time I was eighteen years old, I began to bring complete consciousness into my eating, into everything I put into my body. At that time I had a spiritual teacher and began a serious practice of meditation. As soon as I closed my eyes and truly began to tap into the inner world, it was instantly clear to me that my body was a temple that was housing my spirit, and, therefore, I needed to treat it in the same way I would any sacred space.

If, for instance, one of your great mentors or teachers, or a spiritual teacher, was coming to your house, you know you would run around and clean it up. And if you knew they were going to come eat, you wouldn't put out a bag of chips and a can of soda for them.

The thing is, none of us are any different from that. None of us. We are all really products of and reflections of the Divine; we should honor and treat ourselves as we would our greatest teacher and treat our body as we would our greatest temple or sacred space.

So with that in mind, from the age of eighteen, I have been eating extremely healthfully and with great consciousness and great reverence, not wanting to poison my body or burden it, and then wonder why it wasn't behaving the way it should.

ANTON: Was there ever a time in your life where you actually ate differently than you do now?

BARBARA DEANGELIS: I had a very early start in becoming conscious, but there was also a shift in my early thirties. I began to have some health challenges. At that time, I had been a vegetarian since I was eighteen. I didn't eat any junk, I didn't drink any soda. Nothing!

Nonetheless, I realized I needed to balance my body even more; my body was telling me in a sense that it wasn't happy. It needed a certain kind of purification. So at the age of thirty-two or thirty-three, I became a very strict macrobiotic for about six years. Really strict. As strict as you could be.

I was involved at the time with somebody who was a very well-known macrobiotic counselor, and he said, "You're too yin. You have to become more yang."

I met Michio Kushi [the renowned macrobiotic educator] and he agreed.

So I used food as medicine for about six years, and it had a profound effect on me.

I slowly balanced my diet back out again to be more flexible, but it was really clear to me, as it is today, that if I'm feeling off, I have to look immediately to what I've been eating and understand what my body needs.

I've done a lot of work studying nutrition, studying the body, studying food—as everybody should do. The most essential thing we do every day is take things and put them in our mouths. I always say, "What you put in is going to determine what comes out." And I mean, what comes out of your mouth, what comes out of your brain, what comes out of your pen or your computer, if you're a writer. What comes out of your heart. You can't disconnect the two.

ANTON: Everybody just talks about the physical body, but everything really ties together.

You have this word that's kind of your very own: *wobbly.* Can you explain what you mean by that?

BARBARA DEANGELIS: How many of us have ever gone to a restaurant and sat down and noticed immediately that the table legs are not all equally placed on the floor? One of the table legs is a little shorter, so the table is wobbly. You're trying to eat on it, and it keeps moving, and there's this sense of it not being stable.

Or perhaps you have this beautiful table, but you notice that it's wobbly, that one of the legs is weak, and you think, You, know, I wouldn't want to put my expensive lamp on this table because it might not be able to support it.

In my work, what I've come to is that a lot of us are very wobbly. We have one, or maybe two, legs of our being that are strong, but then there's another leg or two (and, of course, we have many legs to our consciousness table) that are not strong, that are weak, that are cracked, that need to be repaired—and so our life becomes wobbly.

Sometimes I meet people that put all their attention on their business. They're very successful. They're into prosperity. But their emotional life is wobbly. They don't have that same level of sturdiness and mastery in their ability to feel or their ability to communicate, for instance. So they're a wobbly person. They're not balanced.

Maybe they have a very strong sense of a successful life, but they have no sense of their inner life, or they're not taking care of their body, or a combination. I say that, just as you would not put something valuable on a wobbly table, I believe the universe will be very careful about putting a great opportunity onto a wobbly person, where it might crash down to the ground.

This is something I've seen with my own clients when I work with them. When they fix the wobbliness, something shifts.

I met a realtor at Seminar of the Century with Harv Eker. She was very successful financially but was kind of stuck at a certain level. Emotionally she hadn't really done any work on herself, and so there was a real imbalance between her relationship and her success.

We worked together for a year in one of my programs. She literally fixed those other legs, and two days ago she wrote me that she had just closed the biggest real estate deal ever for a townhouse in Manhattan!

I never talked to her about real estate. I know nothing about it. I never even talked to her about her career. But I helped her fix her wobbliness. Then the sense that people had when they met her was, "You are solid. I can trust you," and therefore they gave her more business.

This is my philosophy. It's the work that I do. What you're doing is so important because one of the big places that we get wobbly is with how we take care of our bodies.

Of course body is the *body-mind*, it's not just the body. We think of our body as if it's some kind of thing separate from our consciousness. It's not.

Everything you eat will determine the quality of your self and the quality of your feelings. My field isn't the body—it's the emotional body and the spiritual body. Nonetheless, to not understand there's a link to the physical body is again to be wobbly.

ANTON: When we meet other people, we instinctively respond to whether they're wobbly or not. We know what it feels like to meet someone solid.

BARBARA DEANGELIS: We do unless we ourselves are wobbly in a certain way. Then we will actually resonate with somebody else's wobbliness and think they're really wonderful because they don't challenge ours! That's a whole other topic we can get into (laughing).

If you want to live as an awakened being, it's essential to bring consciousness to everything, to realize that every choice we make, whether it has to do with whom we spend time with, what we decide to take action on, how we choose to eat or drink, what we choose to put in our body—every action is either going to create more freedom or more bondage, more joy or more contraction.

When you choose to do something, it's really not that far-fetched to ask yourself, "Is this for my highest good or not?" and, if you're offering yourself food, is that food a way of saying to yourself, to your body, to your temple, "I love you" or "I don't care about you." That kind of cuts to the chase.

It really has to do with understanding the wholeness of life. We are so blessed to have a human body. We are so blessed to have a human lifetime. Whatever body we get, we should just be so grateful. We waited a long time for it. We should take really good care of it, because it's not so easy to get one.

GET SELF CENTERED

Get centered and clear on who you are and
then bring that out into the world.

The young Max Simon brings a fresh new energy to the world of business and personal development with his casual, authentic approach. He is a master at live events. His productions have transformed the lives of thousands of people and generated millions of dollars.

Max has been immersed in personal transformation, conscious business, and live trainings his entire life. He grew up with luminaries like Deepak Chopra and Debbie Ford. He is the son of David Simon, MD, bestselling author, renowned physician and co-founder of the world-renowned Chopra Center for Well-Being. His mother, Julia, is a forty-plus year Transcendental Meditation teacher.

As Director of Consumer Products for the Chopra Center for Well-being, Max transformed the once small, unprofitable division into a multi-million dollar business in just a few years.

Max is a recognized global authority on teaching entrepreneurs how to create a highly profitable and powerful business that's on-purpose and in-service. Martha Stewart called Max the "Next Big Idea" in *Body & Soul:Whole Living* magazine.

I spoke to Max Simon from the Yampah Hot Springs in Colorado, a really amazing spot on this planet. Three and a half million gallons of perfect mineral water comes gushing out of the ground there daily at boiling temperatures, healing everything it touches.

Max Simon, much like those hot springs, is a healer of spirits. With his youthful mindset and approach to teaching, Max defies many of the fundamental assumptions of older teachers and systems and brings a refreshing vitality to help people find the balance and potential in their lives that can only come from being centered on their True Self.

ANTON: Max, you grew up in quite a remarkable environment.

MAX SIMON: My father is David Simon, Deepak Chopra's business partner and co-founder of the Chopra Center. He's a neurologist by background but really pioneered mind-body medicine in the West. This is a rather interesting time for us. In a totally crazy, bizarre turn of events, he actually just self-diagnosed his own malignant brain tumor. I was raised with total consciousness and wellness and mind-body medicine as part of my world. All of a sudden we're getting this opportunity within our family to see how to put these tools into practice as, basically, my father embraces his own mortality.

ANTON: I'm sorry to hear about your father, but you are passing this beautiful knowledge on to people in a big way. You travel all over the place, teaching people.

MAX SIMON: My past has been in the business world. I have always been an entrepreneur, and I actually helped Deepak Chopra grow his products division into a multimillion-dollar business. I was their youngest lead instructor and travelled around with him and my father for about five years. I then left to start my own business. Since then, we've been putting on these transformational business events.

For anybody that has ever been to a business event, you know that most of them are just about marketing tactics and business sense, that kind of stuff. While their knowledge might be okay, they're kind of boring and drab, and somebody like me really appreciates the more spiritual side, the connected side, the authenticity side of everything we're doing. So we're known to be the ones to merge the kind of experiences that help people get deeper into themselves with strategic tools to help them make hundreds of thousands of dollars doing what they love.

ANTON: Authenticity is a big word with you. You help people discover what truly is in their deepest soul and bring that forward, so they can make money and be successful and help other people doing the things they love.

MAX SIMON: The challenge is that most of the people in the world are not taught, interestingly enough, how to be successful being themselves. We're taught how to be like other people and look up to other people. There's a lot of emphasis on that, because leaders know that it's good for their business to keep themselves on a pedestal.

I actually have taken the reverse approach, not only because I think it's a waste of energy to try to keep me on a pedestal, but also because it helps people more when you can play on the same field as them. The misconception is that if you're not distinguishing yourself as somebody on this high level then people won't buy from you. I have found that it's actually completely the opposite, that the more authentic and real and human and just like them you are, the more people trust you and thus actually feel really good about investing their money in you, rather than coming from a place of fear and scarcity.

ANTON: You radiate this clarity and calm. I went on your website and did the pre-recorded meditation that you lead people through. It was truly centering. It was wonderful. Thank you.

I have a feeling that the way you live your life and the way you eat are right in tune with everything else you do. Is that true?

MAX SIMON: I have four pillars I call The Four Pillars of an Enlightened Entrepreneur. One of those is silence. I think it's important to take time every day just to be still and reflect and quiet the mind. Movement is one of the pillars, and gratitude and nourishment. I have seen the dramatic impact that having a good nourishing daily routine has on people. That very much includes what you put in your mouth, how much water you drink and being very conscious about the fact that the food you eat is the energy that you're putting into your body, so that you have more energy to put out into the world.

ANTON: You have been consciously meditating since you were four years old, but was there ever a time in your life when you didn't eat this way, when you weren't quite so friendly to your body?

MAX SIMON: I had about a nine-year stint where I did everything bad for me that I could possibly do. During my college era, I was eating ninety-nine-cent chicken sandwiches from Jack in the Box every single day, followed by Top Ramen and beer. I had a pretty good extended period of my life, from about twelve or thirteen all the way up until I was about twenty-one, where I couldn't have been any more unhealthy. And, of course, as you can probably guess, it was also the most depressing and the most self-sabotaging, angry, dark period of my life.

Ultimately, when I became twenty-one, I woke up from my stupor one day and said, "This is ridiculous! I know that this isn't the only way to live!" I quickly returned to my four pillars. If you want to get to a space of balance and clarity and focus, you may not know how to get there yet, but all you have to do is the four pillars: daily movement, daily silence, daily gratitude and daily nourishment. If you can just do those four things, your life will turn around quickly. So good food is so, so, necessary.

ANTON: You had a good foundation, so that probably helped pull you back once you went through the dark side, so to speak.

MAX SIMON: I knew where to go. I come from a world that keeps things pretty simple, and one of the philosophies of the world I come from is don't eat anything where you can't read what the ingredients are. Make sure that you're preparing as much of your food as possible, because when you put your own energy and attention into it, it's just going to feel different; it's going to be a different experience.

I am vegetarian most of the time. There is a rare occasion when I feel that my body needs some chicken or fish. I am certainly not opposed to eating meat. It just doesn't really resonate as deeply with me. And I drink lots and lots of water. Ultimately, that's one of the funny, simple things: most people don't drink nearly enough water.

ANTON: There is a big movement of consciousness on the planet right now. People used to say "you are what you eat." Now people are saying "the world is what you eat." What you eat affects how you behave and how effective you are, and then, through the butterfly effect, that affects all the people around you, and all of that interaction spreads to the world at large.

MAX SIMON: One of my trademark sayings is, "The world doesn't need more information, it needs better models." We are always asking, what do we do? I think it's the simplest thing: who do we want to be? It's nothing new, but I think that the more times we say to ourselves, "Okay, if I were being a good model of an enlightened entrepreneur, if I were being a good model of a parent, if I were being a good model of whatever, how would I behave?" I think that's the kind of global movement that's starting to form. People are realizing that all they really need to do is become better models themselves. As we do that, we will shape the world in a new way.

ANTON: We grew up with people saying, "don't do as I do, do as I say." That didn't work very well. People will always do as you do. You recently demonstrated how true that is when you lost your voice to a cold just before a speaking engagement you hosted. Instead of calling off the event or changing it, you simply showed up and did the best you could with your hoarse, whispering voice. The audience had to be more quiet and attentive than usual. You made slight adaptations, on the fly, to the number of participant activities in the program. People recognized your integrity and the example you set by not being defeated by circumstances. In the end, many of the attendees said that was one of your best events ever.

MAX SIMON: I put on this sold-out event. People flew in from all over the world, paid thousands of dollars, and the very first day I lost my voice. All I could really do in that process was just show up and do the best I could. Sometimes that's just the breaking point. We get so much in our own way that we stop showing up. Nothing can ever happen if you don't show up.

These days I feel that everybody is feeling really stretched. Whether you want to call it the universe or the times or whatever, everybody is having an opportunity right now to question what they're really made of. Part of that is seeing how committed you can be to doing the things you know are good for you, and becoming disciplined with what you know you need to be doing for yourself, which includes food, nourishment, movement and gratitude. Then, whenever anything happens outside the realm of your understanding or expectation, you use your tools. You just show up and do the best you can.

I like to keep things really simple. The way I teach is the way I live. Some of these fundamental principles that you're teaching people and that I'm sharing include the understanding that it just doesn't need to be so freaking complicated.

ANTON: Simple is always better. You have a knack for teaching people to quiet their mind chatter. We are all bombarded by our mind chatter, and then we add TV and radio and all sorts of other noise from the world to that. Then we add food that clogs up our arteries; it ends up clogging our brains so we can't think, and we get tired. People are blaming all sorts of things for the state we're in, when, really, it's pretty simple.

MAX SIMON: A lot of us are doing good work. It's very cool. The collaborative model that's showing up is, let's all keep doing good work and supporting each other when we can. There are so many people now doing good work that you have to figure out, How do I support people without losing sight of what supports myself? It's a funny dance, a game to play, but with the right state of consciousness, you just keep getting into the conversation and seeing what unfolds. As long as people are committed to the same goal, which is making the world a better place, then something cool and new will arise.

ANTON: Just being around your optimism and your generosity and your joyful spirit, just hearing you now today, I feel so good. The energy is just coming through.

MAX SIMON: You are a great interviewer. I just want to give you a shout-out after my having done hundreds and hundreds of interviews. You have a really cool interview style.

ANTON: It's easy when you have intelligent, tuned-in, conscious, fun people on the other end.

MAX SIMON: Find the models that you are inspired by, and then do everything in your power to surround yourself with them. I would say that the biggest challenge people have right now, at least the perceived challenge, is what they would call money problems. Nobody ever really has money problems, but they think they do, and so what happens is that they get surrounded by a bunch of other people that have money problems, and then they get stuck in a certain energy and a vibration that just doesn't feel good. They start throwing out all the things that are actually good for them, like eating healthy organic foods or going to retreats.

My philosophy is that whenever something is not working, it's probably because you are *doing* something that's not working. The next step would be to find the person that's doing something that *is* working and do whatever it takes to get to them. Do *something* to spend more time with the people that are good models for you, because as soon as you get into somebody else's energy field that inspires you, it will quickly raise your vibration and make it much easier for you to move forward.

ANTON: I love the name of your company: Get Self Centered. There was a time when people would say that to you as an insult: "Oh! You are so self-centered." But you have turned that around into something very positive.

MAX SIMON: People still say that these days, but I think anything creative will ruffle feathers. One of my mentors used to say, "If you are not pissing people off, you are not playing a big enough game." It's because if you stand for something, if you believe in something, then you're going to bump up against other people's belief systems. And one of my beliefs is that one of the most important things for us to do is to get really centered and clear in terms of who we are, and what we stand for, and our authenticity, and then bring it out into the world.

I would call my tribe, the people I help the most, spiritually-centered entrepreneurs. I think that too many spiritually-centered entrepreneurs are not focused enough on how they bring themselves into the world. They need to get a little bit more centered in themselves and stop being so caught up in the esoterics. I like to ruffle people's feathers a little bit, because those who get ruffled but then see me as a good model will take action. Those who get ruffled and get irritated and aggravated will just make for an interesting dialog.

ANTON: They say that when you're reacting, you're on the threshold of a breakthrough. If you're not reacting at all you're probably just sleeping or dead already. So getting self-centered isn't about selfishness. It's like the oxygen mask on an airplane: first put it on yourself so you can stay conscious to help others. We need to find our center so that we have more to give.

MAX SIMON: Exactly. It's important to get clear in who you are, but then take it out into the world and shake some stuff up.

FEARLESS LIVING

Fear is like water on the fire of your light. The world is waiting for you. You make better choices when you believe in freedom instead of fear.

Rhonda Britten is a globally recognized expert on the subject of fear and fearlessness. She is the author of four national bestselling books on personal growth, including *Fearless Living*, which features her groundbreaking work called the Wheel Technology. She is the founder of the Fearless Living Institute, an organization dedicated to providing the tools to master emotional fears.

Rhonda has been featured on radio and in newspapers and magazines worldwide. She was a repeat guest on *Oprah* and has appeared on *The Early Show*, *The O'Reilly Factor* and *The Montel Williams Show*, as well as her own nationally viewed *Fearless Living PBS Special*. During her three seasons on the hit daytime reality drama, *Starting Over*, Britten was named America's Favorite Life Coach and was dubbed *Starting Over's* Most Valuable Player by the *New York Times*. Her corporate clients include Southwest Airlines, Toyota and Northrop Grumman.

Rhonda Britten is an unusual beacon of light in a world where fear holds people back from discovering and enjoying the benefits of their true full potential. An unspeakable event in her childhood that could have left her a broken human being became a source of discovery and commitment to help others recognize, overcome and free themselves from the obstacles that fear creates.

Rhonda shares her expertise and fearless philosophy worldwide through workshops, online classes and her interactive website.

ANTON: Rhonda, you absolutely stir my heart. You spend every day of your life uplifting people. You give them new wings, give them new life. I have such great respect for you.

Some people are quick to complain. They love to whine while living their lies. They love to blame and have someone else clean up their messes. What happened to you as a child is unthinkable. If there is any complaint anywhere in my body, it just evaporates as a triviality when I hear your story. And yet, somehow you have become this glowing, bright-eyed, cheerful beacon of hope to so many!

RHONDA BRITTEN: You are so kind, thank you. I have worked very diligently. I am not only helping myself, healing myself and overcoming and embracing my past, I have a real desire and drive to help others.

Fear is a killer that kills hope; it kills dreams, it kills relationships, it almost killed me. It killed my parents.

ANTON: Some people teach because they've learned something from books, but you teach because you went through a tremendous experience that most of us won't have to go through. Would you mind letting people know what happened to you so they can appreciate the conviction behind your purpose?

RHONDA BRITTEN: Not at all. I pray that you don't go through anything like it, and I hope that you never have to feel what I felt.

I had the horrific experience on Father's Day, when I was fourteen years old. My parents had recently separated, and I hadn't seen my father for a few months. He had left town and now he had come back into town.

It was Father's Day, so my sisters and I wanted to take him out for brunch. When he came over to the house, he took a gun out of the car, shot my mother twice and then shot himself. I was the only witness.

I was outside when it happened—the only one with them. My father started yelling, "It's your fault, this is your fault!" And my mother was screaming, "No, don't!" And I was trying to say something magical, something amazing. I yelled, "Dad, don't! Don't!" I was fourteen, and I felt *I* had to stop it. I yelled out, "I will live with you, I will live with you!" thinking that he was getting divorced and he was lonely. I was trying to come up with anything.

I took a step off the porch—and he aimed the gun at me. Then he turned it on my mother, shot her and then himself.

It was a moment of complete powerlessness, complete hopelessness, complete helplessness, complete blame. I blamed myself for my father killing my mother and killing himself because I couldn't stop it, I didn't stop it, and I was left standing. I blamed myself for still standing afterwards.

After that event, I became a super-achiever. As you can imagine, I had very low self-esteem and self-confidence. I didn't want anyone to think I was weird or unusual, but this happened in a small town and nobody knew what to do. Other kids weren't allowed to play with me. They weren't even allowed to talk to me. My father's side blamed my mother's side, and my mother's side blamed my father's side. Nobody came to check on us kids. It was completely horrific.

Afterwards I attempted to kill myself three times. After my third suicide attempt I realized something: I'm not good at killing myself, so I'm not going to die. If I'm going to keep living, then I'd better figure out how to live. Because I was miserable. I was not well. I didn't like life. It was so painful to be alive.

I had to get through the joke of having been a witness. I had to deal with forgiving not only my father, who seemed the obvious one, but also my mother, who had stayed in that relationship for years longer than she should have. And then there was forgiveness of myself for not having had the ability, the power, the magic key to stop it. I have done a lot of forgiveness work, a lot of healing about the past, about what I experienced before that happened, the day it happened and then afterwards.

ANTON: What was the turning point where you realized that you have such a tremendous gift for helping people? I mean, I'm sitting here, my face is wet from tears, my nose is dripping and my body is still in a state of chills. I have never heard a story like that. And yet, somehow you are such a shining beacon of joy and light. Because of that story I cling to every word you say—you're truly a no-nonsense person. I mean, how could you not be?

RHONDA BRITTEN: That's true. For me, it took the thought of complaining for any other reason than life and death away. When somebody is complaining and summoning the excuses, that may not feel like life and death to them, but it *is* very important because they are choosing their pathway. One complaint here, two complaints there, three complaints there turn into a lifetime of complaints. The same thing with excuses.

So the two things that I have gained from my life experience and my healing are: the first thing I consider when I encounter another human being or myself is to give them compassion. We all are calling for compassion. The second thing is accountability. The level of accountability that we all need to give to another human being and to ourselves when we are trying to shift the way we think or the way we live or the way we see the world.

My life changed, really, twenty years after my parents' death, when I decided to take responsibility for myself. I had forgiven them a lot over the previous twenty years. But on the twentieth anniversary of their death, I did a very big forgiveness ceremony. I proclaimed that I was no longer going to live as the daughter of a murderer, was no longer going to live as an abused victim. I was no longer going to let my parents decide my future.

I wrote them letters that I burned in this ceremony, which I describe in detail in my book *Fearless Living*. When I walked away from that two-hour ceremony, I was really ready to own my own life.

There was good news in that, but bad news too: there was no one left to blame, no one I could point a finger to. "My father killed my mother, that's why I'm being a jerk today" wouldn't work any more. It was all on me. And it was very freeing and very empowering.

After I did that I started getting really clear messages that I was supposed to support people. I wasn't happy about this in the beginning. I said, "No, I can't do that, I just can't do that! I don't know how to do that." I literally thought God had the wrong person. He must have accidentally sent the message to me, because it really belonged to somebody behind me or something. Seriously, I looked around saying, "I know that wasn't for me!"

ANTON: What I love about you is that you acknowledge everybody. Not everybody is going to go through what you went through. Some people live kind of blessed lives all the way around, but there are still things underneath that are troubling them and that affect the way their life is moving. No matter what the degree, how big or small the problem, you acknowledge it. I think that gives people the love and the trust they have for you when they're working with you. You help people transform. You get them on the right track really quickly. It's like picking up a train with a crane and moving it over to a track that's not even connected.

RHONDA BRITTEN: One of the blessings of my experience is that when I say something, people believe me. I trust my intuition when I'm working with somebody. I trust myself completely. So based on my history and the fact that I trust myself so implicitly, when I say something to someone, they trust me implicitly and they're willing to do what I suggest. And when they do it they get results. They go, "Oh, my gosh! It worked!" It gets them over the hump of not believing they can do it or not believing in themselves.

I'm sitting there holding their hand. I'm not going to leave them. I'm right there. It gives people that extra incentive, that extra courage, that extra sense of fearlessness they need in order to start making a change. Once they get over that hump, the world starts opening up.

That's what people don't really get: there is this whole new world that is waiting for you, and the only reason you can't see it is that you believe fear more than freedom. You make fearful choices versus fearless choices. But regardless of how seductive, insidious and convincing, they are still short of our best choices. When you start making better choices out of *fearlessness*, the whole world literally becomes different, and everything you thought was holding you back becomes possible.

ANTON: I am a big believer in the butterfly effect, that exponential way of how we affect people. When you're doing something great, it's not just between you and one other person. It expands outward through everyone you touch and through everyone that every one of them touches.

You have been very successful with your business, but I know that financial success wasn't your initial goal. Some people set a goal of making a lot of money. You realized, against your own will initially, that what you do now was your calling. You grew into it.

So what has this got to do with cooking or with food? It has everything to do with it.

RHONDA BRITTEN: When I was on *Starting Over* for three seasons, I filmed 185 episodes a year. I worked six days a week, twelve to sixteen hours a day. When people are working at that level, they often say, "I had to grab fast food. I had to because I was just so busy."

When I really want to work optimally, when I really want to be fully alert, when I have to be able to have all my senses turned on, the last thing that I can eat is junk food or fried food. I've got to keep myself so clear and so clean, because that is a direct reflection of my ability to hear my intuition, my ability to keep my energy level up, my ability to stay focused, my ability to keep listening, my ability to be with another human being.

I am basically on a vegetable-driven diet. I do eat protein and I do eat meat still. Every morning I will have eggs and vegetables. In the afternoon, whether I have a California roll or salmon and a salad, I always have some vegetables and meat. I might have some carbs at lunch, depending on what I'm doing and what's going on around me, but normally it's just vegetables and protein. At dinner it's the same thing.

I did the L.A. marathon a few years back while I was doing *Starting Over*. I trained for the marathon while working a schedule of twelve to sixteen hours a day, six days a week. When I am working at that high level, my life consists of two things: one is sleep, my first priority, and two is food. My whole schedule revolves around sleep and food.

I am not in charge of when we film, so I find out when I'm going to be working when I get the filming schedule for the next day. If I'm going to have to drive in at 7:30 a.m. and be there till 10:00 at night, I start making my plan. If I have to leave at 7:30, what time do I have to go to bed tonight? If I have to be on the set all day, I bring these foods with me in my little pack.

ANTON: So you're not eating from the craft services table piled with M&Ms and donuts?

RHONDA BRITTEN: For the most part I don't eat craft services. On some sets they are trying to be healthier, but I usually bring my own food, eat my own food. If I want to work at that high level of output, my input has to be really clean, really supportive and really nurturing.

ANTON: When you are really busy like that, how do you manage to find more time or make more time to organize your food?

RHONDA BRITTEN: I make a bunch of muffins for the week. I put them in bags, two muffins per Ziplock bag. Then I cut all my vegetables for the week, and I put a variety of vegetables inside bags. I'll have carrots, tomatoes, sugar snap peas and red peppers—a variety of vegetables.

The secret is to put a piece of paper towel inside the plastic bag with the vegetables, otherwise they get soggy. They will hold for three, four, five days. I can grab a bag of vegetables five days later and it will still be fresh.

When I wake up in the morning, I grab a pack of muffins and a pack of vegetables. I usually eat one muffin and some of my vegetables, and then on my first break, an hour and a half, two hours later, I'll eat the other muffin with vegetables.

ANTON: Was there ever a time in your life when you ate differently?

RHONDA BRITTEN: Oh please! I'm from upper Michigan and Minnesota. We are meat-and-potatoes people. I grew up eating Cheerios. My whole body is a function of Cheerios. I would say that my back and my spinal cord are made of Cheerios stacked on top of one another. I literally ate Cheerios every meal of the day. When I was in college, I ate Domino's pizza. I still love pizza here and there, but it's not my everyday food.

I just got off the road, touring in fifty cities. I ate much more fast food than I normally do. The good news is a lot of the fast food places have fantastic salads now.

ANTON: I love your honesty about what you eat when you're on the road. Some people won't admit it. There are alternatives. Still, you're definitely doing something right, because you look fabulous. You're beautiful and you're fit.

RHONDA BRITTEN: My whole thing is vegetables, protein and getting my water intake. But again, even before food is sleep. If I don't get my sleep, I definitely make poorer food choices. My senses are down, my will power is down, my discipline is down. If I continuously get no sleep, I have a tendency to go, "I've just got to eat *something*," thinking that the food will solve my sleeping problem.

Food does not solve sleeping problems. Sleep solves sleeping problems. Three quarters of Americans don't get enough sleep. In fact, we're a sleep-deprived nation. When I don't sleep well I have a tendency to be lax on my food, so I have to be even more vigilant. That's why I prepare my food ahead of time.

For me, if I'm eating vegetables, it turns on the *eat healthy* switch in me, and that makes me want to eat healthier and better because I'm experiencing more energy.

When you have better energy you make better decisions. That's the thing people don't get: the food choices you make directly reflect your ability to make decisions. If you're eating five foods every meal, and if you're eating a carb-laden diet without enough vegetables and protein, you don't have enough energy to be fearless.

Your food choices directly reflect your ability to make powerful choices. Start shifting your thinking and the way you see the world. Shift your food in order to support business thought processes.

ANTON: You have a book about food, *Do I Look Fat In This? Get Over Your Body and On With Your Life.*

RHONDA BRITTEN: That is by far my funniest book. I talk about all my food stories, all my body image issues, about me and my clients. Such as this time when I was in a restaurant with my friend and I asked her to compare my butt to the woman at the counter. I walked up to the counter and stood next to her so my friend could compare our butts and tell me what she thought. I think many people have experiences like I do regarding their bodies.

Do I Look Fat In This? is a gentle approach to starting to take our bodies back. I can't tell you how many people I talk to on a daily basis that use their body as their number one excuse for not going for the passion, not going for the career, not getting a raise, not feeling like they belong.

Such a large percentage of Americans are obese or overweight. A lot of us are using our bodies as excuses to live smaller lives. It just doesn't have to be that way. *Do I Look Fat In This?* is maybe a place to start.

ANTON: You give people permission to be themselves. You encourage them to feel safe when you ask them to look at who they think they are.

RHONDA BRITTEN: Some people have to change everything at once, and some people can only do one thing at a time. Changing everything all at once can be overwhelming. You don't have to give up dairy, give up bread, give up gluten, give up wheat, give up sugar—all at the same time. It's okay. Let's change breakfast, or let's change dinner. Let's change one meal and start building from there.

ANTON: I like that. People get discouraged by trying to do too much all at once, then they're right back where they were, and that reinforces their old thinking.

Your whole thing is about being fearless, having people not be afraid. It's scary to change or even succeed. It's very comfortable to continue to fail because you know how it feels. We say we want to get better, but there's comfort in the familiar, even if it isn't a good pattern. Successful people are willing to live a certain way because they have experienced the joy and benefits of stepping out of their box and are willing to do it again. It becomes a better pattern.

RHONDA BRITTEN: One message regarding Fearless Living: there is nothing wrong with you. You are not flawed. You are not a failure. You are not screwed up. It's just fear. When you have been into fear for a long time, it feels like your own voice. I help you separate your own voice from the voice of fear so that you can hear yourself.

Your body is craving and truly desiring more water, more vegetables, the life force of the earth moving and pulsating through it. When those neurotransmitters start flickering on and start connecting at a greater intensity, you're going to feel more alive in so many places. I know this to be true.

I think people give up on themselves because they think there's something wrong with them. They think they're flawed, and they think they're damaged, and they think there's no fixing them. I am here to say as a testament, I once believed that about myself—for twenty years! You do not have to live that way. That's a lie, a big fat lie. It's not true. It's just that you believed it because you believed fear, just as I did.

I want you to see you through my eyes. I just want you for a moment to see yourself through my eyes, and you will be set free.

DANCING ON A HIGH WIRE

There is a direct correlation between diet and success.
Clean food provides the clean energy required to create
and maintain a successful business with clarity and grace.
There is more to life than work.

Christine Comaford has built and sold five of her own companies (for over 700% ROI) and helped fifty CEOs grow and sell their companies for up to $425 million. She has coached two United States presidents and consulted for the White House and 700 of the Fortune 1000. She has been featured in the *New York Times*, *USA Today*, *Wall Street Journal*, and *BusinessWeek*; appeared on *CNN* and *FOX*; and been studied by the Stanford Graduate School of Business. She's also a thought leader on leadership for Forbes.com.

Christine has led many lives, having been a Buddhist monk, Microsoft engineer, entrepreneur and venture capitalist. She claims this gives her a unique perspective on people, performance and business. Her approach to executive coaching and leadership is based on neuroscience techniques to inspire and motivate staff, build cultures and grow companies. She sees business not just as a set of strategies, but also as a complex web of human interaction.

Christine believes that we can do well *and* do good, using business as a path for personal development, wealth creation and philanthropy. She has been a hospice volunteer for twelve years and is keenly aware of how fleeting our lives are. This is why she focuses on helping clients experience profound personal fulfillment while building tremendously successful businesses.

ANTON: Christine, you are an incredibly successful woman, and I'm certain that you have a deliberate approach to how you do everything—including the way you eat.

CHRISTINE COMAFORD: Absolutely! I find that to build companies, you have to have two really important things: mental clarity and stamina. I see a direct correlation between my diet and my success.

My goal is to always eat 50% fruits and vegetables in my diet. It's not always easy. I was at a dinner party the other day with Harvey Mackay. We had a kind of chicken thing, and it was pretty good, and then afterwards this really gnarly looking dessert came, and I thought, *I want that dessert, but I would feel much better if I ate a fresh fruit plate.* So I just asked the catering staff for a fresh fruit plate instead. The whole next day I was just charged with energy. I also drink about a gallon of water a day. For me, diet makes a huge difference.

ANTON: When I am around you in person you are such a bundle of energy! A lot of people think that they need to eat their piece of cow every day to have energy. It sounds as if that is not true in your world.

CHRISTINE COMAFORD: I was a strict vegetarian for thirteen years, but now I am definitely an omnivore. I had about a third of a steak last night, not a whole one. As long as you don't go too crazy eating huge chunks of animals, you can keep your energy high. Mostly I eat fish, but I don't have any issue with eating critters. I just like to make sure that I have lots of fruits, vegetables and water along with them.

ANTON: What you are suggesting is a sense of balance. It's not like the eighties thinking, with this struggle for power where we needed to just blast our way through with as much TNT as we could. You definitely have this sense of balance. Is that from your Buddhist monk days?

CHRISTINE COMAFORD: Yes. It's also from seeing imbalance. For instance, when I was at Microsoft, it was pizza and Coca-Cola. Luckily I never got into sodas, but a lot of the guys lived on pizza and Coke for years. Now several of them have adult onset diabetes.

These are lean guys, but they just ate so much goop for so many years that it really affected their health. So every day you have to eat something that was alive.

ANTON: And diabetes can become a part of your life overnight. It can come on from one day to the next!

CHRISTINE COMAFORD: It's major. You can get away with stuff in your twenties, but seriously, once you hit thirty, in my opinion, you'd better really get on it taking care of your body.

I was getting burned out when I retired in 2002. I have always been good about eating well, eating vegetables and protein, but I realized I had way too much white flour and too much caffeine. If you watch some earlier videos of me that are floating around the net, my energy at that time really came from being wired! There is a difference between being high energy and being wired and strung out on stress because you're not giving your body the right foods. Being high energy has a feeling of balance beneath it.

You can feel the difference and you can see the difference. I definitely burned myself out by working too hard. When I was working too hard, the work, the project was more important than caring for my body. Now I totally get it. I work out three times a week with a trainer, and I dance at least three times a week. I hike on the weekends.

The diet and exercise thing do go together. I really do think you have to blow off that energy, especially if you're building something and you're under pressure and your mind needs to be really clear. If you're an innovator, you have to also add the exercise.

ANTON: You were a consultant to the White House, and you have been featured in magazines and on every major news network—*PBS* has done specials about you. You really live in the fast lane, yet in your food and your behavior, you are actually finding time to still live and be a human being.

CHRISTINE COMAFORD: I meditate every day. That's also really important.

ANTON: I love to quote something from your website. It says, "Christine believes we can do well and do good using business as a path for personal development, wealth creation and philanthropy." You are living your life on purpose and with joy.

CHRISTINE COMAFORD: It has to all work together or else at the end of the day it won't work at all.

Everyone can say, "Oh! I'm too busy to make half of my diet be fruits and vegetables." You don't have to cook them, you know! You can just throw them in your briefcase! My boyfriend (and this is a little extreme for me) will carry bell peppers and cucumbers and tomatoes in his briefcase, and he will just whip one out and eat it!

I want my food to be a little bit more interesting than that, like with dressing or stir fried or something. But there is always a way to eat well. Even if you are in the middle of Podunk, it doesn't matter what's on the menu. Tell them that what you want is a steaming vegetable plate and what vegetables you want on it. You won't get all of them necessarily, but you will get some of them.

It has to be a priority. You have to see that food is a business tool for mental clarity and longevity and energy. Also, you're going to age well. I am forty-eight. Most people think I look about thirty-eight. A lot of the folks that are my peers are not feeling great. They are taking all sorts of medications for high blood pressure and heart stuff, anti-anxiety and depression, and so much that can be controlled with spirituality and food.

I've been diagnosed with ADD, OCD, GAD—you name it! I don't take any meds because I take really good care of my body. I make it a priority. It's really easy to *not* do so, but eating well is what you have to help you through the adventure of this life—or you're not going to have one.

V.

WHAT YOU PUT IN

WHAT WOULD YOU TRADE
YOUR LIFE FOR?

Manage your thoughts to control the beliefs that define your world.
Every day you are trading your life for how you spend your time.
Make the trade worthwhile.

When you meet John Assaraf face to face, he makes you feel as if you are old pals. He is one of the experts featured in the film and book *The Secret*. He has shared his expertise on achieving financial freedom and living an extraordinary life with millions of viewers on *Larry King Live*, *The Ellen DeGeneres Show* and dozens of other media venues worldwide. His commitment to overcome the challenges of his turbulent youth and his intense desire to live a life with purpose and meaning led John to discover his passion for brain research and quantum physics and how they relate to achieving success in business and life. Using the principles he discovered, he has built four multimillion-dollar businesses.

Today John shares his passion with audiences worldwide as a certified life coach and world renowned speaker. He is one of the Martial Goldsmith School of Management's distinguished thought leaders and the founder of One Coach, a company dedicated to helping entrepreneurs build successful businesses and live the life of their dreams by incorporating a powerful belief system and positive affirmations. He is an intensely spiritual man and a dedicated family man.

ANTON: John, you have quite a busy and demanding life, and yet you have plenty of time for your friends and family. How do you find time for everything?

JOHN ASSARAF: It's really a matter of setting out my priorities and my values. I want to be thoroughly used up when I die!

Something that I learned many, many years ago was to really understand what your highest value is and to categorize all your values in order of priority. Then make sure that every day you fit in your first priority, your second priority and your third priority so that your life always has meaning and fulfillment. I start off every day with my gratitude exercises and my meditation to connect to the spiritual essence that I believe we all are. Next, I work out with my trainer and exercise, and then I fit family in. Work comes in after all the important stuff.

ANTON: Life tends to throw us changes in the middle of our best set plans. What do you do when that comes up?

JOHN ASSARAF: For me it's just called life and so you go with the flow. One thing I learned many years ago was not to react to outside circumstances but to be calm and be aware, to observe and then act. If you know that the weather could change at any moment, you learn how to be prepared for the weather changing at any moment. Instead of crying and whining and bitching when it snows or rains or hails, you figure out how to enjoy it.

It's no different than what surfers do with waves. There are some people that go to the ocean and they go, "Damn, look at all the waves. I can't swim." There are other people who go to the ocean, look at all the waves and go, "Wow! How can I ride that?"

It's not a matter of the waves or the weather or the things that happen to you, it's always a matter of your perspective and the meaning that you give things. When you change the way you look at something or when you change the meaning of something, the experience changes dramatically. The only thing you can control is the meaning you give things and your interpretation of things. It's just a skill and an art that you can learn and practice. The more you practice the easier it becomes.

ANTON: You had a pretty radical and challenging youth. On your website you say you could have ended up in jail or dead. What made the lights come on for you?

JOHN ASSARAF: When I was in my teens I thought that the way to become successful was to do illegal things, and I got involved in a street gang. I was adept at shoplifting and doing a bunch of other illegal things. As I got older the risks we took were much more significant, and several of my friends, as opposed to getting the usual slap on the hand that we all got, started going to juvenile hall. A couple of them even went to prison.

I was rescued by a man who became my mentor. He said, "Listen, you're working hard trying to keep away from the law and you're working harder trying to pretend that your life has meaning and that you're a pretty smart kid—but you're not. If you take that same energy and you focus it on really understanding who you are and how to retrain your brain to achieve the things you want to achieve, you'll be able to achieve whatever you choose." He said, "If you are prepared to be *committed* I will help you, but if you're just *interested*, I'm not going to help you."

I took him on his word, because he was very successful philanthropist and a loving, caring man. I was guided by him for about six years, and he transformed my life.

ANTON: I once heard you say, "You are creating a life no matter what. Every day, every moment, you are headed in some direction, so you might as well create a good one."

JOHN ASSARAF: Most people don't recognize or realize that they really have a choice in the matter. What separates us from the animals is our ability to choose, and what I discovered thirty years ago when I was twenty is that whatever I focused on became my reality. So if I focused on lack and limitation or focused on believing that I *couldn't*—because I didn't go to college or whatever the case was, whatever beliefs I had— they caused my perceptions and my behaviors.

What I was taught by my mentor, Alan, was to choose the goal that you want to trade your life for. Every day you are trading your life anyway, so why not make the trade worth it. He said, "Don't ask yourself if you are worthy of that level of success or that goal. Ask yourself if the goal is worthy of trading your life for it."

When he said that to me I said, "Geeze, if I'm trading my *life* for something, it had better be really well worth it!" As soon as I made that paradigm shift, I started to think differently of myself. I started to think differently of the goals I went after and what I would tolerate and what I would accept in my own life. Once I stopped tolerating mediocracy, once I stopped tolerating the lack of integrity that I had with myself and with others, once I stopped tolerating the behaviors that may have been getting me results but made me feel like I was dirty, that is when my life shifted and changed. For me it was really a matter of making a decision to cut off from any option that I didn't want in my life. That's really a key element of growth and change: feeling like your life has the purpose and the meaning that everybody wants.

ANTON: We all live with a huge amount of mind chatter, those noisy thoughts racing around in our heads, and a lot of us believe that that mind chatter is pretty much who we are. You make a big distinction between our thoughts and our beliefs.

JOHN ASSARAF: Yeah, absolutely. When we dig a little bit deeper and we ask ourselves, "Where are my thoughts coming from, are my thoughts original, are they repetitive, are thoughts the same as thinking?" The answer is *no, they are not*.

It's only been in the last twelve years that we really have been able to look a little bit deeper inside the brain. Through fMRI technology, functional magnetic resonance imaging technology, we could start seeing blood flow to different regions of the brain during thoughts, during stress, during activities, etc., and what we discovered is that our brains have these neural networks and pathways. Messages are sent between neurons like a telephone system. One person calls another person, the person on the other end picks up the phone, and then the message is sent across to that phone.

What we recognize about the brain is, once we have certain beliefs, those beliefs come with a paradigm, with the way we look at the world. The way we look at the world creates our stories, and our stories then create the inner dialogue that we have in our heads. The more we have the inner dialogue, the more the neural networks become reinforced and lower the firing threshold of that message. So if we are used to having negative chatter and dialogue all the time, we are actually reinforcing more negative chatter and more negativity. If we are focusing more on positive things, then we reinforce more positive neural networks or messaging within our own brain.

The latest research suggests that we need three to five positive messages per every negative message or thought that we have. The reason for that is our brains try to keep us away from any real or perceived danger, so any negative message that we are perceiving, either in the universe, in our world or within our own brains, causes us to pay much more attention to that than anything positive.

What we start to understand is that when we learn *how* to manage our own thoughts—to stop the negative mind chatter, the negative thoughts that hold us back, the doubts, the fears, the anxieties, the lack of confidence, the lack of certainty we have—we can then start to shift the way our brain works.

Think of your brain in the same way as you do your heart. You can exercise your heart by walking up a flight of stairs, by playing golf, by bicycling or by walking. But what about exercising your brain? What about doing what I call *inner-cising* your brain and teaching your brain how to perceive reality differently, how to change your belief so that you change your results, how to change your habits so that you're much more productive?

Everybody feels they can achieve more and be more. Well, then, why aren't they achieving more and being more? It's not because of their potential, it's because we're creatures of habit, and once we become conditioned to a certain way of thinking and behaving it becomes repetitive and automatic.

ANTON: So when we're blaming our parents and other people in our lives for challenges we face, what we're really doing is digging up old beliefs that we've grown accustomed to live by. It's hard to get away from our histories. You're saying that no matter what great things we learn or get exposed to, our true inner beliefs can still undermine our efforts, will still determine the results manifesting in our lives. But you have a way of teaching people how to reach those beliefs and address them so we can clear away the bad, nonsupportive ones and plant and nurture a new, healthier, more supportive foundation of beliefs.

JOHN ASSARAF: If I asked you: What is a belief? Where are they? How did you get them? Can you get rid of them? Are there easier ways versus harder ways? Can beliefs cause resistance? Can beliefs cause our behavior? Can beliefs cause us to feel? The answer is *yes* to every one of those questions. What I have done is to ask myself and the top neuroscientists in the world how we access the areas of the brain where our beliefs and our habits are, and are there proven methodologies that allow us to make the internal changes so we can win the inner game versus trying so hard to win the outer game?

The answer is, through repetition of certain language patterns, through the repetition of visualization techniques and exercises, through the repetition of self-hypnosis or guided hypnosis, you can alter your brain's programming in the same way you choose what you're watching on your TV. If you don't like the movie, you change the channel or the DVD. Well, guess what? If you don't like the movie you call your life, whether it's your financial life or your relationship life or your health life, why not just change the programming?

It's a hard concept for most people to get, but our brains are like a projector that projects outwards into this space called our physical existence. All we're doing is projecting everything that's in our head, all of our neural networks, onto the physical world. Everyone thinks that they are looking *out* into reality when the truth is that you are actually looking *in* at reality.

ANTON: How do we break that chain? When I think I've done something wrong or bad, I feel there has to be a continuum between the bad event and getting to the good side again. And yet you're suggesting that we just cut that line, that continuum, and start fresh, and do that twenty times a day if we have to.

JOHN ASSARAF: Yes. Do it twenty times a day or two hundred times a day. Interrupt the pattern!

ANTON: When you were talking about fMRI, it made me think there must be some physiological aspects to our brain function and beliefs. I know that you exercise regularly, and I'm guessing you probably have a certain way of eating, too.

JOHN ASSARAF: Without question, how you eat plays into all of this. My wife and I both love food. We both love to cook, and we both love the flavors from different cultures around the world. We also understand that food is fuel. Just like you wouldn't put wax in your car and expect your car to really drive optimally, or at all, you can't expect to put bad fuel into your body and expect it to run optimally.

We know a lot more today about food than in the past. We know that the brain needs certain nutrients. We know that sugar does certain things to our insulin levels. We know that certain foods take more energy than they provide. We know certain foods are harder to digest than other foods. If you look at food as *this is my fuel*, the question is, will my muscles, will my bones, will my eyes, will my brain work more optimally if I give it better fuel? The answer to any logical person is, well of course it would!

ANTON: I always say you can't paint your barn red with blue paint and yet, somehow we seem to think that we can still have the things we know are bad for us and expect our brains and our bodies to work.

JOHN ASSARAF: A rule that I live by is the 90/10 rule: ninety percent of the time I put in just excellent fuel and food for my body, and ten percent I have what I call psychological fuel. I'll give you an example. Two nights ago I was at one of our favorite restaurants, where they have the best carrot cake in the world. It's packed with icing, it's packed with sugar, it's packed with flavor, and every bite I take I close my eyes and have a mental orgasm. For thirty minutes while I was eating this carrot cake I was getting my psychological fuel. But now I won't have a carrot cake for the next two or three weeks.

ANTON: Most of the people I talked with came down to the mechanics of food, how specific types of food affect us, but a number of people also brought up the importance of the spirit in preparing and enjoying food. In his book *Outliers,* Malcolm Gladwell talked about an entire group of people who moved to Pennsylvania from Rossetto, Italy and how it was a mystery why the members of this community are living to be so old and are still healthy and don't have Alzheimer's. They eat food similar to what we're eating. It was found that the spirit, the security and sense of purpose that they had from being part of a truly integrated community seemed to play the biggest part in their successful long lives. There is scientific documentation on how feeling comforted and happy and engaged, including when we eat, has positive effects on our health. It makes me wonder, how do we bridge this chasm between eating healthy, supportive fuel and eating comfort foods?

JOHN ASSARAF: I understand the benefits of comfort food, but there is a huge challenge around people who eat when they have other challenges and use food to comfort their emotions. Emotional eating is one of the biggest dilemmas in our society. So is alcohol and so are prescription pills. We use those to mask other challenges that we haven't really looked at. I've eaten emotionally in the past as well, but I would say it's a matter of *awareness* of your patterns of behavior. I always ask myself which foods make me feel great and help me be focused and clear and full of energy and which foods take me away from that.

I learned a process thirty years ago of studying my goals in writing. I review my goals every morning before the day starts and create my plans for the week on Sunday nights, investing thirty to forty-five minutes planning what I want to do.

My wife and I plan most of our week and our meals. Today happens to be a day that I'm fasting. It's one of my ways to balance out eating that big carrot cake two days ego. So I'm constantly aware of the decisions and the life that I want to live, in addition to free-flowing it as well. I don't want to be so rigid that it causes psychological and emotional stress. I want to have some flexibility. But I also don't want to live a life of excuses and rationalizations, where I'm telling myself rational lies all the time. The only way to do that is no differently than how a captain captains a ship: a constant gathering of information, of the coordinates, and checking to make sure *am I heading in the right direction*?

The right direction for me may be the wrong direction for you. It's all very individualized, and it goes back to *what do you want to trade your life for*? What do you want your energy level to be like? What do you want your physique to look like and feel like? What do you want your emotional life to be like? What do you want your spirit to experience and feel?

Very few people have been taught the art of introspection and the art of being true to oneself and asking themselves the real deep questions.

I found a quote many years ago. I can't remember who it's by, but it says, "Most people tiptoe through life hoping to make it safely through to death." I don't want to tiptoe through life. I want to ask the serious questions. I want to ask myself the meaningful questions. I want to trade my life for what I love so that at the end of whatever time I have on this physical earth I feel like the journey was just off-the-hook phenomenal!

I am prepared to challenge my thinking, to challenge my behaviors, to challenge myself with what I'm doing. I want to be the best that I can be and achieve, week in and week out.

We are capable of so much!

WHAT YOU PUT IN

Music helps inspire and align you to your higher purpose.
Only the best quality of anything that you bring into
your life can produce the best results.

Paul Hoffman is dedicated to changing lives through the power of music. He is a master of branding and wrote many famous jingles that we hear on TV. He has also written music for many Fortune 500 Companies like Budweiser, Nike, Pepsi and General Motors. He has been on the road with such greats as Pink Floyd; Emerson, Lake and Palmer; Blood, Sweat and Tears; and Edgar Winter, and has worked with amazing artists like BB King, Isaac Hayes, Tony Bennett and many others.

Despite his huge success, Paul always felt that music could do more. He founded Success Songs and began using his music as something deliberately designed to help people release their limiting beliefs and move them to discover and unleash their ultimate potential.

ANTON: Your music is so powerful. I don't think I have ever listened to one of your songs without my hair standing up or my eyes tearing.

PAUL HOFFMAN: I appreciate that. With my Success Songs Empowerment Program, regardless of the particular state you're in or particular thing you want to try to create, you can listen to a song that will give you the inspiration and the mindset to follow through.

Self-communication can kill you or it can inspire you to create magic in every moment of your day. I have always felt and always believed and taught that what you put in you, not just food, but the kind of music you listen to, what you read, how you conduct your spiritual practice, how you communicate to yourself, has a direct effect on what comes out of you.

Good Morning Great Day is a fifteen-minute process I developed that you can do every morning when you wake up to get centered and out of your mind chatter and into action! It involves affirmation, visualization, video and focused intention-setting, during which you set your intention for the day, plus three success steps you'll take to manifest what you want during the day. During the day you get two reminders of what you said you were going to do to keep you on point. Then at night you review your day and connect to the highlights and insights of your day in a ten-minute guided visualization. Before you go to sleep you ask the universe one question that you want answered by your non-conscious mind upon awakening.

Everything I do is based on a principle of keeping me in my most optimal state of readiness to create. So even when I eat, I eat for success.

If you're not going to eat healthily, if you're not going to take care of your body temple—and food is an important part of doing that—your psychic energy, your physical energy, your emotional energy and your mental energy will all be affected by it. If you don't do your best in how you treat yourself, you're not going to be working in harmony and in alignment with your higher purpose. Then you won't be able to create from that place of infinite possibility within you.

ANTON: I like that point of infinite possibility, because we tend to think of food on a fairly superficial level. Food affects us much more deeply than just our bodies. The body is the beginning of it, but the repercussions of what we eat affect everything in and around us. I saw a man yesterday, forty-one years old, who was just recovering from a heart attack, and of course we started talking about the direct affect that the food you eat has not only on your own health, but also on all the other people in your life.

PAUL HOFFMAN: It has a lingering effect. Most of us at one point in our lives have eaten something where we said, "Geeze, I really wish I hadn't eaten that." Food is energy, just as money is energy, consciousness is energy, getting proper rest is energy and exercising is energy. Food is energy. There is a life force in the food you eat, and if you don't eat food that can contribute to the well-being and overall good of your life force, then you are defeating the purpose of you being able to create from the highest possible level that you can.

I am sober twenty-one years. I used to be a drug addict and an alcoholic. Now, don't get me wrong—I had a lot of fun. But I almost killed myself. Doing the drugs and alcohol gave me a false sense of power. It helped me fit into the particular world I was in at that time, writing music.

During that part of my life I wasn't really present or aware or, in fact, interested in anything that was remotely connected to spiritually and physically taking care of myself on a conscious level. I was always an athlete, so I was always in pretty good shape and I always had somewhat of a connection to my well-being. But during that part of my life that connection was not as vibrant as it is now.

What I came to realize after I got sober was the importance of maintaining a healthy and vibrant connection to your emotional, your spiritual, your physical, and your mental well-being. This has a lot to do with many different factors, one of them being food.

I was raised Italian. My father is a German Jew and my mother is an Italian Catholic. I was raised on spaghetti and meatballs and all that kind of stuff, but I was a very picky eater most of my life, and I always gravitated towards vegetables and fruits. I ate pasta, don't get me wrong, but meat wasn't a big part of my diet.

I haven't had red meat in over thirty years. I haven't had chicken, fish, or turkey in over fifteen years, and I've been ninety-five percent vegan the last six years.

ANTON: Is that for spiritual reasons or for health reasons? That's a fairly extreme diet.

PAUL HOFFMAN: It's for spiritual reasons and for love of animals. I'm not going to go out and carry placards around the city and tell people not to eat meat, but for my particular beliefs of what I think is healthy for my body, I'm more interested in eating food that has a great life force to it.

I firmly believe that the way animals are slaughtered and the way nonorganic food is sprayed with pesticides have a direct effect on their energy balance. I can't believe that if an animal is going into slaughter and he is in fear, that that fear doesn't translate into the cells in his body as he's slaughtered. The same thing with plants, with everything. They are living beings. Rather than eat things sprayed with pesticides, I choose to eat organically, because I feel it's the freshest and the cleanest food, and I think that's important for your body.

One of the reasons people age and bodies break down has to do with inflammation, which has to do with what you put into yourself. If you continue to compromise your immune system by putting things into in it that are destructive, of course you're not going to feel good.

ANTON: Well, it's amazing what a body can process and what it can put up with, but ultimately, over the long term, there is a cumulative effect from what we put in there.

PAUL HOFFMAN: I wake up every morning and drink a nice fifteen-ounce glass of purified water. Then I make myself some fresh grapefruit juice. I make a juice every day of thirty-two ounces of apple, pear, ginger, carrot, celery, broccoli, radish, cucumber, kale, mustard green, parsley, tomato and broccoli. I drink it all day.

I also make a protein drink every day. I make my own almond milk. I buy organic almonds and soak them in purified water overnight. I have a Vitamix, into which I put raw flax seeds, hemp protein, a complete whole-food health optimizer that's totally plant based (called Vega) and Pure Synergy, the ultimate superfood formula. Then I take the whole avocado with the pit (I don't use the skin) and throw it into my Vitamix and grind it all up. I make enough for two of those a day.

I do an hour-and-a-half workout every day comprising aerobics and and weight training. I'll have my protein shake when I come back from the gym. Exercise is important to keep the body in motion. Something in motion is always moving towards something, and hopefully you are moving forward. During the day I'll drink my juice as I mentioned, and then around three o'clock in the afternoon I'll have the second batch of my protein shake. I'll have one meal at night, which I usually eat before seven o'clock. The meal will consist of veggies, some kind of grain and some kind of protein, beans or tempe or something like that.

ANTON: Food is really an integrated part of your entire day. Does the food that you're describing energize you for something that requires physical strength, like going to the gym?

PAUL HOFFMAN: It's all about feeding my life force, feeding my higher purpose with the highest quality and concentration of good energy that I can.

ANTON: How do you integrate that into your interactions with other people? Say you're invited to someone's house for dinner that may not be aware of the food you eat.

PAUL HOFFMAN: Whenever I get invited somewhere or I am speaking at an event, I always just say, "I'm vegetarian. Please make sure there's something there that's vegetarian," and I'll make it work.

ANTON: So you're not trying to push your beliefs onto other people, you're simply stating what works for you so that you can share that possibility with others.

PAUL HOFFMAN: Absolutely. You and I became instant friends because we recognize the divine in each of us, in each of our cells. So not only is food important, but also the kind of people we hang out with is important.

Your inner reality creates your outer circumstance.

ANTON: I hate to watch the news, and I have been challenged on that a number of times. But I say I like to live in my bubble because the important news still gets through to me. Friends or other people will make those announcements without fail. But when I hear something disruptive it does something to my energy and my day. I would rather be the person who is walking into the store smiling at other people and happy and energetic than the person who is depressed because he just saw something horrible on the news. I am not unaware of what's happening in the world, but I do think that, similar to our choices of food, we have a choice in what we deliberately put into ourselves.

PAUL HOFFMAN: I would encourage everyone to take a good hard look at what's working in your life and what is not, because those are fair questions to ask yourself. The only way we can create better success for our lives, live from our higher purpose and realize our vision is to look at what's working and what's not.

And you have to be able to release and let go of what's not working. In my program The Character of Success, the last virtue is called "Reboot." Reboot is about releasing and renewing. I would encourage you to look at all the areas of your life that play an integral part in it. Money might bring you material things, but money can't buy you happiness; happiness is an internal job. Right now we're talking about food. Try to eat from a place of understanding that what you're eating is playing an integral part in how you feel, what kind of emotions you have and what kind of energy you'll be able to operate from. And, therefore, it gives you the ability to be more conscious, more aware, and more present to what you need to do to create success in your life.

YOU ARE A LIVING EXAMPLE

*Actions speak louder than words. Everything you do
is seen by someone whom you will influence or inspire.
Be congruent with your message.*

Keith Leon authored the best-selling book *Who Do You Think You Are? Discover The Purpose Of Your Life*, and he and his wife co-authored the best-selling *The Seven Steps to Successful Relationships*. Their company, Successful Communications, focuses on helping others improve and optimize their personal and professional relationships. Together they have more than twenty-five years of experience in the field of personal and professional development, and they have worked with leading transformational experts like Jack Canfield, Michael Beckwith, and T. Harv Eker. Their passion is building personal and professional relationships that work.

KEITH LEON: When I was a teenager, the father of one of my friends and also a mentor of mine said, "If you find a job doing something you love, you will never work a day in your life." I didn't remember this phrase until I was an adult, but ever since I remembered it, that's really the way I've been living my life.

I enjoy what I do and I love the people I work with very much. I feel that being able to love my work has made all the difference for me. The quality of my work and my enjoyment level have risen. I choose to work only with people that have a higher purpose. Are they making a difference in the lives of others, or is their main focus money? Money is only a tool.

ANTON: As a teacher and mentor, you're looked up to as an example to help them make a difference in their own lives, but you told me that there was a time when your inner philosophies and outward expression weren't really aligned.

KEITH LEON: In July of 2009 I stepped onto the scale and saw that I was up to 310 pounds. I came to the realization that day that, even though I *felt* I was eating pretty healthily, I was not. My processed sugar and processed food intake was at an all-time high. I love to eat! Some of what I ate was healthy, but it was the amount of food I was eating that was most detrimental to my health.

I would eat until I felt really, really full. The problem with that is that I would end up feeling over-full about ten or fifteen minutes later. The food would settle in, and I'd be bloated and uncomfortable. But this didn't stop me from doing the same thing the next time I ate. I had become compulsive about the way I was eating.

The second realization I came to was that I was not setting a good example for the people that came to see me speak on stage, read my books, or use my coaching and mentoring services. I was telling them about all the goodness available to them and how they could make a difference in the world. In the back of their minds they were probably worried for me because my weight was spinning out of control. I'm sure there were many who thought, *If things are so great with him why doesn't he do something about his health?* And I can't blame them for having thoughts like that, because it took me standing on the scale and seeing that I was up to 310 pounds before I even *noticed* how big I was getting!

I was just living life, enjoying every moment, serving others, being there for my clients, friends, family—and all along the way I was letting my own health deteriorate.

ANTON: I am not sure what our responsibility is to each other, whether to tell people what we think. I believe we *are* responsible to share our thoughts with others when our observations come from love and genuinely good intention. I don't want to stand by in silence and discover that someone has gotten sick or died because I didn't speak up.

KEITH LEON: I've got to be honest, I was scared when I stood on the scale that day. I started sharing my experience with people I loved, and, at that point, they all shared how they had been concerned for me for quite some time, but they had been afraid to tell me because they hadn't wanted to hurt my feelings!

I decided I was going to do something about my weight. I was finally ready to come up with a plan and put this plan into place in my life.

I'm a big fan of the show *Biggest Loser*. This is a show where they take obese people that are really in a danger zone to a ranch. They give them not only an eating plan, but the food to do it with and a place to stay, with a workout facility and trainers to work with. They help them release as much weight as possible within the time of the show.

I knew that if I hit it really hard I could release the weight really fast, but what I didn't want was to set myself up for failure. Since I had been watching *Biggest Loser* for three years, I had noticed that over time, many of the contestants who dropped weight really fast hadn't dealt with the *reason* that they had put the weight on in the first place. These people ended up putting the weight back on after the show concluded.

I was concerned about sagging skin and stretch marks. I decided that I was going to do the inner work as well as the outer work. I was going to change my relationship with the food I ate and how I ate it, really look at why I had eaten the way I had to get up to the highest weight I had ever been in my life. I would take my time and release the weight in a very intentional way.

One of my clients is a master at nutrition and using the mind to intentionally release weight, as well as physical pain and internal anguish. What Dr. Bob Levine helped me do was to get to the root of the issue, to uncover *why* I was eating the way I was. He taught me an intentional way of eating that completely changed my relationship with food. I just want to take this moment right now to thank Dr. Bob for making such a profound difference in my life.

In a few months, I released eighty-three pounds. I was feeling better than I had in a long time. I had healing inside and out, and my business began thriving. Now I feel as if I'm a living representation of what I teach.

ANTON: Your approach is very holistic. It's taking all of you into account. It's not a question of taking a quick-fix drug or eating the latest fad diet. Changing the way we eat is not just a matter of plugging in a new shopping list and recipes. So you're saying you can do whatever you want to on the outside, but it's not going to stick if you don't take care of what's causing it on the inside in the first place?

KEITH LEON: Absolutely. I knew that the internal process was what needed to be uncovered. There is always a reason that we do what we do, and that's the thing that is usually buried deep underneath a bunch of past stories.

I have friend who is just really, really skinny. Always has been, always will be. At one point I said, "I don't understand why you can eat anything and everything you want and not gain a pound!" He looked at me and said, "When you were little, did your parents tell you, 'If you eat too much of that you will get fat?'" I said, "Yeah!" and he said, "My mom never told me that."

How revealing was that statement? He doesn't even consider that if he eats cookies and all of those things that he'll get fat, because he never had that story. He was never told that, so it doesn't even enter his mind. He just eats the cookie and it feels good and he loves the taste and that's it.

ANTON: It's frightening to think how radically we change the direction of the lives of our children and those around us with a few unconscious statements, with things we don't even realize we're saying and doing.

KEITH LEON: You are a living example to everyone around you, whether you know it or not. Most people will not share with you how you have inspired them, how you have touched their lives, or how you have been a walking example for them.

Each good deed is noticed, as well as each cool comment, snide remark or passive-aggressive statement. Everything we say and do is noticed or observed. So think to yourself, "What type of message am I giving or do I want to give?"

Once you have the answer to that question, think, "How am I being in each moment?" Bringing this type of awareness into your life will change everything.

The phrase "you are what you eat" has a new meaning for me now. I never really got the complexity of that statement until I changed my relationship with food. Since I took complete responsibility for my life— how I look, how I act, how I choose to react in any given situation— everything in my life and my business has improved.

Weight can release really fast. You can make just a few changes in your diet and walk around the block a few times and you will create a change. Starting with baby steps and working your way slowly into a life change is the best way to go about it. Drastic changes are shocking not only to the system, but to the psyche. One step at a time with intention is a powerful, powerful way to create change.

Everything you need is inside you. You can do anything that you put your heart and your mind into. Life is good and so are you. You make a difference in this world. No one can be you but you, and you are doing a great job at being you.

WHO'S YOUR WINGMAN?

There are essential qualities to develop and sustain for the heat of battle. When you are aligned with your passion, and with a strong team, you can excel through the toughest times.

Lt. Col. Rob Waldo Waldman is a decorated F-16 fighter pilot with sixty-five missions under his belt. He is also a professional leadership speaker and author of the *NY Times* and *Wall Street Journal* best seller *Never Fly Solo*. A graduate of the United States Air Force Academy, he holds an MBA with a focus on Organizational Behavior. His clients include Hewlett Packard, New York Life, Nokia, and other giants, and he is ranked as one of the top forty business leaders in Georgia.

Waldo has an infectious passion for helping people. When teaching men and women in the civilian world, he uses metaphors based on his experiences as a combat-decorated fighter pilot to show the importance of a "wingman" in our personal and business enterprises to support the team as a whole with 100% commitment, especially when the heat is on.

ANTON: Active combat has to be one of the most insane and demanding jobs in the world!

WALDO WALDMAN: We train in environments that are so intense that when we go to combat, it's almost easier to a degree. When you're prepared, when you're focused, when you're mission ready, then when the missiles come, you know how to deal with them. That's the key. It's less overwhelming when you're mission ready and prepared.

ANTON: I think a lot of people over here have no idea quite how crazy it is in a war zone. My best friend just got back from six years in Afghanistan. From age eighteen to twenty-four he was on the front lines. Some of the stories I heard changed my life and my appreciation for what you guys do over there.

WALDO WALDMAN: No one wants to be over there. Anybody that says they do is kind of crazy. You just live up to the expectations and the responsibilities of your title and your job. When you're called to battle and you're wearing the uniform of your country and your country says *Mayday*, you have to step up and help. I don't think there's more of an advocate for peace than the soldiers who are serving. I commend them, and I commend the husbands and wives and brothers and sisters and moms and dads whose wingmen and women are serving our country.

ANTON: I grew up in the hippy era and I was one of the cynics, but I tell you, not after Mark got back from Afghanistan. Alive. I took my son to a Rockies game and when they played the Star-Spangled Banner, I was shaking and crying just thinking about what you guys do over there. Before hearing Mark's stories, I had no idea.

WALDO WALDMAN: I'm touched. I appreciate your compassion. That means a lot.

ANTON: These missions you guys do are serious life-and-death combat missions. It's so intense. There's no room for error, no room for moods or whining or worrying. You have such intense focus. Other people's lives depend on your ability to perform under pressure and to get that job done and to do it well. How on earth do you prepare for something like that?

WALDO WALDMAN: A lot of it has to come back to that *root passion*, that love for what you're doing. The combat and that stressful environment is a byproduct of the military. No one wants to do it, as I said before, but you ultimately train for it.

At the end of the day you've got to love the feeling of strapping into that F-16, flying that jet and participating in those missions. You've got to enjoy the thrill. You have to enjoy that tension and the pressure. That environment that is very, very stressful at times. If you don't have that passion, then nothing else matters. You won't be able to break through the fear and the obstacles and win any war, on the battlefield or in your life.

At any time in life, you're only tested when things are tough. When life's missiles are being shot at you, such as when you have a health challenge, or when you "go into battle," or when you're possibly going to lose your job, this is when your preparation and your passion for what you're doing really comes to fruition. If you don't have that passion, you'd better find another career, another mission, that really gets you going. If you don't have that, you're not going to be able to get through the tough times.

ANTON: You were right on the razor's edge. You almost didn't make it as, first, a pilot and then as a fighter pilot, but despite the circumstances, you were determined and you pushed through.

WALDO WALDMAN: Passion is a very, very important component of success and whatever you do. A lot of people think I'm crazy when I tell them I had to overcome massive claustrophobia as a pilot, but I was so passionate about flying fighters and flying jets that I was able to deal with it.

I had this latent claustrophobia that only came out after a scuba diving accident, when I almost died and had a massive panic attack. A few days after that incident, while flying, I had this extreme desire to get out of that plane; latent claustrophobia had revealed its ugly head. For the rest of the eight years of my eleven-year flying career, I had to deal with this demon of having a panic attack, of freaking out. It took everything inside me to stay focused, to stay present, and to remember what I'd learned, to overcome the fear of this panic attack.

It took hard work, but I loved the thrill of flying more than the fear. That's the key. We are all going to have fears and panic attacks and obstacles that threaten us, but when you're really in touch with what you love, you can break through that.

ANTON: In your book *Never Fly Solo*, I loved your anagrams for fear. F-E-A-R: Forget Everything and Run *or* Focus Energy and Accept Responsibility. You pulled those out of the same word.

WALDO WALDMAN: We all have that fight-or-flight mentality. Even when you're prepared and focused, if you let your fear take control of you, then you'll forget everything and run away.

It's normal to feel that way. Most of us want to run away from the fear. But a real wingman, a real trusted partner, or a real disciplined, committed individual will focus all his energy and accept responsibility for the fact that he strapped into the jet and made a commitment to fly. Whether you're flying an F-16, flying a mission as a dad, starting a new business, working with a customer, or dealing with your kids, you've got to strap in and accept responsibility. That's what real wingmen do. That's what committed professionals do.

ANTON: The key to what you teach is that we are not in this alone. We shouldn't be doing things alone. The do-it-yourself days should be over.

WALDO WALDMAN: Most of us think we're flying solo. Many times we're flying by ourselves, but we have wingmen. We have a lot of unsung heroes. Our vendors, our partners, our spouses, our friends— the folks whom, when the missiles come, we can count on to be there for us.

ANTON: Most of us have some friend whom we can confide in and who confides in us, who can say what only a friend can say, but we tend to be reluctant to do that in our daily interaction with other people. I think we are shortchanging other people by not doing that.

WALDO WALDMAN: A wingman isn't there just to encourage us and be a cheerleader. Often times a wingman will have to tell you what you don't want to hear but need to hear. Maybe tell you to refocus, or give you a perspective that you may not have. It's important when we're taking on a new mission, a big endeavor, a lofty goal, to find those wing-givers, those cheerleaders and coaches and truth-tellers who put us on the right flight path and maybe even bruise our egos at times. Because sometimes we need somebody to be brutally honest with us when we don't want to hear the truth. But it's important.

ANTON: When you're getting ready for one of your missions, there is so much energy involved in the preparations and in the duration of the mission itself. There is such intensity! How do you prepare for that? I can't imagine that you could eat a massive heavy meal before you go up and fly combat.

WALDO WALDMAN: Absolutely not. You need to be homeostatic. Functioning. Your brain must be functioning. You've got to be in top state. Obviously, when you're flying, adrenaline takes over and that can help you out, but on missions where you fly six, seven and eight hours, you've got to maintain that energy level. If you're going up and down on a sugar high, your adrenaline eventually runs out. You need to sustain your energy and also make sure the neurons are firing in your brain. In combat, you've got to be thinking.

Even as a professional speaker, if I take the stage and I'm not homeostatically in sync and my neurons aren't firing, I can't think on my feet. Even in this conversation I have to have those neurons firing and be very open and receptive to the thoughts coming to me. If your blood flow isn't going in the right direction and to the spots where it's needed, then you won't be able to be in a peak performance state in combat, on the stage or even in a conversation.

ANTON: When you're up in the air for six or eight hours like that, that's a long time, especially where you're using up your physical resources very quickly because of all the adrenaline flowing and the stress of it. How do you actually sustain that level?

WALDO WALDMAN: I used to bring a lot of protein bars in the plane with me. Power bars or whatever. That's a really good fix in intense situations because it's relatively fast and it can fill your stomach up. Sometimes even a banana will work as well. Normally, a good healthy handful of nuts can sustain you. But you can't really bring them in a combat plane, because when you're breathing through your oxygen mask, having those nuts in your mouth and in your teeth could interfere with the oxygen hose.

I like the all-natural green energy bars. Those normally sustain you because they have a good shelf life on a longer mission, they're easy to access and they're not going to mess up the cockpit. On those long sorties you definitely need those types of things in the cockpit. I would even bring hard-boiled eggs with the yolks removed so they made less of a mess. You've got to be environmentally friendly in that F-16 cockpit! And even while I was going cross-country in a non-combat environment, an apple would be really good to sustain me.

ANTON: Did something ever happened when you were flying or on stage where you realized that you were out of balance or didn't have all your resources at your fingertips?

WALDO WALDMAN: If I'm not careful with what I eat, my energy level can drop. There are times that I flew some of those long night missions in the F-16, and I was just trying to stay awake. Getting into the combat zone, your heart is naturally pounding. You're afraid, and that gets your anxiety and stress levels up so you won't fall asleep. However, when you're droning to and from the tanker to refuel in the non-combat zone, or you're flying forty-five minutes to an hour back from the *area of responsibility*, the AOR, to the home base, where now your natural anxiety and natural stress levels are going down, your body just takes a breather and you can become very fatigued.

You've just got to grin and bear it, eat those protein bars, talk to your wingmen on the radio, stay active.

That was ten years ago. I was a younger stud back then. I was in naturally better shape. As we get older we have to take cognizant steps, more calculated specific steps with our nutrition, because our body's natural mechanisms may not be working as well without that support—without the food-wingman and the fitness-wingman to help us.

ANTON: You lived this really intense life for eleven years, and yet you didn't fall apart when you got back here. You're still in really great shape, but you keep working on it. So many people imagine that when they achieve their goal, everything will just stop and they'll be on this plateau and just hover there for the rest of their lives. But it's not that way.

WALDO WALDMAN: It's easy to get distracted. It's easy to slack off on your fitness, to have the extra candy bar. The key is to resist the temptation to ease up on discipline and that commitment to your health and nutrition, because it all accumulates.

My twin brother is a fitness competitor, an all-natural body builder. He is always talking to me about fitness. To have somebody in my life like that to get my vector corrected when I may have gotten off track is important. When we are busy in life it's easy to lose that focus.

I have slacked off a little bit in the last year since my marriage. But I recently hired a fitness coach. He talks a lot about discipline and the *mindset* of staying in shape because we need horsepower. He's always talking about horsepower—horsepower in the gym, working on your core, working on your fitness.

The mind and the body from the inside are a reflection of the outside and vice versa. If you're not taking care of the inside with your health and nutrition, it manifests itself not only in your physical appearance, but also in your energy level and your weight and your ability to execute, be it as a speaker, a salesperson, an author, a writer, a chef or whatever.

The bottom line is this: we have to stay disciplined, but sometimes it takes a wingman, a coach, a friend, a partner or even a book. We need that to keep us on track, because easy things to do are easy *not* to do. And it accumulates. We need to stay focused and disciplined so that we can serve our families, serve our customers and pursue whatever avenue we choose.

I believe in my fitness. Health is important to me. As General George Patton said, "We are always on parade." What we say, how we look, is a reflection of our character, and if we're going to inspire people and lift people up and show them the way, then everything counts.

The biggest thing is, don't be afraid to ask for help. It takes more courage and discipline and maturity to ask for help, but don't wait until you really need to ask to develop relationships with the people that are going to help you.

Build these relationships now. Build a team of people who can be there when those missiles do come. Do that now when you're in peace, so when you have to go to war in your personal or professional lives, you'll have folks there to help you out. That's the key to success. It's helped me be a success in my life. I am blessed with the wingmen in my life who allowed me to take my life to new levels.

VI.

WE'RE IN THIS
TOGETHER

THIS IS OUR WORLD

*Take responsibility and initiative to make this world a better place.
Treat your body temple in a way that it can operate at its highest
level as you give your time, talent and resources. Create the vibration
of abundance in fulfilling your purpose.*

Paul Martinelli is one of the most sought-after international speakers and coaches of our time. Paul is one of the writers participating in the international best-seller *Beyond The Secret*, along with Bob Proctor, Mary Morrisey, and Les Brown. Paul travels the world to talk about the importance of the development of the mind's power to realize and change our desired direction in life. Corporations everywhere seek him out to teach his innovative and revealing techniques to activate and maximize their value and greatest potential.

ANTON: You have led a remarkable life. You went from being a high-school dropout to being a multimillionaire. You had a speech impediment, and now you are an international speaker sharing the stage with people like Bob Proctor, Les Brown, Brian Tracy and Mark Victor Hansen. You are transforming lives at a level and scale that's remarkable.

PAUL MARTINELLI: When I failed out of high school, I was one of the those kids that could have gone either way. I could have gone the wrong way and just stagnated in some dead-end job. Or I could have grown. Under the mentorship and leadership of Curtis Sliwa, in an environment that fostered community service, personal growth and a higher level of conscious awareness, I really blossomed. I blossomed in confidence, I blossomed in purpose.

I love how my teaching partner, Les Brown, says that "kindness and purpose are perfumes of life you can't sprinkle on other people without getting a little bit on yourself."

ANTON: You were part of the Guardian Angels that was getting started when I lived in New York in 1973.

PAUL MARTINELLI: Curtis Sliwa founded the Guardian Angels in New York City. I met Curtis when I joined the group at fifteen. At sixteen, I became one of the leaders. Through the grace of God, I had an opportunity to travel with Curtis for a number of years and be under his mentorship and leadership. He really molded my character. He helped me change the paradigm and self-image I was holding onto. It was a great opportunity for me at that time in my life.

Curtis had a vision of returning to the values where we no longer just sat by apathetically and self-indulgently, looking at the problems facing our community as something we wanted somebody else to solve. There was a time in my grandparents' history when, if somebody was harassing an older person or dealing drugs and doing some kind of damage to the social fabric of the community, these people wouldn't just sit there and write a letter to the mayor. They would get off the stoop and get involved actively in the community, either as role models or through physical intervention.

That was what Curtis did. Young people certainly were contributing to the problem, especially in New York with the gangs and violence and muggings that were taking place on the subways. But Curtis recognized that young people could also contribute to society and be a solution. His vision was to recruit young people and give them an opportunity to identify with a group whose purpose was to act as a visual deterrent to crime and to physically intervene if needed.

We would ride the subway trains and patrol some of the worst, most crime-ridden neighborhoods, neighborhoods that had been taken over by poverty and all the problems that come with that. These were really under siege by drug dealers and criminals. We would go into those neighborhoods and stand guard and watch for those people who were intent on causing harm to the neighborhood or to the people who lived there. If we saw somebody who was being assaulted, we would physically intervene and exercise our right as citizens to place them under citizen's arrest. We did that thousands of times across the country. In doing so, sadly, we lost nine of our members; they were shot or stabbed in the process of defending other people.

We knew that was a risk when we entered into that understanding and into those efforts. Whether it was Cabrini Green in Chicago, the South Bronx, Harvel Homes in Atlanta, or Liberty City, Miami, we recruited young people from those areas and gave them the opportunity to say *yes* to something positive. We gave them an opportunity to stand for something so they wouldn't fall for anything, and we gave them an opportunity to be part of the solution rather than the problem.

ANTON: I find your story of the Guardian Angels analogous to what you're doing today. There was a situation where there was danger, there were challenges. Rather than waiting for someone else to step in and save the day, you showed us that this is our world—and we are here now. We can take responsibility for ourselves and do something about it. The Guardian Angels did that to the degree that some people actually died. They were so dedicated, it makes your hair stand on end! And yet, they weren't paid anything; they were jumping in and just doing it.

PAUL MARTINELLI: It was an all-volunteer force. It was missionary work. The organization is still operating today in over a hundred cities and dozens of countries across the world. It operates on a budget of less than one million dollars, absolutely no federal funding, no state funding, no tax money. It's all by private donation. Curtis's vision was exactly that.

ANTON: Volunteering and giving your time doesn't stand in the way of or detract from pursuing your dreams of success?

PAUL MARTINELLI: Not at all. As a matter of fact, it's part of the success. It's what leads to the success. It's part of understanding that we have been blessed with abundance.

Thomas Troward, writing on the creative process of individuals in *The Spirit of Opulence*, says that, for most people, we start out with the desire to help and we look at our bank account. We say, "I have hardly anything to give." But money is just one resource. The financial rewards we have in life are an expression of something much higher and much deeper. We can also use those resources from that deeper, higher source, the spiritual essence of who we are as individuals. We can give and should tithe our time and our talent and our resources.

If for some reason financially we are not capable of doing that, by giving that which we have, we create the abundance vibration and frequency to our very core. Every single cell of our body gets a message that *I do have*. Although my physical financial resources may be limited, there is still abundance in my life that I can give, thereby adding value to the lives of other people.

ANTON: You are transforming individuals and organizations around the globe. Do you see any parallels in the way you approach food and the way you approach and manage all other aspects of your life?

PAUL MARTINELLI: I was raised Italian, so food is something that's holy in my family. I always say that food is my hobby. I absolutely love to experiment with food. For a long time though, in my teenage years, I struggled with my weight. I have two brothers who are tall and skinny; I always said, "Somehow I got the short, fat, bulgy body." I didn't understand how that happened. I was overweight and had a self-image issue around that.

One of the things I've learned in controlling my weight and understanding the important role that food plays in my life is that most of us make decisions from our IQ, which is how we were trained and conditioned in our school systems. We're taught to *read, remember, repeat,* and we're taught that we know something when we increase our intellectual understanding of things.

We also know that there is an EQ, an emotional intelligence, as well. For many people the battle with making right choices with food is driven by the lower level of emotional intelligence. That was certainly true for me. I didn't feel good about myself while I was growing up, because I had a speech impediment. I believed that I was dumb or stupid or less than other people. I used food as a way to feel good, as a way to reward myself, so I was operating from a lower level of emotional intelligence.

We also have two other intelligences. One is the intelligence of SQ, our spiritual intelligence. From each of us there is something emerging from our soul, from our spirit. Our souls are seeking oneness with Spirit, which is always for fuller expression, always looking to express the highest nature of who we are and what we can become. When we align that spiritual intelligence with the higher level of intellectual understanding of the role that healthy choices in food makes, and with an awareness and expression of higher emotional intelligence, we can then align with the last intelligence, which is PQ, our physical intelligence.

Through just this understanding, by extending my awareness with study and really entering into the experiment of life, I've learned to really listen to my body and allow my choices to be driven from all four of those intelligences: IQ, EQ, SQ and PQ. When they are not in harmony or alignment, there is an immunity to change, a part of us that resists change.

Among my core values and beliefs are that it's important for me that I make right choices when I eat, that I want and value high energy, and that I value having a healthy body so that I can do all the things that I do.

I was in Romania, then flew out to L.A., which is a ten-hour time-zone difference, did three days there, and came back to Palm Beach. I had a full schedule, but I never missed a beat. The reason for that was that during that entire time, although I had all kinds of choices to make, I allowed myself to use those four intelligences to align with what was best for me to be able to live for my purpose.

ANTON: I make notes as we talk, Paul, and I just wrote down IQ, EQ, SQ, PQ. I don't know if you ever noticed that those letters say IESP. *I have ESP.* IQ, EQ, SQ, PQ.

PAUL MARTINELLI: I love that. I can assure you I will use that.

ANTON: Paul, do you have any advice about food and success that you would like to leave as your legacy for people who are still searching to grow and improve their lives?

PAUL MARTINELLI: In my "battle with the bulge" and teeter-tottering with making healthy decisions, I was very much an all-or-nothing kind of guy. I never ate a slice of pizza in my life—I ate the whole pizza! I never ate a piece of chocolate cake—I ate half the cake! What I've come to realize is that when there is resistance to change, I have to identify, "What can I do now? Meal by meal, choice by choice?"

When I was in Paris I was absolutely going to eat some cheese. I was absolutely going to enjoy their croissants. I was absolutely going to enjoy some of their heavy sauces. But I was also going to do that with moderation and a healthy dose of exercise. I was going to pre-determine and pre-plan and pre-decide.

I have a philosophy that I call Crystal Ball Thinking, looking into the future and planning what I'm going to do. Making healthy choices with food is a big part of that, because we have to nourish our body temple. We cannot expect our body to be able to continue, to be able to move us through this life and meet the demands that we put on it, if we're not willing to take care of it and feed it the nutrients and the food it needs to operate at its highest level.

What I have learned to do is, meal by meal, consider what I can do that will allow me to be healthy. I don't want to play an all-or-nothing game. For me that doesn't work. But I do know that at each meal I can say, "I'm going to go ahead and allow myself to experience but not overindulge to the degree that I become stagnant or stuck." One of the things I've realized is that when I begin to eat right, it begins to drive all my other behaviors in a right way too. When I eat right, I tend to exercise right. When I eat right, I tend to sleep right. When I eat right, I tend to study right. When I eat right, I tend to interact with other people in a completely different way. When I eat right, I tend to feel better about myself.

ANTON: There is such grace to your approach, teaching people a tolerance to grow into their new awareness. In a way, changing the way we eat is analogous to weight training. You couldn't go out there and bench press 150 pounds of weight right off the bat the first day. It would hurt you. It would damage you, and you wouldn't make any progress. You start with the little weights and work your way up.

PAUL MARTINELLI: For most people, I think that starting is the challenge. For most of us, we think that we have to start on an extreme level. What I teach people to do is just start from where you are. Is it better to have at least one really good meal today? Can you make a commitment to something small and then build on that? And as you do, not only does your awareness expand but your confidence and your ability to make those healthier decisions are fortified. That's really what we want to do. We want to fortify our vision through our action.

Emerson talked about a person being willing to enter into an experiment of life and just practice. Just by setting the intention to create a change in our life, we begin to change at a cellular level.

WE'RE IN THIS TOGETHER

The more we connect with each other, the stronger we become. The quality of our food and water determines the quality of life we can have and sustain. Protect and teach your children well.

Kieron Sweeney is an entrepreneur at heart. At age eleven he made his first business acquisition and was financially free by the age of thirty-five. Kieron received his degree in Political Science and International Relations from York University in Toronto.

While leading educational trade missions to Europe, he discovered his talent as a speaker and leader, and today is one of the lead trainers at the *Millionaire Mind Intensive* and other courses offered by T. Harv Eker's international Peak Potentials, one of the world's largest and fastest-growing organizations in personal and business development. Kieron teaches what he lives with deep compassion that he says comes from his desire to educate and inspire others to live their lives with clear and deliberate intention.

ANTON: I have seen you command a room of 1200 people as though we were all sitting at a small tea table together. You have such warmth that it defies understanding your power as a teacher and trainer and the amazing amount of success you've had in your life.

KIERON SWEENEY: A lot of that just comes with desire and wanting to make the best out of the 150 years that I'm going to be here on this planet.

ANTON: I see that you're in cahoots with Nick Delgado!

KIERON SWEENEY: I think we are all in cahoots with each other on an energetic level. We are all part of the same thing as far as I am concerned. The more we connect with each other, the stronger we are, the more powerful we are. That is really what we are: energetic beings.

That is why it is important to stay healthy, because your body is just energy and it wants more good energy in it.

ANTON: You are persuasive because you're so comfortable to be around. Do you feel that food plays any role in the success that you've had?

KIERON SWEENEY: One hundred percent. Back in the 1990s when the whole low-fat craze kicked in, I was running an export business. We identified this trend very early. We had all kinds of different products made under a label that had a very Canadian identity, playing on the perception of Canada having a healthy lifestyle and all natural ingredients. Good prairie wheat. Great fruits. Blueberries from Nova Scotia.

We created a whole image about Canadian food under a label called Distinctively Canadian, and we started to market it in the United States. It was very successful early on. That, in fact, became my first really successful business, and it was a business aligned with the consciousness of good food.

I have always been very health conscious; diet has always been an important part of my life. I was an athlete growing up, and I have always exercised. In 1990 I cycled from the top to the bottom of France. The only time in my life when I kind of let it go was when we had four kids in five-and-a-half years. It seemed to be a lot easier just to get something from the store, throw it in the oven and cook it up—but our bodies paid for it! Within about two years we decided that we were going back to the lifestyle we were accustomed to. The good thing was, when you do have a healthy body, if you ever gain any weight, you can actually lose it fairly quickly and get back to the muscle memory, those toned muscles, that you have underneath.

I have always been cognizant of the fact that you must eat well. Today I am fifty years old. I look forty, and I attribute a lot of that to the fact that I eat a lot of organic foods, a lot of raw vegetables and lots of good proteins. I am very careful about what I put in my body. I am lean, 175 pounds and six feet tall—and I feel great. I just can't say enough about eating well.

ANTON: You live such a demanding lifestyle. You seem so casual and alert and comfortable when we're around you, but you're always on jet planes going across the world from Singapore to L.A., back to Canada. You're everywhere. How can you possibly do that? Does the food you choose help you with that energy?

KIERON SWEENEY: Absolutely! When I teach the Millionaire Mind Intensive, I am on stage for a good forty hours over the course of three days. To maintain energy and sustain that, I really need to be eating well. Whenever I go backstage for a break, I'm eating fruit and vegetables. I keep my energy level up that way. I eat a lot of salads, fish, and free-range chickens. But most of my diet is fruits and vegetables. I find it makes a huge difference. I can't eat heavy food, especially when I'm training—it will just weigh me down. You can't process it the same way.

What goes in your body will immediately start to manifest and create energy. You want to create good energy and not drain yourself.

I am really big on water. I drink really good water and make sure it has a good pH level and is completely mineralized and reenergized[1]. It makes a huge difference in your body. Drink lots of water.

I keep my diet consistent. I know what works for my body, and I know what foods work best for me. I've done a lot of research on it. I take a supplement every day, a little shot of a drink I buy from a company in the States that's basically mangosteen and sixty-five different fruits and vegetables. That gives me pretty much what I need for the day.

As long as 95% of your diet is healthy, you can have the fun foods too. It's okay to eat a little chocolate once in a while or have a nice glass

---

1   Energizing water is an electrical process that restructures the water, changing its qualities on a molecular level and making it more effective within our bodies, improving its ability to move through membranes, dissolve substances, remove toxins, and thus promote better health.

of wine or something like that without guilt, because as long as you're maintaining your health with exercise and good nutrition, you'll be fine.

Here's the interesting thing: when you eat this way, if you take a bite of a slice of pizza, you immediately taste the fat, you feel the fat. Your body starts rejecting it from the moment it hits your palate. My body says, "I don't want this." I guess I have trained myself now to the point that I just don't really enjoy eating those foods.

ANTON: More and more these days, organically raised, grass-fed beef is becoming available everywhere.

KIERON SWEENEY: I like meat. I am a meat eater, but I don't eat excessive amounts of meat. When I eat meat, it's good lean meat. We buy direct from the farm so it's good.

I won't allow my kids to eat anything but organic meat. I don't want them getting any of the steroids or hormones, because that stuff all affects the body. I've heard from people in the health community that this is causing people to actually develop quicker around age ten to twelve.

ANTON: Many children are going through puberty at an earlier age.

KIERON SWEENEY: Exactly. You want to keep your kids away from those steroid-induced meats. The best way is just to go organic.

Organic foods are now more affordable. There is no reason that anyone would have to pay more any more. There's enough production right now that it's cost effective for producers. I believe that most of the North American market is going to go organic eventually and move away from the foods we grew up on. We're all probably lucky we're still alive, thinking of all the crap that was going into our bodies over the last forty years.

ANTON: Do you have a hard time getting your kids to eat their vegetables?

KIERON SWEENEY: We started kids early on the vegetables. Our kids are kids. They look at broccoli and go "Yuck," but they eat it. There are different ways of getting fruits and vegetables into kids. My wife will make soups and stews and things like that. That's what my mom did to kind of trick us into eating them. I also have them on a supplement, so they're getting what they need.

My youngest daughter likes kiwis. She will pull a kiwi out, cut it in half, take a spoon and eat it out of the skin like a cup. They're very good at eating fruit. It's not an issue with them.

ANTON: So you just have that around the house where it's easy for them to get to it?

KIERON SWEENEY: Oh yeah, they just grab it.

Make sure you're eating all the right parts of the fruits and vegetables (like the skins) and getting the most minerals you can. We live in an era when we can transport fruits and vegetables from anywhere around the world. A lot of fruits are picked before they ripen. In nature, a lot of the nutrients actually come into the fruit in the latter stages of development. When they pick it early, the fruit hasn't really absorbed all the nutrients you need. Everything is timed. Pick it, transport it, get it to the store in the United States or Canada—and it's got a certain lifespan. The younger they pick it the more time it has on the shelf, but you never really get the best nutrients because they're picked prematurely.

Getting your fruits and vegetables from as close to source as you can is best. That's why in urban centers you're now seeing people raising fruit and vegetable gardens on rooftops and in communities in whatever kind of city plots they can find. That's what's working for people. It's also a lot cheaper.

Your body is a mass of energy and it needs to have good fuel. You can get a low-grade fuel, or you can get a medium-grade fuel, or you can get a high-grade premium fuel, just like you put in your car. I believe that the higher the grade of fuel, the more optimum your performance is going to be.

Food is energy. The best is clean and organic.

ANTON: This is about our being conscious in whatever we do. The food we choose affects not only ourselves but the world we live in and the other people in our lives. Children especially are influenced by our lifestyle choices and the example we set in everything we do, including the way we eat.

KIERON SWEENEY: We have to change the way young people in North America are eating. Especially in the United States. It saddens me when I see young kids that are obese. It is just not necessary. Those kids are unfortunately going to continue to do what they've learned from their parents. Their bodies are going to pay that price for most of their lives unless they can get it under control. We need to do what we can as a society to get our kids back to eating well and eliminating the junk.

I know a lot of schools are very cognizant of it. They are doing their best to have the food programs be much healthier, but we have to do what we can as citizens ourselves to be a good influence.

CONSCIOUS CREATORS

You have created your life. If you don't like it, you can change it.
Becoming conscious in everything you do, including the way you
eat, influences not only yourself but also the entire planet. Put your
awareness on what you want to create.

Janet Bray Attwood is an expert on what it takes to live a passionate life. She is the co-author of the *New York Times* best seller *Passion Test: The Effortless Path To Discovering Your Life Purpose*. She has been a practitioner and teacher of the Transcendental Meditation program for over forty years.

Janet is a founding member of the Transformational Leadership Council and has shared the stage with The Dalai Lama, Sir Richard Branson, Jack Canfield, Lisa Nichols, and other top transformational leaders.

Prior to becoming a top transformational leader herself, she worked in the corporate world as the marketing director for Books Are Fun, the third-largest book buyer in the United States. She is co-founder of Healthy Wealthy 'n' Wise Magazine, one of the largest online magazines in the world.

For her ongoing work with homeless women and youth in detention centers, Janet received The President's Volunteer Service Award, the highest award for volunteer service in the United States, from the President of the United States.

She is president of an organization in India called The World United, whose sole purpose is to promote conscious, healthy and sustainable choices for a better world.

Go into your Zen mind to a place called the "beginner's mind." Listen to this quote from Janet Bray Attwood:

"You are powerful beyond your imagination. You have created your life, and the good news is: if you don't like it, you can change it. Remember, your life is created first in your mind, then in the world."

JANET BRAY ATTWOOD: A conscious creator is someone who is consciously putting their attention on what they choose to create. They're also taking action in a conscious way to create the life of their dreams. What does eating have to do with any of that? It has so much to do with it, because the world is as you are. *The world is as you are.*

I was just in India. One of my passions in the past year has been to travel all over the world, specifically in India and Nepal, interviewing spiritual masters. I even went to the top of the Himalayas, to the source of the Ganges, known as Gomuk, and interviewed enlightened masters up in the mountains. Enlightened masters are conscious creators. I love the way I feel when I'm with someone who is a conscious creator.

I was interviewing this great master in Rishikesh, India. I brought in my camera crew for my video series called *Dialogues With The Masters.* I walked in and said, "I'd like to film you," and he said, "I don't like being interviewed." I went, "Oh dear," and he said, "But you can talk to me until the cows come home." I thought, *Well, that's cool. OK. Whatever. I'm going to stay open. I'm not going to force the issue.*

I said, "All right. What do you feel about the world situation?" He got this big smile on his face and he said, "I am so happy you asked me that. As a matter of fact, if this is what you were going to ask me, you can turn on your film." And I went, "Yes!"

He went on to say that we are at a tipping point right now. The world is either going to go one way or the other. You'd have to be brain dead not to notice that the weather patterns are completely insane now all over the world. The tornados and the hurricanes and the floods that we're having, we can't run away from it any more because for many of us, it's happening in our own backyard.

He said that one of the greatest things that each and every one of us can do in order to create sustainability for this planet is to . . . Then he hesitated for a minute and said, "It's not for spiritual reasons, and it's not for health reasons, and it's not for political reasons. It's because it's the right thing to do." And he went on to talk about the importance of everyone becoming a vegetarian.

It was so beautifully said. He went on to talk about the fact that they're clearing the forests in the Amazon. We all know that the Amazon is being threatened. All that incredible forestation is being cut down, and this wonderful, beautiful part of our planet, which feeds us oxygen all over the world and is the home of so many incredible medicines, is being cut down at an alarming rate. And what are we cutting it down for? We're cutting it down so that we can have more grazing land for cattle, so that we can make hamburgers out of them.

He went on to say that for every one person that becomes a vegetarian, sixteen starving children can eat. This is because of all the energy on all these different levels that's needed in order to create that one Big Mac that we put into our mouths so unconsciously.

What we used to consider a farm, the green pastures and the beautiful barnyard scenes, is a thing of the past. What's happening today is that factory farms and animals are crammed by the thousands into filthy, windowless sheds in confinements in Iowa—where I live!

ANTON: So you're right in the center of the corn country and the corn that feeds the meat factory.

JANET BRAY ATTWOOD: Yes. We have thousands and thousands of these things called CAFOS (concentrated animal feeding operations). They're gigantic, windowless, airless, four-sided housings with no ventilation that they cram cattle and hogs into. They shoot the animals up with all kinds of drugs and hormones, and they don't get to see the outdoors any longer.

ANTON: This is exactly what Michael Pollan talks about in his book *Omnivore's Dilemma.*

JANET BRAY ATTWOOD: It's so intense! They're drugged and they step in their own feces. What's so awful is that they even eat each other. And they're dying. Anyone in their right mind, who wants to be conscious—a conscious creator . . . If you know that we are part and parcel of what we call the *unified field,* that there is no separation, that that we do not exist in isolation, that each and every one of us is part of this collective consciousness, you would never in a million years put another Big Mac in your mouth. Never!

ANTON: Even some of our greatest athletes are vegetarian. We've just somehow been trained to think that we need to eat so much meat.

JANET BRAY ATTWOOD: If you want to know who the famous vegetarians are, just Google it. The most amazing people that we love and admire, that none of us would ever think are vegetarian, are full-on vegetarians. This is not about, *meat is bad.* It's about, *look at what we're doing to have that meat.*

It's not only what we're doing to the animals, but look at what we're getting rid of in order to have that Big Mac. We're hurting ourselves. This is insanity. Just like that master said, it's not for spiritual reasons, it's not for health reasons, it's because it's the right thing to do.

There has been so much scientific research. Be conscious. Wake up. Get out of this mirage that you're in and find out what you're putting in your mouth and at what cost for the third world countries and people that are living on the streets in the United States.

ANTON: Ultimately it will come back to us. Easter Island is an example in history. They eventually ate themselves out of house and home, over-cut and overgrazed everything until, on this most remote island in the world, they died out because they couldn't get away. They used up all their resources. They couldn't even build ships to get away to reach other resources.

We are now in a world that has shrunk, where we can get anywhere and be anywhere on this planet. There are more people and the planet is still the same size. We're sharing this world and its resources with each other. Earth is our Easter Island, only, this time, there's no where else to go!

JANET BRAY ATTWOOD: It's so important if you care anything about sustainability. Google *Why be a vegetarian?* Or go to PETA. That's a little intense, but tell anybody who is strung out on red meat and doesn't want to get real just to find out what we're doing. How we're treating animals. Think about it. My message is mixed. Mine's not as pure as the master's, because I think about it in two ways. I agree with him for the fact that, if one person became a vegetarian, sixteen starving people can eat. But it's also, what are you putting in your beautiful temple, your body temple?

You're not eating the same meat that our grandparents grew up on. Anyone in their right mind would never take another bite of chicken in a restaurant if they knew what they're doing to chickens, how they allow them to live in cages on top of each other and how they peck each other to death.

I was talking to a healer. He said, "Energetically, when these animals die, they know they're going to be killed, and they're totally freaked out. Well, you're eating that freak-out. You're eating that fear."

Everything is energy. There is enough research all over the world to tell you that everything is energy. So you're putting a great big adrenaline shot of fear in your beautiful body temple! And then you're going to try to go out and live a passionate life? No way! Your stuff is going to come up so fast because of the fact that you've fueled your beautifully designed physiology with a ton of fear fuel. It's insanity!

It doesn't have to happen that way.

I'm really going to talk to the youth here. A lot of times, as we get older, we become complacent in our habits. But to the youth: Notice. I want you to notice. Go to different websites and find out what we're doing to the world and get conscious. You know what's happening out there. Look at the fact that you're going to be wondering whether you're going to have an ocean to swim in that's not polluted, or rivers to swim in, or even glaciers to be able to marvel at in this lifetime. Will they still be there?

ANTON: Our world is changing faster than it ever has, and the speed of that change is increasing all the time.

Janet, was there ever a time in your life when you ate differently than you do now?

JANET BRAY ATTWOOD: Sure! I never set myself up to be this way, but I'm very conscious. If I'm going to eat some movie theater popcorn that's genetically engineered, I'm going to go, "OK, I'm aware of what I'm doing. I'm putting this genetically engineered popcorn into my mouth right now."

What I'm noticing is that, the more I allow myself to be conscious about what I'm doing, the less I'm doing it. I'm not asking everybody to be perfect. What I'm asking them to be is conscious. Conscious. Because when I walk into the local Vons or Piggly Wiggly, I can't find very much to eat any more. Think about it. You're eating genetically engineered food. Do you know what that's doing to your physiology? Have you studied it? Have you looked at the research about what happens when an individual eats genetically engineered food?

Google what farmers are saying in India. So many of them have committed suicide because they've had all this genetically modified seed put on their land, which they've had for generations, and found that the first crop looked really good, and then, all of a sudden, after the second or third crop, there wasn't any crop. They weren't growing.

Just be conscious and notice.

Notice when you walk into a health food store that the strawberries and the tomatoes aren't as beautiful as the ones at Vons or Piggly Wiggly— but why are the ones at Vons and Piggly Wiggly looking so good? Why are they perfect? Just find out. Go on the Internet and research it. You're going to be horrified, and you're going to go to the health food store.

If you put a ton of tomatoes together from Vons and Piggly Wiggly and a ton from the health food store that have been organically grown, you're going to know the difference. Blindfold yourself. The ones that are genetically modified don't have a taste, but they look pretty. Because we're so visually oriented, they have to look good.

Notice that this is what you're feeding your kids as well. When you're eating genetically modified foods, they're not getting the wonderful nutrients that we used to get when we were kids.

ANTON: The food that we were given growing up as kids forty years ago was different food than what is available now. Many of the systems that are in place now weren't in place at that time. They were just beginning. Back then we were still getting tomatoes that tasted like tomatoes.

The reason I ask you if there was a time in your life when you ate differently is to show that we're all human. Even our greatest teachers and leaders weren't always where they are now. I think it's important for people to understand they have this option to make a *transition* in their lives, in their own time and in their own way.

JANET BRAY ATTWOOD: And my transition wasn't even that long ago. Maybe twenty years ago. What I did differently that changed my eating pattern was that I changed myself from the inside out.

I started doing Transcendental Meditation over forty years ago. Meditation is just this simple, effortless process to give an individual a deeper state of rest than deep sleep.

There's all this research from Harvard, Stanford, Yale and other top schools in the world that has found that meditation (when you do the type of meditation like TM, where you transcend) gives you a very deep state of rest. You transcend your thoughts. You are no longer in a thinking state. You're transcending the thinking level and getting a profound state of rest. When you come out of meditation, you're clearer, you're more focused, you're more conscious, and you have more awareness. And the more you do that, the more awareness you have.

I lived with Maharishi Mahesh Yogi, the founder of TM, and he said, "Learn how to meditate, learn how to do TM, and what you'll find is that you'll naturally put down your bad habits and pick up good ones."

This is what happened to me. I started to become very conscious and sensitive to what I was putting into my body. It was a natural evolution of just becoming more conscious through meditation.

ANTON: You're suggesting we reach inside ourselves, find the truth inside ourselves, and then that will express itself outwardly, automatically. You don't have to force the change.

JANET BRAY ATTWOOD: In simple terms, who doesn't need to get more rest? Here's an analogy. You wouldn't drive your car all over the world without getting a tune-up, would you? But we drive ourselves, our physiologies, into overload with too much to do and constantly having everything coming at us without getting a deep state of rest. That's why people are so stressed these days.

What all this research has shown is that by just this simple process of TM, of just giving the whole physiology—the mental activity of the mind and the physiology of the body—a very profound state of rest, an individual gains a deeper state of rest than they do at the deepest point of deep sleep. The end result is that you're less stressed. Research has found that the only thing that gets rid of deep-rooted stress is deep, deep rest.

They're doing studies in many of the schools in San Francisco where they're introducing meditation into the school system. What they're finding is that the kids are much more engaged. Their grades are going up. Their happiness level is going up. Their involvement is going up because they're not so stressed. They're not worried. They're not all psychotic about their life and about what's going to happen to them, because they're feeling and experiencing, in a very practical way, the peace inside them.

They're also getting rid of anything that's getting in the way of them being able to experience their true nature. Our true nature is *being centered*. Our true nature is being happy. Our true nature is being healthy and awake and experiencing the world in a really blissful state.

What getting exhausted and getting really stressed out and having a lot of tension in your life do is to create a lot of stress on the physiology. Then all of a sudden, *the world is as you are*. You're not perceiving the world and looking at every moment as a gift any longer. Instead you're saying that the world is just this hard-knock place to be.

ANTON: And of course, food is intrinsically tied to your energy level. You can eat certain foods that might give you a buzz for a moment, but then you find that your energy is constantly drained and so you reach for more and more of these foods.

JANET BRAY ATTWOOD: Yeah. I eat chocolate like a drug, don't you? I mean caffeine . . . (laughs).

ANTON: You're my kind of girl! I love chocolate. I'm not a big caffeine guy, but I have my little piece of dark chocolate every night. But that chocolate piece is only the size of two of my knuckles. That's it. It's good pure organic chocolate and very satisfying.

JANET BRAY ATTWOOD: This is not about being perfect. It's about just becoming conscious and looking at what it is you're eating and understanding what you're putting into your mouth instead of thinking, because that tomato's so red, it's good for you.

There's all this research now about genetically modified foods. "Franken-foods." They're finding all these different diseases coming from genetically modified foods. What is really important for people to start becoming aware of is that 75-80% of all foods sold on the shelves of your markets in the United States is genetically modified. Google "genetically modified food horrors."

What are you doing in your life on a regular basis, and are you aware of what you're doing or are you just turning your head saying, "Oh, it tastes too good; I'm gonna go and have that Big Mac," even though there are third-world countries where kids are starving because you have to have your Big Mac.

I love humanity so much. I know every moment is a gift, and yet I think it's really important that each of us notices what it is that we're up to. That's my message, and it's my passion to spread that message.

It's all about being practical, isn't it? What's in it for me? is what people are looking for.

I want to be the best I can be because my whole life is in service to humanity. It's not an outside-in job. It's an inside-out job. What the world is looking for is teachers who are *living* their teaching. It's also about becoming very aware of knowing that you're part and parcel of the unified field of the world, that we don't exist in isolation, that every single thing affects every other thing.

SUPPORTING HAPPINESS AND LOVE

*Remove the blocks. Do your daily habits support your experience of
the happiness and love that are your essential nature?*

Marci Shimoff is a world-renowned transformational expert and one
of the bestselling female nonfiction authors of all time, with book sales
of more than 14 million copies worldwide in thirty-one languages. Her
titles include *Love for No Reason* and *Happy for No Reason*, and she
is co-author of six *Chicken Soup for the Soul* books. She is also is a
featured teacher in the hit film *The Secret*.

MARCI SHIMOFF: I know a lot of very, very successful people who
have devoted their lives to creating great success. Many of them have
ignored their bodies or put taking care of their bodies, including the
way they eat, towards the bottom of their list. Many of them are very
unconscious eaters.

I also know some people who eat beautifully, because that's their priority
in life. They have great eating habits, eat fantastic organic food that they
prepare themselves—and yet they are not outwardly successful at all.

But a lot of it depends on how you define success.

ANTON: What about you personally? Is food an important part of your
life and your success equation?

MARCI SHIMOFF: Food has played a huge role in my life—and it's
a really important component of my health. In fact, the way I eat is one
of the biggest parts of my ability to focus and to be creative, successful
and happy. When I eat well, I feel great. When I feel great, I am able to
be more productive.

I've been attentive to how I eat since I was seventeen years old, when
I became a vegetarian. I consciously try to stay healthy, so I'm very

careful about eating organic and healthy food as much as I can. But I travel a lot, and eating well is quite a challenge when you're on the road traveling 250,000 miles a year. When I eat poorly, it really shows. I have less energy. I am less motivated. I am less focused.

ANTON: You have a high-pressure lifestyle, yet you're so comfortable to talk to, to be around. Your energy and focus are so clear. When you go out, do you find it challenging to find food that meets your standards? Some people are fanatics about that and some people adapt better.

MARCI SHIMOFF: I have gone through phases of being somewhat fanatical. It's especially hard for a vegetarian to travel and find good food, so I used to travel with a little hot pot to be able to cook my own meals in my hotel room. I'd travel with all kinds of my own pre-prepared foods. Nowadays, of course, it's harder because of security; you can't get certain soups and things onto the airplanes. Still, I always try to prepare my airplane meal at home and bring it with me. I'm very careful that way.

But the biggest shift I've experienced in my life has come from a dietary change. Two years ago I stopped eating sugar. I'm adamant about it: I don't have any kind of sugar. I can't tell you the changes that have happened in my life on all levels as a result. I feel enormously better.

It started when I was on the road promoting my book *Happy For No Reason.* I noticed that I was getting incredibly tired and burned out, and I wasn't feeling that happy. Since I really believe in walking your talk, that wasn't such a great thing.

So I stopped eating sugar and, within a couple of weeks, I noticed my happiness level had soared. I felt younger, more energetic and better able to handle anything that life was bringing me.

I also started exercising more regularly.

Now I'd like to clarify something. A lot of people who hear this may think, "I would love to go off sugar, but I can't." Part of the reason they can't is that they don't have the amino acids or the vitamins to support them going off sugar.

When you want sugar, it's because something in you craves it. There is some biochemical imbalance. So I took amino acids, vitamin B12, vitamin D and other appropriate things that helped me let go of my cravings for sugar.

I don't want people to beat themselves up if they can't go off sugar right away. But I think it's really important to look into. Ask yourself what you can do to support yourself so that you can go off sugar or anything else that's dragging down your energy. There's a great saying, "It is hard to do good when you don't feel good."

ANTON: A few years ago when I had a bout with anxiety attacks, it was quitting sugar that saved me. I can't tell you quickly everything changed.

Was there ever a time in your life when you ate like most of America?

MARCI SHIMOFF: Growing up, my breakfast was Cheerios and my daily afternoon snack was Ho-Hos or Ding Dongs. I don't know how people survive eating things like that. I just don't know how people get through a day. I see why people are addicted to coffee and why we are addicted to sugar. We feel we need these artificial stimulants to keep us going in our lifestyles. I think a lot of it is that we need to look at our lifestyle and ask ourselves, what do we need to change so that we are not relying on the artificial stimulants?

ANTON: Marty Lefkoe talks about our beliefs. I know you have worked with him. It's astounding how quickly things can change in our lives when a few underlying beliefs are approached and assessed.

MARCI SHIMOFF: I have spent years writing books about this and speaking about this: I deeply believe that we are on the planet for a specific reason—to experience greater states of happiness and love—and that success is actually a byproduct of experiencing greater happiness and love.

Happiness and love are not just airy-fairy ideas. They are real, concrete, physiologically based experiences. When we experience happiness and when we experience love, it is because our bodies have the right chemicals going through them, because our brainwaves are working in a particular way, because our hearts are open. This is evidenced in various heart-rhythm tests.

All of this ultimately comes down to, how are you supporting that experience of love and happiness through what you eat, how you think, whom you surround yourself with, and all of your daily habits?

This is my biggest advice: look at your daily eating habits and see how they support your experience of happiness and love. Eat what will support your experience, your long-term experience of happiness and love—not just that instant feeling of happiness you get from eating a chocolate chip cookie, but the long-term experience of being able to live in the state of love and happiness.

Anton: Can you tell us more about *Happy for No Reason* and what you've learned about creating happiness?

Marci Shimoff: *Happy For No Reason* is a book that offers a revolutionary approach to experiencing lasting, unconditional happiness. What I mean by "happy for no reason" is an inner state of peace and well-being that doesn't depend on your circumstances.

You don't have to have the right partner or the right job or the right amount of money—or even the right body or the ideal experience—in order to be happy in life. When you're happy for no reason, you bring your happiness *to* your life experiences, rather than try to extract your happiness *from* your life experiences.

The truth is, this inner experience of joy is our essential nature. It is the truth of who we all are. All we need to do is remove the blocks to that experience. I really believe it's what we are all here for.

I am delighted to be on this life's journey with you. Thank you for the great work you are doing and for all that you are finding out about the correlations between how we eat and our success in life.

VII.

THE IMPERATIVE OF
AWAKENING

THE IMPERATIVE OF AWAKENING

Don't wait until your health is broken to try to fix it. The more effectively you function, the more you can contribute. When you become aware of the effects of the food you eat, you will awaken to reorganizational healing instead of reconstructive healing.

Dr. Richard Kaye has had a multi-faceted and distinguished carreer that has taken him from being an electronics engineer in the field of communications to being named Outstanding Doctor of the Year by the San Diego County Chiropractic Society for his practice in leading-edge health care. He was a founding member of the Board of Directors of The Association of Network Care and is an internationally acclaimed lecturer and author who has appeared on numerous television and radio shows.

Richard is vibrant and clearly lives with a passion to improve and support a better life on earth, by serving on advisory boards for numerous health and educational organizations. He specializes in team-building and super-networking.

ANTON: You are the vice-president of CEO Space, the world's oldest and largest business development organization, where you help businesses of all sizes grow to their greater potential faster by teaching them how to communicate better and avoid common costly mistakes. By helping so many people achieve their dreams, you contribute to the improvement of the rest of the world through the benefits they reap.

RICHARD KAYE: Contribution is a great place to live. I firmly believe in delivering more than is ever asked of you.

I was thinking about the connection between food and living life. In the early seventies, someone set me up on a blind date. When I picked her up I asked, "Where would you like to go to dinner?" She said, "Burger

King." My first thought was, *Oh, this going to be good*. I was eating that crap back then, so we went out and had Burger King.

My life was pretty chaotic, pretty distorted back then. Over the years I have become much more conscious, much more awake in my life as well as in what I eat. As I improved the quality of my life, which came first, I noticed that improving the quality of food seemed to be on a parallel path.

ANTON: It seems to be a common thread that for you to be successful, you have to adopt a certain way of thinking and behaving. You look as if you are fit and live a healthy life. You have a glow about you.

RICHARD KAYE: Thank you. My preference is to eat organic, although I can't always eat whole, live food. I will have chicken or fish. There's a balance. The only thing I would like to be fanatic about in my life is not being fanatic.

When I was practicing as a chiropractor, I would coach people on quality-of-life matters. I would never tell them what they *should* eat, because who was I to tell them what they should do in their lives? But I told them in all honesty, if you act on 80% of my suggestions and recommendations, you'll be doing better than most people.

I remember being at the airport at eight o'clock in the morning and seeing a family. The parents were morbidly obese. That's a clinical distinction: morbidly obese is someone who is 100 pounds overweight. And what were they eating? Glazed doughnuts and coffee. Just shoveling crap into their mouth.

The saddest part is that they had two children between eight and ten, and they were doing what Mom and Dad were doing. Like people who smoke. What's the message they're giving their children?

It's a level of awareness, a level of consciousness.

I remember my very first cigarette. I was probably about seventeen or eighteen. I remember what my body told me. But because I wanted to be cool with the guys and girls, I ignored my body and started smoking. It's the same thing with food. What are we putting into our bodies? If you want to have more vibrancy, more life, more light in your life, you should not be putting certain foods into your body.

I had patients who had lung cancer, had a portion of their lung surgically removed, and they still kept smoking. It's an addiction.

ANTON: Smoking is something that seems so obvious to us. Over the last twenty to thirty years, it's become part of our culture to exclude smoking. Yet we take food for granted. The cigarette seems like an obvious potentially damaging item. But we are less aware of the dangerous and toxic foods we put in our bodies every day. We need food, but we've forgotten the true purpose of food. We don't have to go out and hunt for it as we did thousands of years ago. Now we just drive to the store and pick up what triggers all of our highest sensations, without any regard to what it's actually doing. Would you put Kool-aid into the gas tank of your car just because it's a prettier color?

One of the great tragedies in this country is that we have developed fast and destructive food and food habits. In times of economic challenges, people start eliminating certain things on which they will spend their money. It's ironic that even though quality food is the one thing that can benefit their lives the most, it's often the first thing where they cut corners. Fast food outlets are benefiting hugely from this fact.

RICHARD KAYE: I just saw on MSNBC that one of the world's biggest fast-food chains is making more money than ever because, in today's economy, people are (and they used the expression) "pinching pennies." Of course, what they don't realize is that on some level, they're poisoning themselves.

Years ago I was in a grocery store, and I remember looking at a label on a loaf of bread and starting to laugh. Some people came over because my laughing was contagious. "What are you laughing at?" I said, "Look at this. It's all chemicals!" The quintessential example, of course, is Twinkies, which have an indefinite shelf life because there is nothing in there to decay! It's all chemicals. What astonishes me is that the body can assimilate that crap and still keep breathing.

ANTON: The item is completely dead. It's *designed* to *not support* any kind of life because that's what keeps it on the shelf for two years!

RICHARD KAYE: The body knows how to work that stuff and pull whatever nutrients it can. However, understanding more of the wisdom of the body, the closer to *live* food that you eat (I don't mean a live animal, I mean fresh organic stuff), the less hard your body has to work.

Having practiced leading edge health care and the marvel of network spinal analysis (NSA[1]) for the last fifteen years of my thirty-year practice, I take a look at sickness and disease in our culture today and find it frightening.

Most people don't consume enough water. They are thoroughly dehydrated. Most people don't recognize it. Drink lots of water. Half your body weight in ounces of water a day is healthy. Dehydration shows up as headaches, back pain, indigestion, diarrhea and a litany of diagnosable diseases. I used to teach that in the word diagnosis, *di* means two. *Gnosis* means knowledge. The 'a' before that is a negation. So di-a-gnosis translates to "Now the two of us don't know what you've got."

That's not the true origin of the word, but it makes a point.

ANTON: Was there any kind of event in your life that made it imperative that you change the way you eat?

---

1   Network Spinal Analysis™ is an evidenced-based approach to wellness and body awareness. Gentle precise touch to the spine cues the brain to create new wellness-promoting strategies. Two unique healing waves develop with this work. They are associated with spontaneous release of spinal and life tensions, and the use of existing tension as fuel for spinal re-organization and enhanced wellness. (Definition used with permission from donaldepstein.com)

RICHARD KAYE: The imperative just came from an awakening. Was there a health crisis? No. I just literally *awakened* one day and said, "I can't put this crap in my body anymore." That being said, I still eat red meat twice a year. The first time is to remind myself that it's a choice. The second time is to remind myself why I don't eat it. I was never a strict vegetarian. I would eat fish and chicken, just no red meat for many years.

ANTON: I like that you point out that there wasn't a crisis, because we have a habit in this current time and age to wait until disaster strikes to seek a remedy. We all wait for things to break or go to the limit, and then we try to fix it. You decided not to break in the first place.

RICHARD KAYE: Donny Epstein, whose system of chiropractic I practiced, developed Reorganizational Healing as opposed to reconstructive healing. Most people go to a doctor when they're broken, when something happens. They don't go because they're in pain; they go because the pain impairs their quality of life. No one goes to a doctor because something just started. Look at your own life. I would be fairly confident saying the last time you went to a dentist wasn't because you just started to notice a pain in your tooth, it was because it was so intense that you had to do something about it. That's the way we are.

People come in and say, "Doc, get me back to where I was just before the *it*." I don't know about you, but I don't want to go back to where I was just before. I don't want to go back to where I was a nanosecond or a heartbeat ago.

In Reorganizational Healing the body is reorganizing to a new level of consciousness and awareness and quality of life. That's called growth. Tony Robbins says, "If you're not growing, you're dying."

Take a look at nature. Set the human being aside. In nature, if it doesn't grow, it dies. If it doesn't evolve, it dies.

How many times do we drive up the highway and see somebody (forget the myriad of other things they're doing) chomping on a hamburger or whatever it is they're eating? Part of the food process is the ceremony, just sitting down when you eat. When we eat that crap while in transit, because we're so stressed out, it's devastating to the body.

I have been in businesses where, if you go in before lunch, the sales staff are vibrant and full of life and ready to help you. You go in after lunch and they can't get out of their seats. They have been drugged by the food they've eaten.

Hypoglycemia and diabetes are related to the blood-sugar level in your system. The reason we get lethargic during the day is that the blood-sugar level drops and there's not enough sugar. Sugar is the brain's food. That doesn't mean a Hershey bar will help you. It will, but for a very short time, because then the body compensates for the crash in sugar.

ANTON: Everything that we put into our body, no matter what it is, is transformed by the body into the sugars we need. But refined sugar is too fast.

RICHARD KAYE: It's a fast attack, and then it disappears so we get sluggish. There is a distinction between complex and simple sugars. Complex sugars will nourish the body over time, as distinct from a quick fix and then it's done.

I remember when I was an engineer, I would stop and get coffee and a sweet roll on the way to work. Two hours later my blood sugar level would drop. What do we do in industrial America? The roach coach pulls up, and we get another roll and a cup of coffee. Two hours later when we're dragging, it's lunch time. Then two hours after lunch we're dragging and we get a coffee break. The sugar is a quick fix, but it dissipates very quickly.

Here is something to consider. When I started chiropractic school, we were talking about hypoglycemia and blood sugar. Diabetes is too low blood sugar, hypoglycemia is high blood sugar. We were discussing lab tests. Normal fasting blood sugar was somewhere between 90 and 110.

By the time I graduated school, it was something like 75 to 110. I believe that today normal fasting blood sugar is considered 65 to 110.

What does that mean? Because of the preponderance of sugars in what we eat and our body's adaptation, we have lowered the "normal" to a number that's 25% less than it used to be. Because of our poor diet, now it's "okay" to have very low blood sugar, whereas thirty some odd years ago 90 was considered the low baseline.

ANTON: When I had anxiety attacks years ago, the one thing that immediately took effect and then actually resolved the problem was adjusting my diet. It was astounding to me how my energy started to grow again. I was reborn. And it was delicious, beautiful foods I was eating. It wasn't a restrictive diet.

RICHARD KAYE: That's one of the things I love about Europe. The food is so fresh and alive. It's distinct from all the chemicals we put in it here.

I eat a lot of salads. I will go to the organic food store and buy all kinds of greens and peppers and corns and some chickpeas and just mix up a great salad. Occasionally I will have prepared dressing, but usually I just use good olive oil and fresh lemon, not the stuff you buy in a bottle.

ANTON: It's amazing what lemon can do. Lemon is the key element in most of the things I cook. If you need that zing, put lemon into what you're cooking and suddenly it's satisfying. You don't have cravings.

RICHARD KAYE: Lemon is a great alkalizing item. When I was growing up, folks used to drink hot water with lemon. It's one of the most wonderful things you can do, because even though the lemon may appear to be acidic in the body, it's alkaline. Broccoli is also a great alkalizing product. Go on the Internet and you'll find all kinds of alkaline foods.

An alkaline diet is the healthiest diet you can have. Sickness, disease, germs, bacteria, cancer cannot live, let alone thrive, in an alkaline body.

Red meats, alcohol, and dairy products produce acidic situations in the body. Fruits and vegetables and things that are alive are alkaline.

I came home from a Tony Robbins conference where they challenged us to a ten-day diet change: live whole foods, no alcohol, no dairy, no red meat. I went well beyond ten days. I said to my wife, "I think I've got cancer." She looked at me, she said, "Why?" Well, one of the cardinal signs of cancer is rapid weight loss. I forgot the qualifying expression: *unexplained* weight loss. She said, "Richard, you're not eating anything."

Well, I *was* eating. Salads and live foods. No wine, no dairy, no meat. I lost ten percent of my body weight in two weeks. I was fit, my mental process was clearer than it had ever been. I required significantly less sleep, and I was feeling magnificent.

My energy was so sweet!

GOOSE-BUMP MOMENTS

Our bodies give us visceral responses to help us identify what is most meaningful to us. By finding your heart virtue, you can identify the hero within and live your life with unreserved power and purpose.

Greg Montana is an accomplished speaker and life coach who helps people identify their passion and purpose. He studied quantum physics and energy at the Stevens Institute of Technology, where he received an engineering degree, and subsequently enjoyed great success and all the trappings of a good life—boats, houses, cars, etc. He then gave it all up—to become a monk for eight years.

While contemplating heros, he discovered principles that he integrates into his work today: they all expressed a single virtue they were willing to live and die for. They also shared three elements: they knew who they were and what they stood for, they communicated powerfully and beautifully, and they made a huge contribution to humanity.

Working with his wife, Tamara, his company helps families and corporations identify their "authentic culture" by understanding each individual's Heart Virtues™. They have trained entrepreneurs, psychologists, ministers, Olympic gold medalists, and Academy and Emmy award-winning celebrities at the top of their game.

Greg has a different take on the food we eat. He has discovered something even more profound than the simple mechanics of choosing the kind of food we put in our bodies.

GREG MONTANA: I love when people are living in alignment with what's most meaningful in life and most fulfilling, and I love the work that you have taken on, which is to make sure that people are consuming things that are meaningful and fulfilling. A lot of times people think they have an answer because they've got their outside world fulfilled. But then when they actually get there and that goal is realized, they discover they aren't really being authentic and living in alignment with what is most meaningful to them. When this happened to me, I became a monk and gave away a lot of the glitz on the outside to develop that inner kingdom, a place where I could reside for the rest of my life.

ANTON: But now with the things you've learned and the gifts you give all of us through your training and insights, all that success is just pouring back into your life. Does food play a role in that? Do you think your choice of food actually can affect the way you succeed or even the level of success you might achieve?

GREG MONTANA: I think the choice of the type of food is secondary. However, it's important that the food you choose is food that you *feel* is healthy for you. I remember when I was in the monastery. I was a young monk really striving for self-actualization, self-realization. One day I was once holding a big chunk of chocolate cake and really looking forward to it, because I had been working hard out doors. I was thinking I'd have a more substantial meal later. I just wanted to get some sugar in my system because I was lightheaded.

This older monk came up to me and said, "Are you really going to eat that? I mean, that's filled with such garbage." I looked at the cake, and I looked at him, and I said, "This food in my hand has the exact nutrients I need to make my body perfectly healthy." And I believed it. I was enjoying a meal that I felt so good about that when I put it in my body, it was as if I were eating a bunch of broccoli and spinach.

Now, I don't recommend that people go filling up on junk pretending that it's good food. But I do believe that how you *feel* about the food you eat and choosing food that you respect and you feel contributes to the life you want to have is way more important than the actual food itself that you put in your body.

I think what ruins people is the lack of ease. *Dis-ease* is when my thoughts, feelings and actions are not all lined up. When I am authentic, I am *at ease*. But when I'm thinking, I should be eating *this* food and instead I am eating *that* food, I think that can cause *dis*-ease. We have been able to identify certain foods that are better for our health, and yet there are still no across-the-board rules you can lay out about food.

ANTON: You travel a lot and you have to speak in front of audiences for long times. When I have experienced you like that, you are such a high-energy person. You are not over-the-top high energy. You just have clear, focused, tremendous energy. But it never wanes. What kind of food do you eat before or after doing something like that?

GREG MONTANA: My wife and I both practice an austere diet. In this world, there's a lot of emotional eating; we need to be honest with ourselves about why we're eating. If you're overweight, for example, food can be a great way to act out your dysfunction; if that's what food is being used for, then I urge you to get help, get a good coach, go to a few intense workshops! But if food is something that you're using to *nourish* yourself, and it's not just a way of acting out your issues or the dysfunctions in your life, it's a great way to increase the joy of living. I love to sit down to a nice meal and, my God, you are the master of preparing beautiful meals!

When food is prepared with love, I'm happy to sit down and spend the time to let it nurture me. My wife and I don't eat rich food every day. In fact my typical day, when I am not visiting with someone or on vacation or on holiday with relatives, includes drinking four raw eggs in the morning. I just crack them into a glass and drink them because it's great protein. I follow it up with something that has a little flavor to it, usually a lemon or something—because the taste of eggs is a little weird—but you don't even notice it. You just drink them down. I love that it's just simple, incredibly nutritious food.

The second thing is that my wife and I both will have a very simple sandwich: turkey slices, mustard, and two pieces of bread, and that's something we'll do frequently throughout the day. We find that when we put that food in our body, it feels as if we can be athletic. We've got plenty of energy for the afternoon. We do take some supplements, vitamins and things like that. I also like some of the drinks that are out there, whether it's the goji or the noni or the Univera. And there are a number of drinks that have condensed nutrients in them with a little spirulina or something. But by and large, we are very austere in how we eat.

ANTON: Was there ever a time in your life when you ate poorly and paid the price?

GREG MONTANA: When I hit mid-forties, I started gaining weight. I worked with a trainer that completely changed my mindset. For about two months I ate nothing but incredibly pure food, and I dropped the weight and became very athletic. He shifted my mindset, and I stuck with that diet for about a year so that I would establish the habit. So now I have the habit of eating really healthy food. You've seen me. I'm pretty trim. Now I can go out and eat whatever I want, and I can do that three or four times a week because the majority of the time I eat really healthy food. I'm not packing it in.

ANTON: You once told me that when you went on a very restricted diet it just made you cranky, and then you felt that you were spreading that crankiness in the world. You said that the *joy* of food was important.

GREG MONTANA: The years I was a monk, I tried all kinds of austere things, where I would force myself to sit in meditation for six to eight hours and eat only a particular food, for example. What I learned is that, as a physical being that is in essence spiritual, if I torture my physical existence by trying to do strictly spiritual stuff, I am not balanced, and the animal that I live in gets very angry and frustrated.

When I went to one of the monks in the monastery and said, "I am practicing this diet religiously, but it's very stressful," he said, "Hey, listen. Throw the dog a bone." What he meant by that is to practice everything in moderation. When I left the monastery, one bit of wisdom I took with me is to practice everything in moderation, *including moderation.* So you have a moderate meal most of the time, but then go crazy and eat so you don't torture yourself and hate your diet so much that you can't sustain it.

ANTON: It's very important to create a lifestyle that you can *sustain* because you love what you're doing.

GREG MONTANA: Food is so joyful and, as such, deserves to be respected. Indulge it from time to time, max out and let yourself experience that indulgence. It will likely result in your reaching the point where you say, "Wow, I can't eat all that much. I've learned my lesson." I am sure everyone has overindulged in a food that they just couldn't touch for years afterwards because they had done that.

ANTON: You have lived such an exciting and intense life. You really live your life with the pedal to the metal. You're so genuine and such a joy to be around, and you give that to everyone you encounter. It's one of the most outstanding traits I see and feel when I'm around you.

A lot of people are still struggling in their lives, and food is part of that struggle. You have a shortcut exercise to help people find what is truly meaningful to them, to find what their "heart virtue" is. Would you mind telling us about your goose bumps list?

GREG MONTANA: Not at all. Even in the sense of food, or *any* experience that you have, the body gives us visceral data like, "Oh my god! That's so incredible. It gives me goose bumps!"

Everything from food to work to play to the people that we spend time around can give us goose-bumps moments. Knowing what's meaningful to you means taking an inventory of those goose-bumps moments and paying attention to yourself, paying attention to how you feel. My diet changed dramatically when I looked at how I felt after eating a bunch of junk food or fast food! You're way better off eating a decadent sweet on occasion that is prepared with intention and love than you are eating something that continually makes you miserable.

The thing that leads to the best lifestyle is to know what's meaningful to you, whoever you are. If, for example, you're overweight, and you're overweight because you feel compelled to eat food, know what's meaningful to you that's *so meaningful* that it's causing you to eat like that, and don't let the symptom become your life.

Learn what's most meaningful to you and live in alignment with it and design your life around that. The fact is, it's not about living someone else's plan or program.

When people understand themselves, when they are self-actualized or self-realized, that's when they start to really enjoy the dance, the relationship with the animal they live in: a spiritual being living in a human form. Then they can enjoy the five senses in appropriate environments and have incredibly beautiful food and indulge! And then practice, most of the time, moderation.

When you know what's meaningful to you first, everything else falls into place.

THE RAW TRUTH

You may not even know something is missing, but once you have experienced feeling great, you will never want to go back to just feeling good. Food is the most direct way to influence your sense of well-being. Discover the "Naked" lifestyle through whole raw foods.

Diana Stobo is a classically trained Cornell culinary artist and raw food advocate who healed herself through food. An inspirational and motivational speaker, she also teaches the raw food lifestyle in classes, retreats, and live presentations on television and in markets and health clubs. Her delicious and fully accessible recipes make maintaining the raw lifestyle easy and fun to incorporate.

Diana is a person who has taken her food to the extreme in the raw food movement. When you see how gorgeous this energetic mother of three is and how much her life changed from the days when this goddess weighed 247 pounds and was riddled with health issues, you begin to realize the true impact that your choice of food has on your very being. We're not talking vanity diets here. We're talking about life and death.

Diana is a bundle of energy, beauty, kindness, and joy. We filmed a cable TV episode for my show, *Cooking With Anton*, virtually—Diana in northern California and me on my ranch outside Aspen, thanks to the wonders of modern technology. Even from 1,000 miles away, you could feel her generosity and life energy beaming through the air!

We hit it off the moment we met. We had both been through some of life's worst moments and not only survived, but thrived. The only thing beyond the impulse of spirit to be here for our children that really made it at all possible was revisiting the food we put into our bodies, first to heal and then to grow.

Diana is now on the forefront of teaching people the transformational magic that gently integrating raw foods into our diets can have on all aspects of our lives.

ANTON: Diana, on your website you say, "Give me seventy-five minutes, and I'll give you a lifetime of health." That's a wonderful promise. You help people solve some of their greatest challenges by taking them by the hand, guiding them through the process of assessing where they stand, and helping them acknowledge how to come alive and live the life of their dreams—all through expanding their awareness of the food they choose.

DIANA STOBO: People want their hand held. I certainly did. You are taking them blindfolded and guiding them through a path. They don't want to take the blindfolds off.

It can be a lot of work. You want to say, "This process isn't that bad!" But they'll ask the same questions over and over again. And that's what I'm here for: just to say, "Hey, I know it's tough."

ANTON: I think it's tremendous that you acknowledge that and are willing to do it without embarrassing them. You encourage them and help them along. People can get brain freeze. We are so inundated with information in our modern lives that our brains actually lock up. We no longer know what to do and have stopped making good assessments about how to make good choices for ourselves. In the brain's inability to process all this information it simply falls into a kind of paralysis.

DIANA STOBO: There is no room for embarrassment, because that's judgment, and judgment will just turn everybody inward. Then there's no way they will ever get to a place of health, vibrance and beauty.

ANTON: You are gentle and kind in your approach, inviting people to discover this knowledge that you experienced firsthand. From the way you look now, it's hard to imagine how sick you were and that you once weighed 247 pounds. What happened?

DIANA STOBO: The very first book I wrote is called *My Body Naked*. It's my life story. The struggles of life, of childhood, of trying to please your family and eat everything on your plate because of money issues, self-esteem issues, and anorexia. And then there's drugs and then there's sex and then there's how do you appeal to the man and how do you appeal to the woman and how do you make everybody happy with who you are and still make yourself happy?

Just a lifetime of struggling and going on fad diets and trying to fit into the right look and the right jeans and the right hairdo. And it goes on and on! Maybe for women more than men, although I've had a lot of men read the book and say, "I totally get it. This is exactly my life."

All these things led me to a place where I became really toxic. It's not like I was raised on McDonalds and sat home and watched TV and ate bonbons all day. I was living what I considered a healthy lifestyle for the standard American ways. But my body couldn't take it.

It's not just about food. It's about a way of life. It's about judgment. Self-love and self-loathing. My body finally got to a point where it was overwhelmed, exhausted—and it retaliated.

It retaliated, and I started to swell. I had enormous amounts of edema and I was just back-loaded. A lot of it also had to do with medications I was taking in order to heal issues that were occurring. Little things that people take for granted: thyroid, chronic fatigue, a pain in my shoulder. Bursitis or fibromyalgia. I had a pill for everything, and my body couldn't take it. On top of that, when I struggled to get pregnant, I used fertility drugs in order to conceive my children. So I was just overloaded with toxic waste. That's basically end of story. That's how I got to 247 pounds. Years of abuse.

ANTON: In our culture, once TV caught our attention and the industry realized they had a captive audience, we no longer saw our lives for what they were. We started shaping our lives in expectations of looking like what we saw. We were trying to be life imitating art, and suddenly we became this culture of people who believed that we were this Jetson society and that there was a little pill to pop for anything.

You actually went into kind of a hellish time in your life. What happened that triggered your saying, "Okay. Enough. I need to make a change here."

DIANA STOBO: It's unfortunate that most people have to get triggered. A lot of people make changes in their lifestyle *after* they find out they have cancer or they have a near-death experience or they lose somebody close to them.

One day, out of the blue, I started violently throwing up blood. I didn't know what was going on, and I had my three children sleeping in the house. My husband was traveling. I thought, *What am I going to do?* I was trying to deal with the situation, but I was more concerned with what was going on at home than my own health, because this is what we've been taught to do, right?

I ended up getting to the hospital, where they gave me morphine. I remember lying there and going, first of all, calm. My eyes were fluttering in the back of my head, and I was thinking, *Okay this feels good. I wonder what I have.* They said, "The doctor will be back in an hour." The doctor comes back, looks at me and says, "You have a bleeding ulcer." And I said, "Great, what do we do about that?" He says, "Well, the nurse is going to give you another shot of morphine."

As he is saying this, she shoots me up with another shot of morphine. You might as well have killed me then. I looked up into the sky, eyes fluttering back again, and I thought, *What's the point of living? This is it. I mean, here I am drugged out. Is this my life at thirty-five years old? And I'm going to be taking drugs for pain? Seriously?*

I got home. I had a huge hangover like you can't imagine. I still had to deal with kids the next day, trying to get to a gastroenterologist for the next step in this process. There was a three-month wait in a facility that had eight different doctors. Three months of waiting to heal my gut—and eight different doctors on staff! And I thought, *All right, this is not my life. I am not going to sit in the doctor's office waiting for that next drug.*

So literally, God shined his light on me. My sister called me and said, "You've got to read this book." It was *The Body Ecology Diet* by Donna Gates, who also wrote *I Just Shrank a Tumor by Changing the Way I Eat.*

So I read the book and researched tons of other books and came up with the Six No's that you see on my website: "Knowing the No's." These are the foods that cause your body illness and disease, and when I took them out of my diet, within ten days I lost ten pounds. I got off my medication within six months and never saw a doctor again. I changed my life. I chose to take my life into my own hands.

Once off all medication, I was down to a plant-based tyrosine thyroid product, which is an herb product. It has a lot of algae in it. In fact, there's a lot of algae and silica and great things that we can put into our body now to aid our thyroids. Our thyroids are overwhelmed because our digestion can't handle the foods we're eating. Then everything starts to get out of whack. Everything starts at the gut. When the gut's not working properly, everything starts to turn to disease.

It's kind of like working backwards. We take a pill for the thyroid before we heal the gut. We need to deal with the intestinal issues *first*, and then everything else starts to clear out.

ANTON: So food was at the foundation of your discovery.

DIANA STOBO: Absolutely. But I was also teaching meditation and yoga. I was working as a spiritual counselor. A lot of things I was doing were working for me. It was not just one avenue.

On my membership page I have an expert panel that I interview. I introduce all my members to other ways of getting healthy besides food. Imagine a circle of life, of transformation. If you find one entry point, whether it be through yoga, exercise, breathing techniques or food, they are all going to feed into one other. You just have to find your entry point. Because I'm a trained chef and have a passion for food, I chose food.

I was actually on a quest in India with a friend, and he asked me, "What's your greatest passion in life?" I said, "Healing people through food." That sparked my whole business, because when he asked me what my passion was, *I had the answer*. Most people spend their whole life looking for that, and I had it on the tip of my tongue. This is why I am doing what I am doing.

ANTON: It never ceases to amaze me that we go searching down every convoluted path we can think of when the answer is sitting right there in front of us, under our noses, at the stores we visit every day. Granted, not every grocery store has the best food in our best interests, but at most grocery stores we are able to find at least the foundation to begin a new life with good food, and you teach us how to do that.

You've become quite successful. Your life is just exploding. You are all over the Internet. You are working with some really great people, and you are teaching everybody how they can turn their lives around. I look at you, and I see a direct relation between food and your ability to succeed. Do you think that food actually plays a role in whether we even *can* succeed?

DIANA STOBO: Oh yes! You *are* what you eat. You eat for success. I love the title of your book because it's true. If you are clouded—if your body is clouded, if your mind is clouded—there is no possible way to be successful with full integrity. But success, in my opinion, is not just about becoming a *millionaire*. It's about living life to its fullest, enjoying life and having a well-rounded lifestyle. I believe food is an integral part of that.

ANTON: One of the focuses on my show is that cooking isn't something that has to interrupt or add a burden to your life. It's actually your oasis of joy, a place where you can escape and say, "No one can bug me for the next hour, because I'm in this beautiful place and this time is for me. It's mine."

When you and I cooked together, we had so much fun. And our families love cooking with us. They love what we produce. As you just said, we need to *live* our lives, not just be constantly aspiring to *some day* when we can achieve whatever that brass ring out there in front of us is.

DIANA STOBO: This is true. We love food. However, I know a lot of people who adhere to a raw lifestyle and who are trying to teach how to gain health through superfoods, but who are not looking at the whole picture, which includes the *enjoyment* of food. So what I do is re-educate in the kitchen. I take all those delicious, familiar things that bring you happiness, and I show you how to make them in a healthy way. It's a substitution without losing the taste, the flair, the look of really good, exciting cuisine.

ANTON: I love how you don't try to bowl people over or force them to change the way they look at things. You are simply introducing them to a new mindset, a new way of thinking. You let them gently head into their new lives. Sometimes we make changes the same way we make New Year's resolutions. We try to do too much at once. We are all gung-ho, but then we exhaust ourselves and give up!

DIANA STOBO: We get scared sometimes when we hear information about our health. We become overwhelmed and then we freeze. We think, "Where do I start?" Someone who has had success is my husband who, bless his heart, grew up on Twinkies, Coke and white bread. He would do anything for a bagel dog and Coca-Cola. This was his whole lifestyle.

I kind of nudged him to try green juice. I was drinking quarts of it every day, and I said, "Just try it." He literally had to plug his nose to down it, because this guy had probably never had a vegetable in his life.

Now, he is so addicted to that green juice that when he goes to the ball park with my son and tries to eat a sausage sandwich, he is literally in pain. He has shifted his body *to desire healthy food* without actually saying, "You can't have it anymore." He comes home and says, "You know, I don't really think I could eat that anymore!" It's a process.

I'm a foodie. If I'm out to dinner or if I'm out to lunch, I am going to dive into that delicious menu item. I am hoping it doesn't affect my body in a negative way, but I'd say at least 75% of the time it does. I try. I bless it, I do everything I can to eat it with loving intention. But my body reacts. So my comfort food is a smoothie, a green juice, a salad. It makes me feel great.

I don't even sleep that much or need a lot of sleep. I can stay up until one o'clock in the morning and then get back up at six and feel excellent. I don't need coffee or anything. That is not the case for probably 95% to 98% of Americans.

When I eat out, when I eat food that is not within my "Naked" lifestyle, I can't get up the next morning. My body just doesn't have the ability to detox all that junk while I'm sleeping. I get up the next morning and guess what I crave? Coffee! It's a cycle. I feel, "I'm in the cycle. I'm not in the cycle." You have to decide which cycle you'd like to be in: the cycle of good feeling and health or the cycle of toxicity and just getting by.

You talk about success. I think food does play a part, because when you wake up in the morning ready to go and your brain is sharp, success is waiting for you all day long.

ANTON: Most of the people I've interviewed are on airplanes constantly, and they are talking to huge rooms full of people. They can't afford to have a lapse in energy, and somehow they manage to keep up that energy! It always comes down to the same thing: they eat foods that keep them light.

You have a slogan: "Stripping away the foods that weigh you down." That's exactly what you were describing in this unbounded energy that you have.

We love eating comfort food or eating because we feel bad and we want to feel good. But we can actually change the very foods that give us comfort and make us feel good. You have experienced it, I have experienced it—where you actually wake up feeling great because your body has cleaned itself out and it's happy! You actually start to crave these new healthier foods. It's an astounding reward! You no longer crave the doughnuts and other garbage that you used to think made you feel good.

DIANA STOBO: And the beauty is, you don't ever have to take them out completely. That's where people get stuck, and that's where my forgiving way is so accepted. Sometimes you just want to do it and when you do, that's great. Don't beat yourself up. There are a lot of people out there telling you, "This is the only way to eat. You have to eat this way! Constantly, and nothing else!"

I'm saying no. Consistency is key. If you are eating a certain way and then you have a blip, you have a craving and you just want to go for it, go for it. Just remember, in the long term, it's about consistency. It's not a short-term diet that gets you where you want to be. It's a lifestyle. In order to sustain that lifestyle means allowing yourself to indulge when you want to indulge, but recognizing that it is, in fact, an indulgence.

Remember when we were kids and they said, "We'll give you a treat if you are a good kid"? We do it to our own children. The truth is that treat is usually bad. We're teaching people to put bad stuff in their bodies. I always thought, what if we change the word? What if we said, "Mommy is going to give you a treat. Mommy's going to give you a little bit of toxicity for being a good kid today."

If we change the words, suddenly it changes the whole way we think about it.

ANTON: You know, it sounds funny. I'm sure that some people will think this is an exaggeration.

DIANA STOBO: Well, I'll tell you, my parents think this is crazy. My mother is basically anti-raw—and everything I have been working for. She says, "A friend told me that if you become a vegan, it could change the structure of your body!"

And I said, "That's cool. Isn't that what we want to do?"

The people who are resistant to hearing this information are scared. I was scared. I wasn't raised this way. This is something I had to learn through my own body. I'm not even against meat. In my book I talk about knowing the no's and knowing what's wrong with meat. But I'm not against it. Certain people need animal flesh to survive. It's their blood type. There's a certain type of person who actually needs it.

My point is, be aware of the foods you're putting into your body. Don't just go to the nearest market and buy that on-sale beef that's been sitting there. Get yourself a good piece of organic meat. Know the cow it came from so you are not putting more junk into your body.

ANTON: When you talk to people who are addicted to eating a lot, "moderation" sounds like, "Okay, here come the chains and shackles! I'm already miserable. That's why I'm eating and now you're just going to make me more unhappy."

Yet, once you cross that line where your body rewards you with feeling good for treating it right, you never want to go back!

Our bodies are these wonderful machines that are constantly healing themselves, almost no matter what we do to them. It's just that we happen to have somehow figured out how to beat our bodies and, unfortunately, beat them down beyond their limits! Your way of eating and living actually creates the space where our bodies get a fighting chance. And then a person can experience the joy and the energy and the feeling of being alive that you are teaching people. And how to get there!

DIANA STOBO: So often people say, "No, this isn't for me." Then, three to four months later, they've been checking out my site, listening, reading what I've been writing, and they come back and say, "Okay, I'm ready." Three to four months later they go from absolute "No" to "I really want to learn." That's because they're hurting. They are actually recognizing now that they don't feel as good as they could feel.

The other thing is that, from most people who have done this program, who got "Naked," the one thing I hear over and over again is, "I didn't even know that I didn't feel good until I felt good! I didn't realize I wasn't feeling great until I felt great." That is really key.

ANTON: It's just like you have those moments where your mind is so crystal clear, it stuns you, because you realize that you have been living in a fog.

DIANA STOBO: It's awareness. It's *consciousness* that is creating success in your life. All we are doing here is trying to create a successful life and a successful environment on this planet. One of my tag-lines is "Loving your body is loving the planet." It's true because we're all in this together, so start now. It permeates out into the world, and it's a beautiful process when we're doing something good for our world. Don't you think?

FREE TO CHOOSE THE BEST DAY EVER

We have access to more foods today than ever before. Even in large urban areas we can make the best choices for everything from superfoods to fresh living water straight from the earth. With choices we become free.

David "Avocado" Wolfe is a health, eco, nutrition, and natural beauty expert. He is a best-selling author and speaker, having shared the stage with Anthony Robbins, Mark Victor Hansen, Jack Canfield, Buzz Aldrin, T. Harv Eker, John Gray, Les Brown, Barbara DeAngelis, Brian Tracy, and many more.

With a masters degree in nutrition and a background in science and mechanical engineering, he is considered one of the world's top authorities on natural health, beauty nutrition, herbalism, chocolate, and organic superfoods.

David champions sustainable agriculture, living in harmony with nature, and ethical global cooperation. He has founded several all-green and eco-friendly businesses that continue to lead the world with the most innovative, highest quality, organic superfoods and healthy-lifestyle related products and information.

He is the co-founder of TheBestDayEver.com online health magazine and the president of The Fruit Tree Planting Foundation, a non-profit organization with a mission to plant 18 billion fruit trees on planet Earth, including thus far, locations spanning from Africa to Canada, from India to Hawaii.

His message includes how the body is affected by the stresses of today's fast-paced, over-worked, and unbalanced lifestyle, but he shows us how to make new choices about our lifestyle and take our health back into our own hands.

The barefooted David Wolfe is taking the world by storm with his trend-setting sense of eco-chic style. He's a ground-breaking businessman and entrepreneur who lectures extensively. He is a man who walks his talk—a man on a mission to change the way the world eats.

DAVID WOLFE: I started out just like everybody else, eating standard American food. I grew up quite different from most people, because I'm the son of two medical doctors, so I have a background where I was exposed to hospitals, doctor's offices, and emergency rooms. Nevertheless, I ate the same kinds of foods everybody else ate and gradually, step by step, discovered different options.

Things have changed over the last few years. There has been a tremendous interest in natural foods, natural healing and natural living. My mission is to make raw and living foods, superfoods, super herbs and living water a choice for everybody on earth. I'm excited to share the things that I've been graced to learn about and experience in my life.

ANTON: You have such a powerful message. And you're able to touch many famous people who can spread the word through their art and celebrity.

DAVID WOLFE: I touch an interesting, eclectic group. A lot of them are actually in Hollywood, like my friend Dr. Luke. He's a jet-setting thirty-something, the guy behind Brittany Spears, Kesha, Avril Lavigne, and Katie Perry. He's the producer/songwriter who does all their mixing. Amazing guy. Those are the kind of people I'm reaching these days.

When you're in that area of work, culture is being created. In Hollywood, for example, we're starting to see changes in the way movies are being made, what's in the background of films. It's great to actually get into the layers of culture that are starting to bring us a whole different direction for our world. As the message of eating better and living more consciously reaches more people, we're able to have more impact.

ANTON: Your energy and your excitement are contagious. Your casual appearance is as inviting as it is disarming. In truth, you're a scientist, and you're pushing us to experience and understand how to go beyond our limitations of thought and lifestyle.

DAVID WOLFE: And that's it, actually. It's just limitations of thought. All my recommendations are actually easy things that anybody can do. It's not really about a diet or saying "you can't eat that anymore, you have to eat this." It's really about opening ourselves up to the amazing choices that are before us and taking advantage of the outrageous potential of those choices.

For example, the greatest herbs of Chinese medicine are available to everybody in the simplest forms ever—as powders, capsules, teas. Whatever you like, however you like to do it. It's available to you instantly in any form you prefer.

We can say the same about the great superfoods of the world, whether it's aloe vera or goji berries or chocolate. Whatever great superfood you really like, the forms are available now for you to access.

There is a litany of 150 years of American history and research by great scientists in the field of health and longevity, including the areas of raw and living foods. There is an outrageous amount of research on raw foods and how important it is to eat some raw food in your diet, because it's real and it's natural and it's original. The thing we don't eat enough of is vegetables.

ANTON: You also advocate that we drink living water. What exactly is that?

DAVID WOLFE: We once had an intuition or an instinct that we now tend to forget about. In the old days we used to be able to survive on waters that were naturally available, naturally purified by Mother Nature. We could survive on spring water that gushed out from the sources of springs in mountainous regions all over the world.

We still have this instinct, to drink water this pure. I guide people to the sources of springs in their local areas, whether they live in Los Angeles,

Toronto, or New York City. Within two hours of any of those places are great, free spring water geysers. Water gushing out of the earth at full speed, twenty-four hours a day, seven days a week, completely pure right at the spot.

There can be no giardia or bacteria in water when it's ice cold, gushing out of the ground. It can only pick up those things later as it goes down a stream and animals drink out of it. We can drink that water and that water is free. It's original, and it's purified by the earth itself. These are considerations I'd like us all to look into. We're throwing huge amounts of plastics into landfills and huge amounts of plastics into our oceans, and what are we doing it for? A lot of it is the bottled water industry [creating the demand for a product that is exacerbating the problem of worldwide pollution].

You can go to a wine, beer or ale supply store and get glass bottles with corks and go get your own spring water for free. It's perfectly pure original water, and it tunes us into our eco system. It gives us greater understanding about the nature of water, and ultimately, it teaches us that part of living is drinking living water.

All our water is either dead (it's been coming out of a faucet that's been ruined by conventional sewage treatment), or it's been bottled in plastic and has been treated other than consciously. In many cases it's been ozonated or exposed to UV light. It's been killed, essentially, so it can stay in the bottle without forming any kind of algae or anything.

Real natural spring water is actually a revolution in North America and Canada at the moment. There's a huge upsurge of people who aren't willing to go buy bottled water any more, who want to get the original water in their local eco-system. They are finding out where the local springs are.

ANTON: I was on a rafting trip down the Colorado River with my family, and one of the things I found really remarkable was how productive Mother Earth is for us at all times. We passed by this one spring that was producing over three million gallons of water every day, and it has been doing that for hundreds or thousands of years. So these resources are available.

And you've pointed out that these resources are within reach of the masses—not just in more rural areas, but even to the people in great urban areas like Los Angeles and New York.

DAVID WOLFE: Living water is available. It's one of the great resources we have access to. But when we point out the opportunity to take advantage of choices like this, people can choose to say, "This is for me, that is not." That's what freedom's about. Having those choices.

People come to me all the time asking, "What do I do about water?" and I turn them on to their local spring water. Later, they contact me and tell me, "You know, this is the most incredible thing I've ever done, not only for my health, but I absolutely love the exercise! I love getting out, getting my bottles filled up, going and filling them up every two weeks, bringing them home. That whole idea of bearing your own water. You know, the Age of Aquarius. Aquarius is the water-bearer. Let's start living in the Age of Aquarius by bearing our own water.

A young guy who lost a leg four years ago has been a big fan and supporter. He told me that going to get the local spring water is actually the best thing he's ever done for his health. Not just physical health but mental health. There are a lot of aspects of health: there's physical health, but there's also mental, emotional and spiritual health.

ANTON: You're a very successful man and growing more so all the time, because you have such a great message that people are starting to really want to hear.

DAVID WOLFE: There is a parallel with success. You are what you eat. Because I spend so much time selecting the best things for my body, I'll also select the best things for my home. I'll select the best things for my lifestyle. I'll make the best business choices I can make. I don't always make the best choices in every case, but that's life. Nevertheless, I'm very happy with the success I've had in my life.

I've been able to pioneer an area of nutrition, living water, superfoods and herbalism that no one has really ever successfully pioneered before. All of those things go back to my lifestyle.

Sometimes I have to work an extra two or three hours in the middle of the night when everybody else is asleep. The energy that I have is there because of the way I take care of myself. It's very important that, no matter what we've ever dealt with, whatever situations we've come across, however we've been injured or hurt in our life, that we realize we are still on the planet and that it's time to start investing in this life. And start to have a little investment in our health, so that we can get to those areas of peak performance and access those dormant qualities we may not know are there.

At times, I've had to burn the candle at both ends and been able to get away with it—but only because of the healthy lifestyle and healthy eating that I'm such a fan of and that I support so much.

ANTON: I love how you just pointed out that, basically, no matter what we've done, where we are, what choices we've made, we're still here now and we can still make other choices and go forward.

You always say, "Have the best day ever." To me that rings of someone saying, "Five minutes ago something happened, but now we're going to turn it around, we're going to go forward. Ten minutes ago something great happened. Now we're going to take that even higher." You always seem so optimistic to me, David. There's such power in your enthusiasm and optimism.

DAVID WOLFE: Thank you for that, by the way.

"Today is the best day ever" is the summation of all my research into success.

I'm a big fan of success books and success tapes and listening to people talk about success and how to transform your life and spiritual success. Just like anybody else, I've been faced with tremendous hardships and unbelievable obstacles. I realized a long time ago I face some problems because I'm so ambitious, but I just can't stop. I take that with a grain of salt and keep going forward.

We've all had those experiences where something challenging happened to us or to loved ones. I have had experiences where the worst thing happen to me in the morning, unbelievably bad news.

To say "Today is the best day ever" is you thinking: "How do I make today the best day ever? What can happen today to make this the best ever?" And then experience a remarkable, shocking turnaround in the day to the point where you sense a Higher Power at work. I sense that, if you put affirmations like that out there, higher powers will come and support you and help you. In my twenty years of experience, using that phrase has proven to me that it's true. There are forces out there that are forces of good, and all you've got to do is intend to make this [day or situation] the best ever, and those forces will come to work for you and help you out.

ANTON: You immediately reminded me of someone very important in my life with your optimism. When my mother was about ten days away from death with breast cancer, she said something that just blew me away, because she knew that in a few days she was going to be gone. And yet she was worrying about helping this family where the mother and daughter had just been killed in a car accident. A friend of hers. And she pointed out, even in the throes of death, that there was always somebody who had it worse than we did. That way of thinking, of always seeing upward and brighter—you have that. You spread that. It's really a gift. Thank you.

DAVID WOLFE: Thank you. That's brilliant. I'm sorry to hear about your mom, and she was right. There is always someone who's had it worse than us and, check this out, not only is there someone who had it worse than us, often the someone who had it worse than us figured it out, cracked the code and turned it all around.

We can always look at amazing athletes, amazing people in our culture, amazing individuals in every field, and we can see that some of them were fed with a silver spoon and some of them weren't. And some of them made it with a lot of hard work and a tough road up, but if there's a will, there's a way.

ANTON: Well, David, that's funny: there are people who could say you lived your life with a silver spoon because you lived in a successful, intelligent and powerful family. How did that affect your life?

DAVID WOLFE: I was very blessed with my childhood. At the same time, I had an absentee father, I had a broken home, my parents got divorced early, and I had a lot of troubles.

When you don't have a father, what can happen is that you're raised by the street gang, the local kids of the neighborhood. We got into a lot of trouble when I was a kid. So I've had those ups and downs as well, just like everybody else. Somebody said, "Look at your family." And it's like, there is no family. Everybody's had some kind of a screwed-up situation of some sort or another. We've got to be honest with ourselves and move forward with joy in our hearts anyway, in spite of all the tragedies and everything else that happens, because there's a lot of good happening in the world.

There's so much good happening in the world, and there's so much more good happening in the world than bad. We need to focus there more, because it's really the truth. If we're into exploring the truth, the truth is people are generally good. Good things are happening every day. We're wonderfully blessed and graced in our lives all the time. Miracles happen all the time. Let's focus on that more. What we focus on increases.

Get as much understanding about the quality of food that's out there as you can. Look at the conventional kind of factory-farmed food we've normally grown up on. Often it's junk food and that kind of stuff. Let's put it in its appropriate place and say, "Can I do better?"

People always say to me, "What's the problem? Is it overpopulation? Is it this? Is it that?" Really what it is is that we're not bringing enough consciousness into every moment. Bring more consciousness into every moment, instead of having some super meaner leaner whey protein powder fuel or some amino flexo powder that we got somewhere but don't even know where it came from or what the heck is in it.

Let's have real superfoods, like the simple goji berries or maca, the great superroot from the Andes, the great adaptogen superfood. It's the 17-of-18-amino-acids, hormone-building superfood. And let's have some spirulina. Let's have some bee pollen. I just got two beehives at my house. I want to put word out there about bee products instead of just having all of this "protein."

Let's go after the highest quality possible at every moment. When you do that, right there at the moment of choice, instead of potato, select sweet potato. Sweet potato has four times as many minerals, is actually supportive of healthy hormones, and doesn't spike our blood sugar like a potato does. It doesn't take much work. It's almost the same thing. And with that moment of consciousness we upgrade our quality choice.

That's what I really want to share with everybody. With choices we become free.

I want to recommend for everybody to start shopping at organic health food stores and availing themselves of the choices and possibilities that are out there.

You always have a choice for better quality. Go for it. You deserve it.

YOUR FUEL FILTER

The purpose of food is to nourish. Our greatest responsibility
lies in educating ourselves and our children about how our food
choices not only affect our individual potential but ultimately
determine the future of this planet.

Berny Dohrmann is Chairman of CEO Space International, Inc., an organization dedicated to helping entrepreneurs and executives grow their companies through workshops based on high-level networking. He has been a coach to the coaches of corporate training (such as Tony Robbins and Jack Canfield) for the past three decades. On his national radio show, *American Dreamers Broadcasting*, he has been interviewing guests like Mark Victor Hansen, T. Harv Eker, Lisa Nichols, and John Gray since 2003.

A master of innovation, Berny developed the Super Teaching program, which revolutionizes the way children learn through a system that accelerates and increases retention. Berny is a dedicated family man and a prolific author committed to helping others achieve greater success in their lives.

BERNY DOHRMANN: The First Lady of the United States is on a campaign to get children to have the future we want them to have by getting food knowledge. Your program on food knowledge is on the level of a Red Sea parting, a voice bringing illumination to the dark in an area that is most needed in the world today: our choice of the foods we eat.

ANTON: We have seen in our own lifetime huge changes in the difference diet can make. We aren't talking about the latest diet that you see on the news and supermarket stands. We are talking about diet as simply the habit of how we eat.

Berny, you have such a great love of children and a huge belief in raising our kids to give them the best of the world as a promise for a better future for our world. You are the inventor of Super Teaching for public and private schools. How did this come about, and how does it impact what kids learn about the food they eat?

BERNY DOHRMANN: Basically, we wired the brain for thirty-five years to see how to turn the brain's *record* switch on. We were horrified to find that everything they'd been using traditionally in education doesn't really work. We developed Super Teaching to change this.

Super Teaching uses advanced technology and techniques ranging from immersion to relaxation to improve a student's retention. In Super Teaching we create a virtual theater in the existing classroom where three screens are projected behind the teacher. The teacher puts up any kind of media he or she wants: the Internet, videos, PowerPoint, etc.

The content includes nature scenes. The nature scenes are vital because they cause the brain to rest, which causes *posting*. When you get *super-posting* it creates the recording in our brains that allows us more efficient recall so we can pass a quiz or an exam. Super Teaching activates 300% more places than the brain is normally using for storing. The depth of the electricity is so much higher.

With Super Teaching we have a fun way to teach our children to eat for fuel and not just for gratification, and to show them the difference between the two. It's much easier to show them visually how they are contaminating their fuel. We talk about the fuel and fuel filters for the things they like, such as RC (remote control) cars. We ask them, "Don't you want to use clean fuel?" They get it so quickly. Then they start thinking, "What will the fuel I eat do to my system? What will it do to my motor? What will it do to my engine?" They start going home and making their parents think that way! We were just never really trained that way growing up.

Super Teaching also helps with eleven learning disorders. Our children are not slow learners and are not, in many cases, ADD or dyslexic. The dyslexic can learn in a normalized way in the Super Teaching classroom. They don't need special ed. That's very powerful for the schools that are outfitted with it. The system only takes about five minutes for a teacher to learn to use.

ANTON: We came out of the era in the fifties when television was born. Then TV started filling up more and more of our lives in the sixties, and now it's gotten to where electronics have become the surrogate family. I love how you are using electronics and knowledge in a deliberate way, not just plopping kids down passively in front of any old program where they get bombarded with advertising for some very compelling but toxic food products.

Through much of the traditional media, we have gotten used to not paying attention to how the larger industries train us for their profit and not for our own good.

BERNY DOHRMANN: A lot of research has gone into studying how people respond in the superstores. As we walk in, that's where they put the most toxic stuff. It smells wonderful. It's filled with layers of frosting and all of these thick raisin swirls. We are looking at that oozing out, starving, and it triggers an impossible-to-resist impulse to buy—and we start buying the gratification foods. They put them right at the front door before we even get into the main part of the store, because that's where they make much more money, much higher margins—all because we just can't help ourselves. It's very difficult to go and get that lean chicken and broccoli just because of how they've laid out their stores for when we walk in.

When you go to Whole Foods and other organic stores, this is not the case. They are actually trying to help you make a fuel decision instead of a gratification decision. You can still have a lot of gratification when you eat for fuel—but smart gratification.

I divide the way we eat into dumb gratification and smart gratification. Dumb gratification is your fuel going into your motor without a fuel filter. Without a fuel filter in your mind, you're going to have diabetes and create about 90% of your illness.

Your illness is primarily a result of toxifying your water system. You are a water creature, and if you're putting in bad water and bad fuel, when they combine they gum up your motor and all of your organs. We have the knowledge today to change that with programs like yours, and changing it in the public's mind is an *attitude first* state of mind.

The first thing is that you as a family decide you're going to talk about your food attitude. Put it up on the refrigerator: "Eat for fuel, not for gratification." Now you have a filter that causes you to ask, "Is this for fuel or gratification?" and you start making and eating foods that are healthy and smart. Healthy sleep patterns will return, your stress loads will be reduced, your energy will be consistent all day long, you'll reduce your entire illness load, and you won't be spending your money on pharmaceuticals and going to the doctor.

When you're sixty-five and up, as I am, most of the meds people are taking is just a matter of lifestyle. If you exercise properly and fuel properly, you can get off your heart medication, your cholesterol medication. You're medicated because you are eating only for gratification and you're not exercising your equipment.

ANTON: When we eat better foods, the energy levels are sustained better. When you start to feel better like that, you actually begin to enjoy these changes that automatically reprogram your brain.

Parents today are so busy and they're racing around so fast that they're just handing their kids the quick fix, the quick sugar, the quick energy, the quick shutter-upper.

BERNY DOHRMANN: They are tired and under stress so they give the kids that are nagging for addictive foods whatever they want, such as diet soft drinks. It gives them a caffeine carbonated rush, and it's toxic in the sense that it's not the ideal, clean, alkalized water we need. Water should be not acidic. Nothing overcomes disease like your body being a basified water system. That comes from eating healthy and having good water.

Look for pH-balanced waters and let the kids have those. The pH is a measure of the acid versus alkaline quality of something. Hard water is low pH and contains potentially hazardous minerals. High pH waters are more alkaline and support better health. There are some good-flavored pH waters that are very gratifying. You'll miss your soft drinks at first when you go off them, because of the rush and the addictive qualities built into them, but after drinking healthy drinks for a while, the soft drinks begin to taste bad. You won't like them, and that's because your body is actually telling you what's right.

First clean up the water system of your body. You have bad water right now, and you need to clean up that water system. It's the first thing that will make your brain alert and full, change the way you make decisions, and give you a better life.

Make healthy eating and your intake of clean water your number one habit. Nothing will change your journey through life more.

ANTON: We have been raised to think of food as just this pleasure vehicle, whereas it really is our fuel. That doesn't mean we can't enjoy it, but when we make better choices with the food we eat, everything in our lives begins to change: our relationships become more harmonious, the energy in the house is more even, the kids aren't as crazy, the creativity goes up and the joy in our lives increases.

BERNY DOHRMANN: You will have less arguing and fighting with spouses. Almost all of the stress loads that go into the difficulty in relationships begin with food quality.

ANTON: How do our better food choices affect not just our bodies and personal health but the world at large?

BERNY DOHRMANN: A sobering comment from Chuck Vollmer in his book, *Jobenomics*, quotes a Citibank paper that came out in 2010 saying that we are no longer a democracy in the USA, that 1% of the wealth is controlled by a class and the 99% percent of the wealth of the rest of the population doesn't equal the wealth of the one percent.

(*Jobenomics* is a very important read for everybody, and it includes food information. Vollmer is a top speech writer for some presidential candidates, big in the Beltway and a former Booz Allen consultant.)

It used to be 30/70 just twenty years ago, so it shows you the consolidation of wealth in our country. This causes grave difficulties for our culture. They say Congress is controlled by the banking and hedge fund lobbies and the pharmaceutical industry.

What that means is that all of us are spending most of our life paying taxes in one form or another. In our working years, these are taxes such as credit card and other fees we pay to the financial industry, the banks, and the government.

Then in the final part of our lives, whatever we have accumulated goes to the pharmaceutical industry. They take the rest of it. That's the journey of our life! They are taking 90% of us that way. That is where the wealth is concentrated, and the degree by which it's accelerating is enormous.

We can change all of this by first, never sending an incumbent back into office. Put people in for four years and that's it. Public service, period. If we do that, we've got our country back. Second, eat differently. Begin to eat for fuel and not just for gratification. Make that your mantra. Put a big sign on your refrigerator.

Begin to make your meals and everything around them enjoyable. Enjoy a healthy lifestyle and your pharmaceuticals come down. You reclaim enormous amounts of money and you begin to be free of this kind of system; you step into full partnership again with our whole world. If our kids and our adults would get on that wavelength, it would change the nation.

Remember, they *will* give us healthy foods. Everybody is putting a lot of advertising money into what consumers *want*. We are voters when we buy, so start voting for healthy foods and watch us change the industry. If we buy toxic foods, we are voting for that. When we buy from that toxic food source, we extend it in the market. If we buy organic, fresh, wonderful foods, they will only advertise that because that's what the buyers want.

ANTON: We can see the proof of that even now. Fifteen years ago the organic branch of the supermarket wasn't as big as it is now. Even in regular food stores, we see that the organic areas are expanding.

BERNY DOHRMANN: Wal-Mart has 72% of consumers in the United States. Wal-Mart's fastest growing food space is the fresh and healthy, organic food space—by buyer demand! They don't want to lose out to the new emerging healthfood industries that have now gone into the billions. They are seeing their customers walk in and be loyal to higher priced offerings in the healthy and organic area, so they are trying to offer quality equal in the organic area to health-food stores and do it at a lower price point.

Still, it's a very small part of Wal-Mart. In other words, the traditional toxic food area, because it's been the biggest part of buyer public conditioning, is still dominant. But it's changing through knowledge. It's changing through radio shows. It's changing through education.

People are starting to understand that they're not making the best decisions because their brain chemistry is off. They're not having the best relationships; they're fighting too much because their brain chemistry is off. They aren't having a life of freedom and the things that they need because, with their stress loads, it is very addicting to come home and have a big sugar rush with a bunch of appealing candy and things that are very toxic for you. It's very gratifying.

Now, a little bit later you wish you hadn't done it. You feel terrible. You feel bloated. You feel sugar rushed. You feel sleepy. You don't have the energy, and you are doing things that gum up your pistons, gum up your motor, and it's because you don't have a fuel filter in your brain saying, "Is this gratification or is this fuel?"

I found that sentence changes the world for one person at a time.

There is a lot of fast food you can get, by the way, that is healthy, but you have to enjoy *ritual* with eating. You have to *enjoy*. I don't think that we should eat in a place we call the family room, for example, that really isn't a family room because we're just watching a flat screen addictively and not having conversations any more.

Meals are times for us to take time in our lives. The most important ship we ever sail has got to have full sails on it, and that ship is relation-ship. We need to be *in relationship*, and we do that over meals, at a beautiful mealtime where we're with each other and enjoying each other. That's the thing we have to begin to do.

ANTON: When we moved back to my hometown when my mother got cancer, the very first thing she did was buy us a table and chairs. We said, "You don't need to do that." She said, "I *do* need to do that. Remember how we raised you." We were raised around the dinner table. There was no TV going during mealtime. The family would sit down together and we would talk about our day. We learned our entire history and became the people we are and filled our lives because of sitting at that table.

And now we do that with our children. When we make exceptions, the energy in the entire household goes kind of crazy, gets out of whack. By not honoring that, the hectic nature of our daily lives becomes even more hectic and out of focus. Mealtimes are such a good time to regroup and regenerate.

BERNY DOHRMANN: Even if you are alone, make your eating time a time to be with yourself.

We had nine children in our family. When Father came to the table, we had to be quiet. We had to say grace, and then he would go around and ask what every child was doing, who their friends were, what was going on in their life.

We learned about our family history. We could ask questions about Great-grandfather. We learned how our ancestors came over from Europe.

We got lessons in our culture, the depth of what it was, and we were taught that the most important thing was family. Family was everything. Protecting and being there for your family. Being there for your brothers and sisters. There was never a time that that wasn't extremely important.

I think we have lost something very precious by not eating for fuel. We ate fresh farm produce that they got from the markets. Even without the education, our family was particularly interested in eating this way. Dad was always wanting the best natural produce. He had orchards and vegetable gardens on the property. The staff would go out and get fresh food from our garden. We didn't put DDT on our list of things to buy. The result of that shows up in who the adult children are today, what they're doing in the world, and how they're raising their children.

In our family, my wife, September's, first priority is how she buys our food, what our children know about food, and what their eating habits are. Now, I have nine of my own. The last being raised are eight and twelve. In the first group of young adults, because I wasn't as aware of food addictions, I really made some mistakes, and I have apologized to my childen. I didn't translate my own father's wisdom. With the second chance I was given to raise children, I've done a better job and become very conscious of this problem. Early on, before the First Lady took it on, I really worked my buns off to make sure these kids have that knowledge. We talk about it all the time.

ANTON: You work very hard. Your schedule is absolutely packed. You have people running that schedule so you're in the right place at the right time, and yet you still make a priority of finding time for your family, for your kids. You have such a demanding life, and yet you still remember what is important, why we do any of it, ultimately.

BERNY DOHRMANN: Let me give you an example. I was in an important conversation with one of my faculty members, who is the bestselling author of *Integrity IQ*. I told him, "I have to get off the phone now." This was our scheduled time, but I had something I had to take care of with my children. He understood. It put us back a little bit late on our radio interview, but I put the kids first.

I had an issue where the stepfather of my kids was picking up his sons for his time with them. We are close friends. We had a very big conversation about some of the kids' eating habits and the need for the twelve-year old to get this lesson down. We needed the father's input. He came into it with both feet. We wanted to make sure that we didn't have a child who was geared to going into the teenage years by eating his way through emotional stresses. That's how he releases. We wanted him to release in another way and learn that this rule we have in our family about fuel versus gratification is absolute.

And he wants it. He wants to win with that. But there's peer pressure, and you've got to work on it. I had to get off a very important call and go back to it later in order to make the children the priority. I think it's so important. Most of the time I think people wave the children off instead of making them the priority.

ANTON: You're a real innovator. You have a different approach to most things you do. Your business success is based on cooperation versus competition.

BERNY DOHRMANN: I think that's the future. We got stuck in a competitive model.

At CEO Space events we're taking people that are dreamers and making them multimillionaires. We're giving them financial freedom by giving them the tools and information that school didn't give them. We're in the entrepreneurial age, and we give them entrepreneurial tools. Many of them are in this food area, which is exploding with growth.

We believe that competition is the mother of all viruses on the human brain. We used to think competition was good, but it isn't. It means, "I beat you." You're home having tears, and I'm celebrating with a warm, very toxic meal.

If we get into cooperation, then we can begin to celebrate all diversity. We celebrate everything that's different about us, and we all are working for what's called Full Partnership. What we want is that when someone gets ahead financially, they reach back and bring someone else up. We help each other up. If the other person gets ahead first, he reaches back and helps the other person. It's all about full partnership. It's all about celebration. It isn't about "leechism."

In food, that is the way we get to collaboration and cooperation, to be voters who passed our ballot for very healthy fuel with a fuel filter that makes us have good fuel going into our system. We get rid of the toxicity, and the result is that we won't see the dollars flow toward the unhealthy, toxic, prepared, sugar-rich foods.

And we reduce the health care costs in America so that we're OK. It's the biggest cost that we as taxpayers are paying next to [income] tax. If we don't all cooperate to bring that cost down by moving our fuel compass over, our GPS for *fuel vs. gratification*, we aren't going to be able to take a legal U-turn in our eating pattern and get onto the healthy longevity on-ramp that the GPS could take us to. We're going to be in a place of repeating the past and having record health care costs that are going to break society apart as we age.

We must all be in this together. If we do it and cooperate, our appearances will change, our lifestyles will change, our longevity will change, and we'll have so much more opportunity financially. I can't express how important the subject of food integrity is to the world.

APPENDICES

EATING FOR SUCCESS GUIDELINES

EATING FOR SUCCESS GUIDELINES

If you give someone a fish, they will eat today. If you give them a
fishing pole and teach them how to fish, they will eat every day.

Originally I wanted to include recipes and food logs from the people in this book, but it occurred to me that I would only be giving you the fish instead of the fishing pole. I decided it would be of greater value to summarize the key principles of Eating for Success, which you can carry with you in your head and in your heart for all time, anywhere you go, so you can make the best decisions possible, no matter how busy you are, no matter where your life may take you.

You can still find recipes, food logs and daily meal plans to guide you on **millionairesdiet.net** and **cookingwithanton.com**. It is there you will also find guides and recipes for the Mediterranean Diet and the Candida Diet, among others.

> Note: I am not a docotor or nutrtitionist. The information below reflects what I have experienced and found useful in my own life, which I share here for illustrative purposes only. You should check with a health care professional before making any changes in your diet or exercise.

Although some of the information you will find below may be new to you and might even seem extreme at first, know that these are called *guidelines* for a reason. Be brave and give yourself the opportunity to try something new, but don't beat yourself up or give up if you find it too difficult to stick to all of these guidelines at once. Love yourself. Push yourself beyond your comfort zone, but move at your own pace. It will be better to take baby steps and celebrate and build on your achievements than to try too much at once and give up altogether. Even two steps forward, one step back is progress.

As these guidelines become more and more a part of your life, you'll begin to experience their truth and power in your amazing new-found energy; the clean, clear feeling in your body and mind; and your uplifted spirits. This will have you Eating for Success effortlessly, joyfully and without a second thought. It will become an easy and welcome part of your life to feel and function better than you ever thought possible.

KEY ELEMENTS TO EATING FOR SUCCESS:

1. INTENTION
2. BREAKTHROUGH
3. WATER
4. BREATH
5. SUGAR
6. FAT
7. SOURCE
8. QUALITY and VOLUME
9. LOVE

INTENTION

To achieve anything that lasts, there must first be a genuine desire and intention. When your intentions are aligned with your true self, your efforts become easier and more fulfilling. Any kind of change and growth requires effort and determination, but doing anything that is not in alignment with your true self makes life feel as if you're constantly swimming upstream. You don't have to.

Wanting something better than what you have now is the first sign of your intention. If it is no more specific than that right now, at least that is a start; you have taken the right fork in the road. Through Janet Bray Attwood's Passion Test or Greg Montana's Heart Virtue you can come closer to recognizing your true life purpose, and the clearer you are on that, the more focused your efforts can be to get you where you want to go.

But *do not wait to get started* if you don't know those answers yet. Sometimes it's easier to get somewhere by process of elimination. Every moment every day, treat every step of the way as a fork in the road that will get you closer to where your heart wants you to be. Simply go toward the good and away from the bad. Quiet your mind-chatter. Your gut, your intuition, is always there to guide you. Listen to it.

BREAKTHROUGH

Breakthrough is when you go beyond the limits of your comfort zone to expand your world. If you are not uncomfortable, you aren't pushing through those walls that confine you. This path may be new to you, but it's not new in the world. By trusting and following those who have gone before you, you can practice the experience of a new way of doing things until the neural pathways in your body and brain become paved with the rewarding habits of Eating for Success.

Have singular focus. As you distill the clear water of your soul, do not tolerate exceptions and distractions. Imagine you want to paint a barn red. You might open a can of primer first to build a strong foundation, but, after that, why would you even open a can of blue or yellow paint?

Change, like birth, always involves a certain amount of pain, but the gift of life is worth it. Be willing to go beyond your comfort zone and leave old habits behind while you ingrain new, supportive ones. Once you have gone through the Breakthrough Zone, your new experience of life will be so rewarding that Eating for Success will become effortless, second-nature and easy to sustain.

WATER

The single most important aspect of Eating for Success is to always be well-hydrated. Water is the vehicle that transports good nutrition inward, keeps all your systems well-lubricated and flowing so they can do their job, and then helps carry the wastes and toxins out and away from your body and brain.

Fluid alone does not count for hydration. Many beverages that are common to us, especially soft drinks, actually toxify and dehydrate the body. Sugars, artificial sweeteners, caffeine, and alcohol do the most damage. Chlorinated city water is just as bad. Many of the products added to our city water supply are called safe because they eliminate a life-sustaining environment for harmful bacteria—but the things that can kill any living organism can also kill you. Chlorine is also a known carcinogen.

When you are filling up on plenty of water to keep yourself hydrated, you are also putting everything else in that water into your system. David Wolfe can tell you where to find safe, fresh water right from Mother Earth, even if you live in a huge city like New York or Los Angeles. Still, your tap water can be a good source of water if, at the very least, you install a simple and affordable filtration system to eliminate the chlorine and other harmful chemicles. Health food stores sell trace mineral replacement that you can add to excessively filtered water, such as water treated by reverse osmosis.

Drink plenty of water all day long. A rule of thumb is half your body weight in ounces. For example, half of 150 is 75. If you weigh 150 pounds, you want to drink at least 75 ounces of water per day. You will probably urinate more often. This is good. Keep your system moving, drawing in the good, supporting the smooth operation of all your systems and flushing out the bad.

BREATH

Like water, the air we breathe is part of a system that draws in life energy, circulates it through our bodies and brains so they can do their job, and then carries toxins and waste products out and away from us. We can live without food for many days. We can live without water for a few days. We cannot live without air for more than a few minutes.

Just breathing air is not enough. The quality of the air we breathe is as important as the quality of the water we drink. With every breath, as with every swallow, the bad as well as the good enters our bodies and must somehow be processed. Pollution from the environment, including exhaust from our cars and factories as well as from pesticides and cleaning products in the home and work place, all contribute to what becomes a part of us through the air we breathe. Pet dander, mold, smoke, and dust also contribute to what we draw into our bodies and what remains behind, blocking our ability to absorb what we need and getting stuck in our cells.

The volume of air that we get and circulate through our bodies is also important. The best way to get more life-giving air into our systems is to regularly get physical exercise and to learn to breathe more deeply and effectively through breathing exercises.

There is a form of exercise suited for everyone at every age and fitness level. The idea is to get yourself to breathe harder and to get your blood to flow more quickly. Anything from weight lifting and cardio to dancing and good sex will do. Walking is one of the best forms of exercise. It promotes circulation and blood flow without putting demands on the body and joints that come from more strenuous forms of exercise, like running.

Learning to do full, deep belly-breathing will benefit you on all levels, from mood, mental clarity, libido, and strength to how well the rest of your systems function. In the sedentary lifestyle that comes from sitting in cars and in front of computers for so many hours of our days (and nights), many of our internal systems are deprived of the oxygen they need to operate optimally. As a result, we become more susceptible to mental and physical imbalances and disease.

Remember, if your body and brain operate like an old jalopy, you cannot expect to enter the Indianapolis 500 and win—or even qualify to compete. But you do have a choice. Your goal may not be to fly around the world like Richard Branson, but even if your goal is to be available to your children or grandchildren, you will have more to offer—and enjoy yourself and your life more—if your body and brain are tuned to your personal best.

SUGAR

We hear about that old evil sugar all the time and have become numb or indifferent to the warnings. After all, it has been our lifelong reward for being good, and it gives us bursts of energy when we're dragging. Many of us, however, haven't experienced the difference that having no refined sugar can make. The first and most interesting effect of becoming sugar-free is the amazing increase in energy that we feel. But perhaps most important is that sugar feeds everything from candida and destructive bacterias to cancers and all sorts of other evils that want to grow inside us.

Sugar is an addiction. When we don't have it, we can clearly feel the symptoms of withdrawal as we become tired and depressed, so we quickly give our blood sugar a jolt that gets us high until the next withdrawal. This may sound like an exaggeration, but if you give yourself the opportunity to get past the withdrawal stage of being tired and cranky (which could take about two weeks), you will begin to discover a higher and longer-lasting form of energy that you may not even have known existed.

The trick is getting past the Sugar Wall, and I'll admit, it's not an easy obstacle to conquer. I've been there myself. But getting past the Sugar Wall is probably the single-most important challenge to meet in Eating for Success. It will make you feel so great that once you feel its benefits (more energy, better concentration, calmer nerves, better sleep, higher libido) you will never want to go back or have anything less ever again.

Glucose is the sugar that all your cells need to operate, but it is something that *your body makes for itself* from the foods that you give it. Giving your body sugar directly interferes with its natural responses and ability to make and manage the proper sugar levels that make it run effectively. Mess them up too much and you can experience anything from diabetes to Alzheimer's disease. The external sugars that create these challenges for your body come in many forms: refined sugar, white flour, and even some fruits and vegetables. The Candida Diet (see millioinairesdiet.net) is a great way to get past the Sugar Wall and clean and build your new body.

The Candida Diet also eliminates the use of anything containing yeast, since yeast and sugar feed the candida (a natural part of our internal culture) in our bodies, making it so prolific that it actually creates a barrier and inhibits the effective assimilation of nutrients. Yeast is a topic you might consider looking into if you experience chronic fatigue and depression.

Artificial sweeteners are also a topic in themselves. Saccharine causes cancer, and aspartame has been known to cause problems ranging from dementia to death. And to think you have been giving sugar-free gum to your kids, thinking it was better for their *teeth*!

Alcohol is pure sugar that is quickly assimilated by the body. It upsets our sugar-balancing insulin responses and, like sodas, can lead to diabetes and Alzheimer's disease. It interferes with neural and mental function and causes inflammation, the culprit of a long list of other system malfunctions.

Sugar also lowers testosterone. Besides reducing libido and sperm count, lower testosterone levels reduce your ability to build and maintain metabolism-supporting muscle (and we're not just talking to the guys or about looking like Arnold here). Lower testosterone compromises physical systems, like immunity, and mental function, like memory, clarity and problem-solving skills. Your chances of success are greatly improved when your ability to make good decisions is improved.

FAT

The three macronutrients that provide energy for your body are protein, carbohydrates, and dietary fat. Dietary fat is essential to your health because it supports a number of your body's functions. Some vitamins, for example, need fat to dissolve and nourish your body.

There are good fats and there are bad fats. Animal fats tend to be bad, while the oils of vegetables and nuts tend to be better. Good fats support the health of the membranes of every cell in our bodies and protect us from many health threats, while bad fats can clog our arteries and other systems, depriving us of the oxygen and nutrients needed for the optimal function of our bodies and brains and, ultimately, to keep us alive.

Good fats include polyunsaturated fats like omega-3s found in cold-water fish, fish oil, and walnuts, for example. They help reduce the risk of heart disease and stroke and can reduce the symptoms of things like high blood pressure, depression and ADHD. Omega-3s support better brain function and also promote the production of body chemicals that help control inflammation. You can find omega-3s in wild-caught salmon, for example.

Omega-6s are another type of essential fatty acid that supports skin health, lowers cholesterol and helps make our blood more *sticky* so it will clot. But they must be used in proper balance with omega-3s (roughly four parts omega-3s to one part omega-6s.) These can be found in eggs, cereal, poultry, and certain vegetable oils.

Bad fats are are the saturated fats found in things like burgers, french fries, and partially hydrogenated fats designed to have longer shelf life (but not human life). These are the fats that clog your veins and arteries. If you do eat meat, it has been found that wild meats, like elk, grass-fed beef, and range-fed poultry don't pose the same level of threat to our health as corn-fed CAFO beef filled with hormones and antibiotics. (Read Michael Pollan's *The Omnivore's Dilemma.*)

I have learned which fats are welcome on my shopping list and which are not. Extra virgin olive oil, coconut oil, and avocados are among the tastiest and most useful. I use butter (animal fat) in moderation, but never margerine, which is actually toxic.

If you're going to eat dairy, select reduced-fat and organic dairy products from grass-fed cows whenever possible. Also select lactose-free products even if you don't think you are lactose intolerant. Once milk gets pasturized, it becomes indigestible to us. You may find this a fine point, but you may discover you have more energy and clearer thinking when you reduce or eliminate lactose from your diet, and you no longer have indigestion and gas.

Yogurt is a form of dairy that your body can readily process because of the healthy bacteria it contains that support a balanced culture in your gastrointestinal (GI) tract. Certain cheeses, like cheddar, are supported better by your body, while highly processed cheeses, such as American cheese, are not.

The idea is not so much how these fats affect your size and weight as how they affect your body's ability to function well. Your body will find its own stable healthy weight quite naturally when you make better choices in the sugars and fats in your diet, combined with a healthful level of exercise for circulation.

SOURCE

The closer to source that your food is, that is, the closer it is to its natural, raw, unprocessed state, the more nutritional value it will have. Some foods, like brocolli, actually become more digestible by being slightly cooked, but the less you do to food, the less food you will need to reap more nutrition from it.

Whether we can support the food needs of the world's explosive increase in population with all-organic methods remains to be seen, but in the present, we do have a choice. Buy organically raised fruits and vegetables whenever possible. Nowadays you can find beautiful organic produce, but their slight imperfections are a signal of the perfection to be found within. The more perfect-looking non-organic produce available in most markets looks that way because its growth has been artificially hastened and it has been harvested before its full nutritional value has been achieved. It has also in most cases, been treated with pesticides and waxes. The amount of pesticides may be minimal on any one item, but the cummulative effect of ingesting these over a lifetime is significant. Statistics showing the ever-increasing levels of disease in modern society coincide with the industrialized methods of increased food production. (These statistics are measured in percentages; they are not just higher numbers because of higher population.)

QUALITY and VOLUME

It took us a while to acknowledge that smoking was killing us. Food, like smoke, goes in and becomes part of our bodies. It affects every part of our being.

We are so used to thinking of food as something that fills us when we get hungry that we forget why our bodies tell us they're hungry. Our bodies are pretty smart, but the conscious thought of our prefrontal lobe gets in the way. It's no surprise. We are bombarded with messages deliberately designed to confuse and entice us, and not primarily with our true needs and well-being in mind.

Starchy, over-processed and deep-fried foods fill us up but don't contain the nutrition we need, so we feel compelled to eat seconds and desserts and are still left wanting more. It's no wonder that obesity is such a problem.

Fresh fruits and vegetables contain more nutrients, flavor, and water, and will actually trigger the proper hormones in your body to alert you that you have had enough. Even grass-fed beef and other free-range meats will give you more nutrition, flavor, and less dangerous fats than their production-line counterparts.

The better the quality of the food you eat, the more nutrition you will derive from it and the less of it you will need. It has been found that eating more often during the day is more beneficial to your health than eating large meals that fill you up and weigh you down in the morning when you first get up and in the evening before you go to bed.

When you get more nutrition from less food at more frequent intervals during the day, your body doesn't have to work as hard to break down and assimilate the food. The result is that you have more energy, which results in clearer thinking, lighter moods and more success in everything you do. You feel better and you look better.

LOVE

Man cannot live by bread alone.

We all want and need love in our lives. Through emotionally cruel experiments with Korean prisoners of war and with orphans in an experiment in the Soviet Union during the Cold War, it was proved that touch and love are essential in supporting life itself. A lack of either has physiological repercussions beyond the emotional aspect.

Children who are touched and acknowledged grow differently from those who are discouraged or abused. As adults they contribute to the positive energy and spirit of the world we live in.

People in supportive loving relationships, be they with friends, colleagues, or lovers, function better, make better choices, and live longer, healthier lives.

It has been proven that even merely *witnessing* acts of love and kindness changes our physiology and body/brain chemistry.

Emotional eating can spell disaster when the unfulfilled emotions that we try to resolve through food are actually the *result* of food choices that don't support the optimal functionality of our bodies and brains.

So now we find we have come full circle. By making better food choices, we create more energy and better health physically, mentally, and emotionally. These all support clearer thinking, which leads to us making better decisions, which creates more joy and reward in our lives, which alters our body and brain's chemistry, which raises our immunity, which makes us stronger, which encourages us to believe in our ability to be more effective and do more. With heightened energy, strength, and spirits, we gladly eat what made us feel this way and steer clear of what weighed us down, physically and emotionally.

In essence, Eating for Success becomes not just a cycle of life, but an upward spiral.

SEVEN STEPS

TO THE LIFE OF
YOUR DREAMS

SEVEN STEPS TO THE LIFE OF YOUR DREAMS

"You don't have to be brilliant. Just be willing."

1. FEEL THE PAIN:
   Where does it hurt? What is missing from your life? Where are you
   denying yourself what you want out of your life? Where are you
   compromising your true wishes? What makes you mad? How are
   you disappointed? What are you avoiding that you know to be true
   in your heart? You have one life to live, here and now, not *some
   day*. What do you need? What does someone else need that you can
   provide?

2. ACKNOWLEDGE YOUR DREAMS:
   What is it that you want or hope for? What makes your heart sing?
   What brings a tear to your eye at the movies—not because it is sad,
   but because it gives you a sense of the beauty possible in life? What
   do you find easy to do? What do you love doing so much that you
   lose yourself in time? What makes you feel good? What do you
   have to offer? Where can you do the most good? All dreams are
   created equal. To be a good parent is just as important as becoming
   a mighty business mogul. Measure your dreams with your heart, not
   with what you think are the expectations of others. Choose to pursue
   what is truly in your heart.

3. SET A GOAL:
   To get from anywhere to anywhere, there must first be a goal.
   Whether you are going to the grocery store or reinventing your
   life, choose a target. See the target. Aim for the target. You may
   not be a perfect marksman now, but your aim will improve as you
   adjust along the way. If you just shoot random arrows they will go
   somewhere, but the chances of hitting a bulls-eye are just about nil.
   Set your intention and commit to it. *Where attention goes, energy
   flows*. When the going gets tough, the tough get going—*when it is*

in their heart. Choose a goal that is aligned with your heart. If it is, you will be unstoppable.

4. ASSESS YOUR POSITION:

To go anywhere, you must first know where you are now, so you can see where you need to go and what you will need for your journey. Are you high up on a mountain or deep down in a cave? Are you naked and free or buried under a pile of rocks? Knowing where you are now will help you see what your next step is to get closer to the land of your dreams.

5. CLEAR THE CLUTTER:

Clutter holds you back. It blocks the way. It is difficult to see through and to navigate through. Get rid of old and excess baggage. Clear the table. Wash the windows. Take out the trash. Lighten your load. Mental. Physical. Emotional. Get clear. Get ready to fly.

6. PREPARE YOUR PLAN:

Even though this is your dream, you don't have to reinvent the wheel. Others have gone before you who can help show the way. Draw a line on the map. List specific steps and schedule specific goal-times along the way. Pack your bags, your toothbrush, your passport, and your wallet. Don't over-plan. Take only what you need.

7. START THE CAR:

Don't delay. Don't wait for perfection. Head out now and make adjustments along the way. There is no way to know everything the future will hold. Just keep your focus on your goal. When you encounter surprises, you can adapt to get back on track. Remember to celebrate each step along the way, no matter how great or how small. This will give you the courage to persist through rain and shine.

When you achieve your goal, you will not be the same person you are now. When you achieve your goal you will have grown up to new dreams and new courage for your next adventure. The goal is not to arrive at some plateau and stop. The goal gives you direction, but the life you live and love is the journey.

READING TOOLBOX

I highly recommend going to the websites of the people in this book. You will find very powerful and focused resources in all areas of expertise brought forward in this book.

Below is my personal list of if-you-don't-read-anything-else-read-these books (different from those authors already included in this book). If you really want to get to the point without getting lost in the vast amount of material available, this is a great place to start to find the key basic tools to move your life forward.

Follow Your Passion, Find Your Power
Everything You Need to Know About the Law of Attraction
Bob Doyle
There are a lot of books about the Law of Attraction. This one will make all the others make sense.

Secrets of the Millionaire Mind
Mastering the Inner Game of Wealth
T. Harv Eker
There are a lot of books about creating wealth. This one will reveal why you are where you are and how to release the chains that bind you. This will give you the criteria for a solid foundation before you read any other books on wealth.

You Are Your Own Gym
The Bible of Bodyweight Exercises
Mark Lauren with Joshua Clark
You don't need an expensive gym membership to build the body of your dreams. Your body is all you need. Now available to everyone, this system is used by Navy SEALS and men and women in SpecOps.

The Relaxation Response
Herbert Benson, MD
The classic mind/body approach that has helped millions conquer the harmful effects of stress. Meditation and breathing.

The Multiorgasmic Man
Sexual Secrets Every Man Should Know
Mantak Chia, Douglas Abrams Arava, Douglas Carlton Abrams
Not just for men. Includes chapters for women. Discover the world of healing and creative energy through the ancient Tao. Integrate body and spirit. Enjoy and celebrate life. Why else are you on any quest for success, material or otherwise?
Also: *The Multiorgasmic Woman; The Multiorgasmic Couple; Awaken Healing Energy Through the Tao*

Just One Thing
Developing a Buddha Brain One simple Practice at a Time
Rick Hanson, PhD
Not a religious book. Brain-training practices to protect against stress, lift your mood, and find greater emotional resilience. Beautiful, simple, and effective exercises, including how to use your mind to change your brain, be good to yourself, enjoy life, build strengths, engage the world, and be at peace.

A New Earth
Awakening Your Life's Purpose
Eckhart Tolle
A spiritual manifesto for a better way of life—and for building a better world.

Quantum Warrior
The Future of the Mind
John Kehoe
Athletes of the mind. What is reality, the subconsious, the power of your beliefs and conscious evolution.

CONTRIBUTORS

Daniel Amen, MD

Brain imaging specialist, *New York Times* best-selling author
Company: Amen Clinics, Inc.
Location: Newport Beach, CA
Focus: Brain health; innovative neuroscience research; diagnosis and treatment for a wide variety of neuropsychiatric, behavioral, and learning problems in children, teenagers, and adults. World leader in applying brain-imaging science to clinical practice. ACI has world's largest database of functional brain scans related to psychiatric medicine (more than 70,000 scans) and patients from ninety countries.
Books: Twenty-eight books, including the *New York Times* best sellers *Change Your Brain, Change Your Life* and *Magnificent Mind At Any Age*. Also: *Healing ADD* and *The Brain in Love*. Co-author, *Healing Anxiety and Depression* and *Preventing Alzheimer's*. Author of fifty-four professional articles.
Website: amenclinics.com

John Assaraf

New York Times best-selling author, life coach, international speaker, lecturer, consultant, entrepreneur
Company: Praxis Now, LLC
Location: Rancho Santa Fe, CA
Focus: Change people's lives by changing their belief systems through brain training and specialized neuroscience techniques. Helps entrepreneurs and small-business professionals grow their revenues to achieve financial freedom and live extraordinary lives. Life and business success consultant to Hollywood stars, politicians and CEOs worldwide.
Books: *Having It All* and *The Vision Board Kit*. Co-author, *The Answer: Grow Any Business, Achieve Financial Freedom* and *Live an Extraordinary Life*
Websites: johnassaraf.com, praxisnow.com

Janet Bray Attwood

New York Times best-selling author, transformational leader
Company: Enlightened Alliances
Location: Fairfield, IA

Focus: Help others discover their true passion and open to their full potential. Co-founder of one of the largest transformational online magazines (healthywealthywise.com) and co-owner of Enlightened Alliances, a marketing consulting firm. Chris Attwood and Janet Bray Attwood regularly interview transformational leaders on their passions.

Books: Co-author, *The Passion Test: The Effortless Path To Living Your Life Purpose*; *From Sad to Glad: 7 Steps To Staying Open In The Midst Of Change*

Websites: thepassiontest.com, healthywealthywise.com, janetattwood.com

Lee Beymer
Acupuncture physician, holistic practitioner
Company: Radiant Health, Inc.
Location: Aspen, CO
Focus: Understanding energy and facilitating balance and harmony through computerized biofeedback of the meridians and energy field. Facilitates the spiritually awakened toward attaining health, well-being, longevity, enlightenment and immortality.
Websites: radianthealthcenter.net, quantumemotionalclearing.com, phoenix-institute.com

Arnold Bresky, MD
Alzheimer's and senior care specialist, obstetrician/gynecologist, author, speaker
Company: Brain Tune Up, LLC
Location: Woodland Hills, CA
Focus: Cognitive assessments and attention training. Preventing Alzheimer's disease by modifying lifestyle risk factors. Wellness and preventive medicine. Owned a hospital, runs a hospice care unit. Created many successful and innovative health systems.
Books: *Brain Tune Up: Guide To Caring For Yourself* and *Brain Tune Up: The Secret For Caregiver Success*
Website: mybraintuneup.com

Rhonda Britten
Best-selling author, actress, international speaker, life coach
Company: Fearless Living Institute
Location: Boulder, CO
Focus: Living fearlessly with compassion and accountability to achieve one's goals in business and personal and professional relationships. Self-love. Founder of the Fearless Living Institute and FearlessWorld.com. Emmy Award winner, *Oprah* guest, 600 episodes of reality television in over twenty-five countries.
Books: *Fearless Living*; *Fearless Loving*; and *Change Your Life In 30 Days*; *Do I Look Fat In This? Get Over Your Body and On With Your Life*
Website: fearlessliving.org

Christine Comaford
Executive coach, *New York Times* best-selling author
Company: Christine Comaford Associates
Location: Mill Valley, CA
Focus: Specialist in corporate strategy, execution, and behavioral alignment among top executives, teams, and emerging leaders. Consultant to two American presidents, four billionaires, seven hundred Fortune 1000 executives, and more than three hundred entrepreneurs.
Books: *Rules For Renegades*
Website: christinecomaford.com

Barbara De Angelis, PhD
Best-selling author, motivational speaker, coach
Company: Shakti Communications, Inc.
Location: Santa Barbara, CA
Focus: Relationships and personal growth. Dedicated to bringing transformational education to the world through all electronic and print media. Author of fourteen best-selling books, over eight million copies sold worldwide in twenty languages. One of the most influential teachers of our time in the field of relationships and personal growth. Frequent guest on *Oprah*, *The Today Show*, *Good Morning America*, *The View*, *Geraldo*, and *Politically Incorrect*. Regular contributor to *E! Entertainment* and *Eyewitness News* in Los Angeles.

Books: *How Did I Get Here? Finding Your Way to Renewed Hope and Happiness When Life and Love Take Unexpected Turns*; *Secrets About Men Every Woman Should Know*; *What Women Want Men to Know*; *Confidence: Finding It and Living It*; and *Real Moments: Discover the Secret for True Happiness*
Website: barbaradeangelis.com

Nick Delgado, PhD, CHT
Anti-aging guru, author
Company: The Delgado Protocol For Health
Location: Newport Beach, CA
Focus: Anti-aging, fitness, wellness. Natural approach to preventive health care, healing and anti-aging. Medical research, anti-aging speaker, wellness coach, personal fitness, libido, whole foods, natural supplement formulator, life-style education.
Books: *Grow Young and Slim*; *Be Fit and Pain Free*; *Zero Cholesterol Weight Loss Cookbook*; *How To Stay Young*; and *How To Look Great and Feel Sexy*, plus twelve scientifically reviewed books focused on anti-aging, hormones, herbs, and lifestyle therapies.
Websites: delgadoprotocol.com, nickdelgado.com

Berny Dohrmann
Author, chairman
Company: CEO Space International, Inc.
Focus: Help entrepreneurs and executives grow companies. Reduce time and cost to achieve growth goals, based on high-level networking. Coach to corporate training coaches, such as Tony Robbins and Jack Canfield. National radio show host, *American Dreamers Broadcasting* (with guests like Mark Victor Hansen, T. Harv Eker, Lisa Nichols and John Gray). Developed the Super Teaching program for school children, which accelerates and increases retention.
Books: *Grow Rich With Diamonds*; *Money Magic*; *Super Achiever Mindsets*; and *Perfection Can Be Had*
Website: ceospaceamerica.com

Richard Duree
Somatic energy psychologist

Company: Neuroenergetic Psychology Institute
Location: Jacksonville, OR
Focus: Core transformation via session work and experiential training in body/mind integration. Solving conflicts between brain maps, body sensation and mind. Thirty-eight years in the field of specialized kinesiology. Served as head of Research and Development for Dr. John Thie, creator of Touch for Health Program. Instructor/trainer for Touch for Health Foundation with Shanti Duree. Co-creator of the One Brain System with Gordon Stokes.
Books: Contributed to numerous books, including *Touch for Health* (2nd Edition) by Dr. John Thie; *Stay Young* by Dr. Ivan Popov, MD; *Energy Medicine* by Donna Eden and David Feinstein, PhD; *Neuroenergetic Psychology Series 1-6* by Richard and Shanti Duree.
Website: neuroenergetic.com

John Gray, PhD

New York Times best-selling author, speaker, trainer
Company: John Gray's Mars Venus
Location: Mill Valley, CA
Focus: Hormones. Body/brain chemistry. Relationships. Combines specific communication techniques with healthy, nutritional choices to create the brain and body chemistry for lasting health, happiness, and romance. John's books have sold over 50 million copies in fifty different languages. Guest appearances on *Oprah, Barbara Walters, Dr. Oz, The Today Show, CBS Morning Show, Good Morning America, The Early Show, The View,* and many others. Profiled in *Time, Forbes, USA Today, TV Guide* and *People* magazines.
Books: *Men Are From Mars, Women Are From Venus; Venus On Fire, Mars On Ice; The Mars and Venus Diet and Exercise Solution; Why Mars and Venus Collide; Mars and Venus On a Date;* and *Mars and Venus in the Bedroom*
Website: marsvenus.com

Jennifer Read Hawthorne

#1 *New York Times* best-selling author, book editor, inspirational keynote speaker
Company: Jennifer Read Hawthorne, Inc.

Location: Vero Beach, FL
Focus: Help writers transform their writing, authenticate their message and empower themselves as authors. Has appeared on hundreds of national, regional and local TV and radio shows. Her books have sold more than 13 million copies worldwide and been translated into thirty-one languages.
Books: *Chicken Soup for the Woman's Soul*; *Chicken Soup for the Mother's Soul*; *Life Lessons for Loving the Way You Live*; *The Soul of Success*, and others
Website: jenniferhawthorne.com

Paul Hoffman
Visionary/CEO and Chief Creative Officer
Company: The Success Creation Institute; Paul Hoffman Music, Inc.
Location: Santa Monica, CA
Focus: Human potential trainer and program developer. Wrote many famous jingles in TV advertising. Uses music to inspire and empower others to create desired changes in their lives. Keynote speaking, leadership training, team building, creative problem solutions.
CDs: *Step Into Your Power*; *Sonic Access Four Seasons*; *Love Is All Around Me*; and *Whole and Free*
Website: successsongs.com

Dave Jensen
Sports medicine chiropractor
Company: WIN Health Institute
Location: Basalt, CO
Focus: Sports chiropractic. Enhance productive energy flow and focus through physical alignment.
Websites: myremedyshop.com, winhealthinstitute.com

Richard Kaye
Director
Company: CEO Space
Location: San Diego, CA
Focus: Accelerated business growth at reduced cost through networking.
Website: ceospaceamerica.com

Jim Kwik
Transformational keynote speaker, author
Company: Kwik Learning
Location: White Plains, NY
Focus: Teaches speed-reading, memory improvement, and accelerated learning to individuals and organizations.
Books: *Kwik Learning*; *Kwik Recall*; *Kwik Reading*; *Kwik Thinking*; and *SuperheroYou*
Websites: jimkwik.com, kwiklearning.com, superheroyou.com

Keith Leon
Speaker, best-selling author
Company: Successful Communications, Inc.
Location: Long Beach, CA
Focus: Support authors in writing and marketing their books.
Books: *The Seven Steps To Successful Relationships*; and co-author *Who Do You Think You Are? Discover The Purpose Of Your Life*
Website: keithleon.com

Paul Martinelli
Transformational speaker, trainer
Company: The Martinelli Group
Location: West Palm Beach, FL
Focus: Workshops, retreats, seminars, webinars, coaching services, and keynote speeches to train personal development coaches and platform speakers. Teach power of purpose, vision and goals to unleash one's true potential and the power of what the mind can truly accomplish.
CDs: *Power Principles with Paul Martinelli*; *From Here To There Volumes I & II*; and *Paul Martinelli – Journey From High School Drop-Out to Millionaire: Conversations With The Best Entrepreneurs On the Planet*
Website: paulmartinelli.net

Greg Montana
Author, speaker
Company: Emerald Echo/Heart Virtue, Inc.
Location: Miami, FL

Focus: Help people create more fulfilling experiences in life by discovering their inherent talents and what is most important to them (their "heart virtue"). Background in engineering and quantum physics. Created a successful artificial intelligence company. Monk for eight years.
Books: *Your Pain Is Your Credential: Unlock Your Heart Virtue*
Websites: heartvirtue.com, gregandtamaramontana.com

Mark Romero
Transformational speaker, trainer, company founder and CEO
Company: Mark Romero Music, Inc.
Location: Laguna Nigel, CA
Focus: Sound therapy technology. Help people optimize their personal energy and get back in harmony with their magnificence and unlimited potential. Composer, musician.
Music CDs: *Suenos Infinitos*; *Beyond the Wall*; *Health & Vitality*; *The Vibrational Success Music System*; and *Self-Empowerment for Children*
Website: markromeromusic.com

Marci Shimoff
#1 *New York Times* best-selling author, transformational leader
Company: The Esteem Group
Location: San Rafael, CA
Focus: Keynote addresses on self-esteem, self-empowerment, and peak performance to corporations, professional and non-profit organizations, and women's associations. Top-rated trainer for numerous Fortune 500 companies. Her books have sold 14 million copies and been translated into thirty-one languages.
Books: *Happy For No Reason*; *Love For No Reason*; *Chicken Soup for the Woman's Soul; Chicken Soup for the Mother's Soul*; and others
Website: happyfornoreason.com

Max Simon
Transformational teacher, speaker
Company: Big Vision Business
Location: San Diego, CA

Focus: Marketing and coaching services for Big Vision Entrepreneurs. Support, tools, and resources to help entrepreneurs grow their business and get their message out to the world.
Website: bigvisionbusiness.com

Jill St. John
Actress
Location: Aspen, CO
Focus: Feature films and television. Lightweight comedy, spirited adventure, and spy intrigue. One of Hollywood's "royalty," perhaps best known as Bond girl in the 1970s feature film *Diamonds Are Forever.* Took over for Julia Childs as TV chef on *Good Morning America.*
Books: *The Jill St. John Cookbook*

Diana Stobo
Author, motivational speaker, wellness coach
Company: Diana Stobo, LLC
Location: L.A. Jolla, CA
Focus: Lifestyle that strips away harmful foods that produce toxins within our bodies and lead to many harmful side effects, both emotional and physical. Classically trained Cornell culinary artist and raw food advocate. Healed herself through food. Teaches raw food lifestyle in live classes and on the Internet.
Books: *Get Naked Fast! A Guide to Stripping Away the Foods That Weigh You Down*; and *Naked Bliss: Naughty and Nutritious Dairy Free Milkshakes that Make You Feel So Good*
Website: dianastobo.com

Kieron Sweeney
Inspirational speaker/trainer
Company: KieronSweeney.com
Location: San Jose, CA
Focus: Shift clients' mindsets with respect to money, belief patterns and unveiling the purpose of their lives.
Website: kieronsweeney.com

Brian Theiss
Health consultant, body engineer
Company: Theiss Institute of Health and Fitness
Location: Westlake Village, CA
Focus: Preventive health care and fitness for executives. Combines cutting edge technology and a holistic approach to produce quantitative, measurable results in maximizing a person's potential for better health, greater energy levels, enhanced self-image, overall confidence, fitness and strength at any age. Saving and changing lives through controlling the rate of aging and disease.
Books: *How We Live Is How We Die*
Website: theissinstitute.com

Terry Tillman
Leadership seminar leader/speaker
Company: 22/7 Company
Location: Santa Monica, CA
Focus: To support and facilitate people and organizations to "hear" and respond to their call, so they can live purposeful lives of joy, fulfillment and contribution.
Books: *The Writings On The Wall*; *The Call*; and *Magic Miller* (forthcoming)
Websites: 227company.com, wilderness.227company.com

Lt. Col. Rob "Waldo" Waldman
Professional leadership speaker, author, F-16 combat pilot
Company: Wingman Enterprises
Location: Atlanta, GA
Focus: Teamwork. Leadership. Inspire people to overcome obstacles, adapt to change, and take life-changing action during adverse times. F-16 combat pilot for eleven years. Transformational speaker. Focus, discipline, integrity, teamwork, leadership, overcoming your fears, and maintaining a commitment to excellence. Believes the key to winning lies with your "wingmen"—the men and women in your life who help you overcome obstacles.
Books: *Never Fly Solo*
DVDs: *Wingman Team Building*
Websites: yourwingman.com, neverflysolo.com

David "Avocado" Wolfe
Nutrition expert, best-selling author
Company: David Wolfe
Location: Kilauea, HI
Focus: Superfoods, superherbs, living water. Committed to making raw foods, superfoods, superherbs, living spring water, and advanced healing technology a choice for every human on Earth.
Books: *Superfoods: The Food and Medicine of the Future*; *Naked Chocolate*; *The Sunfood Diet Success System*; *The Longevity Now Program*; and *Eating For Beauty*
Websites: davidwolfe.com, thelongevitynowconference.com

ABOUT ANTON

Anton Uhl is an artist. His private art commissions include works in bronze, glass, paintings and murals in the homes of people like Arianna Huffington and Ringo Starr.

He is also the third generation in a restaurant family. The chalet housing his grandmother's home and café was actually *inside* the 1936 Olympic Stadium in the Bavarian Alps. His mother's restaurant, *Gretl's*, was arguably the most famous restaurant in Aspen, Colorado in the sixties and seventies, praised by princes, movie stars, moguls and ski bums alike.

In a determined effort to escape the food industry, Anton fled to New York, where he became a set designer for opera and theater. People like Luciano Pavarotti have graced the stages he worked on in Europe, Canada, and the United States. He also worked as an art director on feature films, television, and music concerts for many years in Hollywood.

Following a severe health crisis in his early fifties, Anton's focus returned to food when it became the first successful tool used in his recovery. This book is the direct result of the very real concepts that he has applied in his life to become twenty years younger biologically than his chronological age.

Anton hosts and produces *Cooking With Anton*, a cooking show that has aired on local cable TV in Aspen for the past two years.

Anton speaks four languages and has lived in eleven cities around the world. He currently lives on a ranch in Aspen with his wife, their two children, and two dogs.

You can learn more about Anton at:
AntonUhl.com
CookingWithAnton.com

www.ingramcontent.com/pod-product-compliance
Lightning Source LLC
LaVergne TN
LVHW011217080426
835509LV00005B/174